# OPENING NEW MARKETS

# OPENING
# NEW MARKETS

*The British Army
and the Old Northwest*

Walter S. Dunn, Jr.

PRAEGER

Westport, Connecticut
London

**Library of Congress Cataloging-in-Publication Data**

Dunn, Walter S. (Walter Scott), 1928–
    Opening new markets : the British Army and the old Northwest /
Walter S. Dunn, Jr.
        p.  cm.
    Includes bibliographical references and index.
    ISBN 0–275–97329–8 (alk. paper)
    1. Northwest, Old—History—To 1775.  2. Northwest, Old—Economic conditions.  3.
Illinois—History—To 1778.  4. Trading posts—Northwest, Old—History—18th century.  5.
Merchants—Northwest, Old—History—18th century.  6. Fur trade—Northwest, Old—
History—18th century.  7. Great Britain—Colonies—America—Commerce—History—
18th century.  8. Great Britain—Armed Forces—Northwest, Old—History—18th
century.  9. Great Britain—Commercial policy—History—18th century.  I. Title.
    F482.D87   2002
    977′.01—dc21        2001058045

British Library Cataloguing in Publication Data is available.

Library of Congress Catalog Card Number: 2001058045
ISBN:  0–275–97329–8

First published in 2002

Praeger Publishers, 88 Post Road West, Westport, CT 06881
An imprint of Greenwood Publishing Group, Inc.
www.praeger.com

Printed in the United States of America

The paper used in this book complies with the
Permanent Paper Standard issued by the National
Information Standards Organization (Z39.48–1984).

10 9 8 7 6 5 4 3 2 1

# CONTENTS

# PREFACE

This work is the third in a series describing the British Army and the American frontier in the years preceding the American Revolution. Readers looking for a survey of all the secondary books and articles that have been published in the last 150 years will be disappointed as I have used primary source material almost exclusively in an attempt to create a picture of life and events in the 1760s on the frontier, the buying and selling that occupied the lives of individuals, many of whom played dominant roles in the events of the time. I have attempted to depict business activity on the colonial frontier centering on the four crucial years from 1765 to 1768, using a mass of detail that will enable the reader to visualize the frontier merchants, traders, farmers, and others; their surroundings; and their everyday activity. These years marked the failure of British economic policies in America and led to political disaster.

Although the sources consist primarily of letters written to and by the participants, one must keep in mind that often these letters were the result of long discussions and served as a summary of what had been discussed. As a result the letters sometimes read like minutes of a meeting, as indeed they were, intended to provide the recipient a review of what had been discussed. Quebec, Montreal, New York City, Albany, and Philadelphia were small towns, and the leading merchants probably saw each other on a daily basis and lunched together frequently or visited coffee houses to discuss business affairs.

One of the greatest obstacles in writing eighteenth-century business history is understanding the monetary system. Dealing with eighteenth-century currencies was a problem even for contemporaries. Each colony issued its own paper money in pounds (abbreviated by the symbol £) and even lower denominations. The pound contained twenty shillings and each shilling twelve pence. The abbreviations took several forms: £10.2.8 represented ten pounds, two shillings, and eight pence. A more frequent abbreviation was 8/6, representing eight shillings and six pence. The letter d signified a penny and was written 10d for ten pence. British currency was called sterling and the rest by the name of the colony, £10 sterling or £10 New York. In addition the livre was used in Quebec and Illinois. Spanish and Portuguese coins were favored because the silver and gold had intrinsic value. Each had a relative value that varied by location and in time. However, for the convenience of readers, I have converted many of the amounts into the equivalent value in 2001 U.S. dollars at the rate of $200 per pound sterling. Other currencies have been converted by using average eighteenth-century rates of exchange; for example, the New York pound has been converted at the rate of $126 per New York pound. The value of this exercise is that the reader may mentally compare amounts and values by using a common denominator and not have to make complex mental calculations each time a sum is mentioned. For the purists the original figure always precedes the dollar equivalent, which is placed in parentheses.

Prices were crucial in all business dealing and are especially of concern in this attempt to quantify the significance of frontier commerce. The critical price was that charged when a product was sold to the consumer, in this study the Indian, the British army, and farmers on the frontier. Only the British army paid in money; because the others paid in products, it is difficult to determine price. A shirt made from English cloth in America was valued at 10/- New York ($63) and was bartered for two beaver ($123, three pounds at $41 per pound). Some plain shirts were bartered for only one beaver. An Indian gun produced in England for about £1 sterling ($200) was sold to American merchants for £1.10 ($300). The merchants passed the gun down to traders in frontier posts, who exchanged the gun for perhaps six beaver weighing nine pounds valued at 6/6p New York ($41) per pound each ($369). The beaver was sold in London for 3/6d sterling per pound ($70). Prices fluctuated widely, and some fur shipments were sold at a lower prices. Transportation reduced the profits, but the business was still profitable. The estimates given in the text should be considered as approximates rather than definite amounts.

The volume of source material is enormous. Most of the research was done from 1959 to 1970, but I have continued to add to my files in the last thirty years; for example, I compiled a biographical file of over 20,000 individuals mentioned in the source materials that has enabled me to identify quickly individuals mentioned in correspondence. As each reference was added to the cards, a useful brief biography was created. Knowing who the individuals and their connections were explained many vague references in the correspondence.

In 1998 Greenwood published my *Frontier Profit and Loss: The Fur Traders and the British Army, 1760–1764* which detailed the early efforts of the colonists to exploit the fur trade after the French Army had been defeated in Canada. In 2000 *The New Imperial Economy* discussed economic changes on both sides of the Atlantic during the same period covered by this work.

The current study focuses on the changes that occurred in the way business was conducted in four areas, the country northwest of Michilimackinac, the lower Great Lakes area, Pennsylvania and the Ohio River valley, and Illinois and the Mississippi Valley. The study details the efforts of the colonists to reap some of the profit from the frontier despite the firm grasp of the French on the fur trade.

The reader should also keep in mind that colonial America was a comparatively small economy with a population of 1.6 million free Americans and 325,000 slaves. The impact of the £700,000 sterling ($140 million) activity that I have estimated as the value of frontier commerce was significant, equal to about one-half of British imports to America.

Every author owes much to many. I would like to thank the members of Professor Jensen's seminar in the late 1950s who tolerated me and shared their enthusiasm. The staffs of the State Historical Society of Wisconsin, the University of Wisconsin Library, the Pennsylvania Historical Society, the Minnesota Historical Society, the Burton Historical Collection of the Detroit Public Library, and the New York Historical Society were particularly helpful.

This book would never have seen light without the patient and persistent editing of my wife, Jean, who continued to offer encouragement when matters were not going well.

# INTRODUCTION

The American colonies were in a state of flux in the period 1765 to 1768. Volatile changes took place as British, French, and colonial merchants sought to take advantage of the opportunities offered by the opening of the frontier to commerce; at the same time the British government was determined to stem the flow of English funds to America by collecting new taxes and increasing the enforcement of old levies.

The policies of the British government from 1765 to 1768 were detrimental to the interests of American merchants doing business in Canada as well as in the lower Great Lakes area, Pennsylvania, the Ohio Valley, and the Mississippi Valley, while favoring the interests of British merchants and French traders in Canada. The result was a continual escalating conflict as large sums of money changed hands.

What was the significance of the financial transactions on the frontier from 1765 to 1768 to the colonial economy? Investigators tend to "follow the money" to find the motives, who was involved, and who were the leading characters. Following the money indicated that those merchants who lost substantially in frontier commerce by 1768 saw Britain and particularly the army as responsible for their losses. These same disgruntled merchants, who previously had close ties with England, became leaders in the Revolution.

To understand the impact of economic changes in the late 1760s that altered the lives of the colonial merchants, one must not only translate the 1760 pound sterling to $200 U.S. in 2001 but also factor in the differences in the size of the two economies. There were only 2 million colonists, compared to 280 million Americans in 2001. The value of frontier commerce, £700,000 sterling ($140 million) in 1765, was equal to a $19.6 billion business in 2001 on a per capita basis.

The prominent customer on the frontier was the British army. The British treasury spent an average of £400,000 sterling per year, more than the total value of furs obtained on the frontier, to maintain an army in America from 1765 to 1768. The British withdrawal of frontier garrisons after 1768 to reduce costs deprived frontier merchants of a share of the profitable business of supplying the army.

British regiments had been sent to America during the Seven Years War to defeat the French in America. French resistance ended in 1759, and a large number of British regiments were sent to the West Indies in 1762, when Spain entered the war. After the Spanish possessions were taken, the British regiments returned to the colonies. Fifteen regiments were left in America, presumably to contain the French, defend the new possessions, and control the frontier.

Why did Britain leave the army in America? There had been no need for a regular force before the war, when the French in Canada posed a continual threat. One theory is that the regiments were left in America to maintain a standing army without arousing opposition in England. Keeping the regiments in America made possible obtaining colonial funds to pay for them. Another theory is that the fifteen regiments provided appointments for friends of George III: the position of colonel of a regiment was a sinecure. The colonel remained in England, receiving a large income with no duties. A lieutenant colonel actually commanded the regiment. These theories could well be true, but the result was a large British army stationed in America for the first time during peacetime, whose presence had a considerable impact on the colonial economy.

The British army stationed in Michilimackinac, Detroit, Fort Niagara, Fort Pitt, and Illinois formed a unique market for provisions and liquor. An average of fifteen regiments of the British army were stationed in America from 1765 to 1768: four regiments in Newfoundland and Nova Scotia, three regiments in Quebec and Montreal, one regiment divided between Michilimackinac and Detroit, one regiment in New York, one in Pennsylvania, four in Florida, and one in Illinois. The numbers fluctuated during each year as regiments were rotated from America back to Great Britain and replaced by regiments from Europe.

The army remained a good customer for frontier merchants until 1768, when the British began to move the regiments to the coastal cities to reduce the cost of feeding and housing them. This move substantially reduced the colonists' income from sales to the army, which were paid in sterling that could be used to pay for colonial imports. Stationed on the coast, the army was much cheaper to maintain because of the lower price of rations and the elimination of the expensive transportation to the frontier.

The other means of payment of debts in England was fur. Before the Seven Years War took the British army to America, the French merchants in Canada and Louisiana were primarily concerned with the fur trade, having over a century of experience dealing with the Indians. The colonial merchants also traded with the Indians on the New York and Pennsylvania frontier and to a lesser degree in the south. When the French in Canada capitulated in 1759, colonial merchants attempted to take over the fur trade both by selling goods to the French traders in Quebec and Montreal and by sending traders with pack horses laden with rum and other merchandise into the country north of the Ohio Valley to deal directly with the Indians.

There were five segments of the frontier market: Canada and the Northwest, the lower Great Lakes, Pennsylvania and the Ohio Valley, Illinois, and the army, all outlets for European manufactured goods, colonial provisions, and liquor. The proximity of the areas and the differing composition of the merchants created competition for the furs and deerskin.

The conduct of frontier commerce was determined to a large measure by the geography as rivers and lakes provided the cheapest routes for the movement of furs and goods. The Indians were concentrated along the rivers and lakes for the same reason. Because of the overwhelming influence of geography on the trade, the Canadian trade continued in the same channels as under the French. In New York and Pennsylvania, the removal of the French military threat enabled traders to extend westward into the Great Lakes and down the Ohio River.

British and colonial merchants competed for the Canadian market, which was expanding northwest of Lake Superior. The French Canadian traders conducted most of the business with the Indians, making annual voyages from Montreal and serving the upper lakes. New York and Albany merchants dominated the lower lakes market, which was conducted by colonial traders in Oswego, Niagara, Detroit, and smaller posts serving the lower lakes. A third market comprised Philadelphia merchants who supplied the colonial traders based at Fort Pitt and other posts in western Pennsylvania and the area of present Ohio. A fourth market were the Mississippi and Missouri River valleys served by French merchants in New Orleans and during this period by Philadelphia merchants. The French traveled up the Missouri River, the upper Mississippi, and the area south of Lake Michigan.

The French traders encouraged the Indians to resist the colonial traders, who were destroying the native culture with rum. Pontiac gladly obliged. Many colonial traders were killed and robbed during Pontiac's Uprising in 1763, but the Indians were unable to take the forts at Detroit, Niagara, and Pittsburgh. Two British and colonial armies were sent to pacify the Indians and received their promise to remain peaceful. Trade, which had been prohibited while the Indians were openly at war, was reopened in 1765. The Indian Department under Sir William Johnson tried to enforce the Plan of 1764, which restricted trading to army posts both to protect the merchants from robbery and to protect the tribes from dishonest and unethical traders who used rum to cheat them. This rule worked to the advantage of the French as the colonial traders were no longer able to travel freely among the villages while the French safely ignored the rule and received the lion's share of the fur. Eventually some colonial traders either received special licenses to leave the posts or did so illegally, but they did not regain the dominance enjoyed for the few years before the uprising. The colonial merchants presented many memorials objecting to the rule restricting trade to the posts, which was prejudicial to them, and viewed the army unfavorably for enforcing the rule against them while doing little to prevent the French from trading in the Indian villages.

Furs were a valuable commodity that was easily transportable and had high value per pound. Beaver sold at the equivalent of $78 per pound on the London market. The profit margin on fur was far greater than on other commodities that were sent to Britain, and the demand for fur in Europe far exceeded the supply.

Before 1760 the French hat makers received the total output of the Canadian fur trade, as well as fur exported from New Orleans. From 1760 to 1768 the French struggled to supply the French hat industry through illegal exports from New Orleans while colonial merchants profited from smuggling out of New York City and Philadelphia furs that eventually reached France. By 1768 the French in Canada and New Orleans along with some British merchants in Canada controlled the fur trade almost to the exclusion of colonial merchants. The loss of both the army contracts and the fur trade forced into bankruptcy even the leading mercantile house in Philadelphia, Baynton and Wharton.

When the colonial merchants were deprived of the profits from both the fur trade and supply of the army, their ability to pay for British imports was diminished. Lacking the ability to pay for the imports, the colonists ordered fewer goods and British manufacturers lost a portion of their market. By the late 1760s America was a lucrative market for British manufactures, which were available in unprecedented quantity. The British economy had exploded during the Seven Years War to meet the military needs of Britain and her allies in the same way the United States economy expanded during World War II. The thirteen colonies were not a self-sufficient economy in 1765 and depended heavily on British imports for such basic commodities as clothing, housewares, all forms of cloth used by individuals and in industry, most metal products, firearms (with the exception of a few American-made rifles), and a lengthy list of other manufactured items.

The American economy in 1765 was predominantly rural. Most of the 1.6 million white Americans and 325,000 slaves lived near the sea on either small farms or plantations. American dependence on British imports was fostered and encouraged by the English government by opposing the growth of American industry. An example was the prohibition of steel making in the colonies but the encouragement of the export of cast iron to England. Hat makers were limited in the number of apprentices to prevent the growth of an American hat industry.

The policy of making America dependent on British imports had one flaw: the Americans were hard pressed to find exports to pay for these goods. No economy can sustain an adverse balance of trade without some mitigating circumstance. Suppliers had to be paid within a few years in the eighteenth century; otherwise they refused to ship more merchandise. The colonists had to find some means to pay the negative balance of trade (see Table I.1) with Britain, which hovered around £800,000 sterling ($160 million) from 1765 to 1768.

The colonial deficit was overcome in part by supplying the British regiments in America. In the late 1760s British military spending in America provided about £400,000 sterling annually, about half the amount needed to balance the

Table I.1
Balance of Trade between the American Colonies and England[1]
(£ sterling in thousands)

| Year | Exports | Imports | Deficit |
|------|---------|---------|---------|
| 1765 | £1,151  | £1,944  | (£793)  |
| 1766 | 1,043   | 1,805   | (762)   |
| 1767 | 1,096   | 1,901   | (805)   |
| 1768 | 1,251   | 2,157   | (906)   |

trade with Britain. The military expenses were paid in the coveted sterling bills of exchange that were sent to England to pay accounts.

The other half of the colonial deficit was overcome by the favorable balance of trade with southern Europe and Africa, about £345,000 sterling in 1769. The tonnage for that year was about the same as for the years 1765 to 1768, so there is no reason to believe that 1769 was an abnormal year. The merchants in Lisbon, the primary port for the region, were able to pay for most of the provisions sent from Philadelphia with English bills of exchange obtained from the sale of port and sherry to the British aristocracy.

However, some additional source of payment to the colonists from southern Europe was probably required. Legal imports of commodities such as wine were approximately £20,000. There was no noticeable influx of specie (gold and silver coins), although there is frequent mention of one or two Portuguese and Spanish gold coins. the context of the letters mentioning these coins implies that transferring money in this way was not usual. A Portuguese "half jo" (a half of a Johannes with eight pennyweights of gold) was valued at £4 Quebec ($560). In October 1767 George Morgan gave Joseph Dobson fifteen half joes ($8,000) to use in Illinois.[2] A Spanish doubloon was valued at £2.14 Pennsylvania ($310). John Askin in Detroit paid one of his debts with three doubloons, four Spanish pistoles ($78 each), and four Spanish dollars along with thirteen small bills of exchange totaling £88.11 New York.[3] Therefore, Portuguese and Spanish coins did circulate, but the addition of any significant number of gold coins annually would have been noticeable.

The third option for the southern Europeans was smuggling illegal European goods from Lisbon and the West Indies to pay for the bread, flour, rice, and fish sent to southern Europe. Practically all of the shipments to southern Europe went to Lisbon, which was open and free, having few restrictions on what landed and what left. About £200,000 sterling worth of bread and flour was sent to Lisbon each year, almost entirely from Philadelphia, and the only products that returned legally were wine and salt. The salt, of little value, was often carried as ballast. There was ample opportunity to unload illegal goods before entering the port. Most ships returning from Lisbon entered the port of Philadelphia without a full cargo.[4] Another source of illegal goods was St. Eustatius, a center for illegal shipments of Dutch gin, brandy, and tea to the colonies.[5] William West sent out a handbill in Philadelphia listing all of the luxury items carried in by a Dutch ship to St. Eustatius. The extent of smuggling is difficult to assess for one seldom finds details of illegal activity in official records. Baynton and Wharton ordered silk handkerchiefs, china, silk stockings, and velvet along with wine from Lisbon. Willing and Morris placed an order for illegal Dutch tea worth £2,000 sterling ($400,000), but the normal orders were for smaller quantities.[6]

With illegal goods coming in, some illegal goods would be expected to go out. A few facts do support the contention that smuggling of fur out of the colonies was far greater than usually assumed. When the British cut off the fur supply to France, the Continental hat makers had to find an alternate source. A beaver pelt made one "castor" hat. The demand in Europe was great. The castor hat was highly prized in Europe and the demand exceeded the 100,000 beaver exported from Quebec before 1760. When the British took Canada, the only legal ways for the French to obtain beaver were to buy it at high prices in the London market or to import it from New Orleans from French merchants, some of whom obtained the beaver pelts illegally in British territory. We have knowledge that both French and Dutch ships visited New Orleans, presumably taking away fur and deerskin obtained west of the Mississippi, but even the official documents question whether most of the pelts were of British origin.

The French must have found an alternate source of beaver because the flourishing hat industry on the Continent was reducing the demand for hats made in Britain in the 1760s. There was no unusual demand for beaver on the London market that would have driven up the price.

Some furs used on the Continent were from Canada by way of England, but few were from the colonies. The legal exports of beaver from Philadelphia were only £4,000 sterling annually, less than before 1760. Smuggling took place in the approaches to New York City and Philadelphia, both major legal fur exporters before 1760 and minor sources in the late 1760s. From contemporary accounts we know that by a wide margin more fur and deerskin entered Philadelphia from the frontier than was legally exported. The American market was probably less than 6,000 hats annually, and far more beaver was unaccounted for in the official records.[7]

Baynton and Wharton repeatedly comment that fur could be quickly sold in Philadelphia in small lots for cash. Shipment to England of such small lots would have been uneconomical because of the transportation and handling charges. Fur and deerskin, which were in demand in Europe and of high value (beaver was $78 per pound on the London market), would have been an ideal form of payment for the smuggled Dutch merchandise. Colonial currency was useless to the Dutch, and sterling bills of exchange would have been difficult though not impossible to negotiate in Amsterdam.

Because the smuggled merchandise was comparatively small in volume, ten tons of merchandise worth about £1,500 sterling ($300,000) could have been unloaded before entering Philadelphia, and the remaining legal cargo of wine from southern Europe would have entered the port without raising suspicion. After leaving Philadelphia with a cargo of sixty tons of fish, bread, or flour bound for southern Europe, along the river the smuggler would take on two tons of fur valued at £1,500 sterling.

In the period from 1765 to 1768 there was a sharp decrease of legal exports of fur from Philadelphia and New York, from more than £50,000 sterling to £30,000 sterling, despite an increase in the amount of fur from the Great Lakes and the Ohio Valley entering the ports of New York City and Philadelphia. One must suspect that the Dutch were taking away a considerable amount of fur illegally, as it was the one commodity that was light in weight, high priced, and immediately salable in Amsterdam. The sharp decline in legal fur exports from New York City and Philadelphia serving the Great Lakes and Ohio Valley areas cannot be explained simply as a reduction in the supply of animals as a result of overhunting. Thousands of Indians continued to live in those areas and consume European goods, and fur and deerskin were the only products they could use to obtain the goods.

The British customs officers were aware of the smuggling and the merchants complained of their ships' being carefully examined. The customs officers also requested smaller vessels that could investigate the small coves near New York City and Philadelphia because the Royal Navy vessels were too large for this work.[8] Therefore, one has to assume that a considerable share of the returns from frontier commerce did not appear in the official records.

Legal returns from the frontier were in the form of sterling bills of exchange from the army, fur and deerskin from the Indians, and produce from the farmers in Illinois and Detroit. Only the bills and fur could be used to pay debts in Britain. American exports in 1770 totaled £3,437,000 sterling. This value was assigned by the British customs service and did not represent the true value in London. The exports were distributed as indicated in Table I.2. The amounts have been rounded off to the nearest £1,000 sterling, and some categories have been combined. The leading exports were tobacco, fish, bread and flour, lumber, and rice. These five products totaled more than £2,348,000 sterling or two-thirds of the total amount. More than half of all the exports went to Great Britain.

The colonial farmers produced most of their needs but had little cash to purchase necessary British manufactured goods. Rural America formed a large market but had very little means to pay for its purchases. Few of the products of the thirteen colonies other than tobacco, indigo, rice, and fur, none of which

Table I.2
American Exports in 1770

| Product | Value | Britain | South Europe | West Indies |
|---|---|---|---|---|
| Tobacco | £906 | £906 | | |
| Indigo | £131 | £131 | | |
| Iron | £67 | £67 | | |
| Flax seed | £35 | £35 | | |
| Whale oil & fins | £94 | £94 | | |
| Fur | £91 | £91 | | |
| Deerskin | £58 | £58 | | |
| Rice | £340 | £170 | £85 | £85 |
| Lumber | £200 | £79 | | £121 |
| Wheat | £131 | £26 | £105 | |
| Horses | £60 | | | £60 |
| Poultry & hogs | £25 | | | £25 |
| Bread & flour | £504 | £50 | £202 | £252 |
| Fish | £398 | | £250 | £148 |
| Corn | £43 | | £14 | £29 |
| Beef & pork | £66 | | £6 | £60 |
| Rum | £21 | | £3 | Africa £18 |
| Candles | £23 | | | £23 |
| Peas & beans | £10 | | | £10 |
| Other | £234 | £163 | £27 | £36 |
| Total | £3,437 | £1,870 | £692 | £849 Africa- £22 |

was produced by small farms, could be exported in large quantities to Britain. The farmers sold some of their produce to colonial merchants, who in turn sold the produce and other American products to the West Indies, Africa, and southern Europe. The returns were used to pay for British imports.

The export of fur and deerskin to Britain was but a fraction of total exports. The amounts are the official values given by customs officers and in the case of beaver represent less than half of the sale price in London. Other commodities may also have been assigned lower values by these officials. The sale price of the fur and deerskin in London was probably about £200,000 sterling. Another £100,000 worth of fur and deerskin was illegally exported.

Potentially the receipts from the lucrative frontier market were as much as £700,000 sterling ($140,000,000), equal to a third of the value of the imports from Britain to the thirteen colonies in 1765 of nearly £1.9 million sterling ($400 million). The conservative value of British manufactured goods, colonial products, provisions for the army, and French merchandise to each of the markets can be estimated as follows:

| | |
|---|---|
| Canada and the Northwest | £185,000 |
| Lower Lakes area | £94,000 |
| Pennsylvania and Ohio Valley | £33,000 |
| Illinois | £113,000 |
| Florida | £67,000 |
| Total | £492,000 sterling |

About £105,500 in British manufactured goods was traded, while the French in Illinois continued to import about £30,000 sterling in merchandise from other European countries. Agricultural products and rum from the colonies, Canada, and Illinois worth about £356,500 sterling were sold to the army and the Indians.

The returns for this investment included legally exported fur and deerskin (£90,000), illegally exported peltry (£128,000), merchandise sold to the French in Illinois (£20,000), and bills of exchange from the army (£400,000). A conservative estimate of the revenue was divided as follows:

| | |
|---|---|
| Canada and the Northwest | £250,000 |
| Lower Lakes | £99,000 |
| Pennsylvania and Ohio Valley | £49,000 |
| Illinois | £150,000 |
| Florida | £90,000 |
| Total | £638,000 sterling |

Beginning in 1760, the colonial merchants did well until 1763, when Pontiac's Uprising brought the western trade to a complete halt. The Indians, encouraged and supported by many of the French residents, killed and robbed the colonial and British traders while leaving the French unscathed. The revolt had been engineered by the French traders and merchants in Canada and Illinois to protect their markets from the British and colonial intruders.

To restore peace to the frontier, the British agreed to limit settlers to the area east of the mountains with the Proclamation of 1763 and to restrain the colonial traders with the Rule of 1764, limiting them to dealing at the posts while the French were allowed to continue trading in the villages. With the restoration of peace and the reopening of the fur trade in 1765 the colonial merchants and the French and British merchants in Canada began a concerted effort to expand their markets on the American frontier. Their efforts were fueled by the unprecedented availability of British-made merchandise resulting from the expansion of the British economy during the Seven Years War.[9]

The British economy had heated up during the war to supply the British army and navy as well as to subsidize the Prussian and Hanoverian armies in the struggle against France. After the war the British had large quantities of goods to sell and turned to the consumers in the colonies. The colonial economy was fueled after 1764 by the availability of large quantities of low-priced British manufactured goods and a growing population that had acquired expensive tastes during the Seven Years War. The colonists were just as eager to buy and found new sources of credits in the trade on the frontier with the Indians and the new French subjects. The colonists had merchandise to sell, a market in the Indians and the British army, and the rivers and lakes to transport the goods. The military road from Philadelphia west to Fort Pitt added a second entry to the frontier in addition to the Hudson River path.

Business was going well on the New York and Pennsylvania frontier as a result of the encounter of two relatively prosperous economies, the Indian and the colonial. The Indians of the Northern Department, the area north of the Ohio River, had access to highly desirable fur from animals living in the cold climate. In the Southern Department deerskin was the primary product. The Indians were eager purchasers of European goods, especially firearms and steel traps, which provided the tools to gain ascendancy over their neighbors to the west as well as making hunting and trapping far easier. Also the Great Lakes and the rivers flowing into the lakes provided a superb transportation network. The Indians had both a highly marketable commodity and an excellent system to take it to market. With two groups of consumers, the Indians and the colonists, each having products desired by the other, and the transportation system to exchange their products, commerce increased dramatically.

At the same time, from the west French merchants and traders from New Orleans and Illinois were striving to expand their markets to replace the supply of fur cut off by the British acquisition of Canada. With the peltry from Quebec then going to Britain, the French hat makers needed an alternate source.

A major blow to the colonial economy was the failure of the colonial merchants to recapture a major share of the fur trade from the French after Pontiac's Uprising. The colonial merchants on the frontier could not compete with the French traders, who lived in the Indian villages and sold their fur to British merchants in Montreal for shipment directly to England or to French merchants in New Orleans, who shipped the fur to France.

The merchants from New York made a futile effort to compete with the French in Detroit and Michilimackinac but were frustrated by the British army rule that they must remain in the posts and wait for the Indians to go to them. Even if the merchants had ventured into the tribal villages, there was a constant threat from the Indians, who were encouraged by the French to rob the colonials. The merchants from Pennsylvania suffered from the same limitation at Fort Pitt and Fort Augusta. Nevertheless, Baynton and Wharton, one of the leading firms in Philadelphia, made a concerted effort to capture the Illinois market, in order to divert from France to Britain the furs from the Mississippi and Missouri valleys either directly or through Philadelphia, even though they also would have continued to flow through New Orleans.

Fundamental to this struggle to expand markets was the need to sell both product and brand name, to use modern terminology. To sell a product one must find new consumers and convince them to purchase the new product, in this instance, British merchandise. To sell a brand one must convince consumers to switch from one brand of a product to another. In the north, the French traders looked for new consumers among the western tribes while, encouraging the Indians northwest of Lake Superior to switch from the British Hudson Bay Company factories to the French traders from Michilimackinac. In the Great Lakes area and the Ohio Valley the colonial traders sought to switch the Indians from the Illinois French merchandise to British and colonial products from New York City and Philadelphia via Albany and Fort Pitt. The Illinois French found new consumers in the Missouri River and the northern reaches of the Mississippi and competed fiercely to maintain their older market areas north of the Ohio River.

Although all the factions were competing to expand markets, their motives differed. Rather than selling a maximum amount of merchandise, the French Canadians were mainly concerned with obtaining the maximum amount of peltry for the least amount of merchandise. They sold the British merchandise available to them at the highest price possible, even at the sacrifice of expanding the market. The French were quite content to have the Indians with whom they traded act as middlemen reselling the guns, ammunition, cloth, and metal goods to tribes farther west at even higher prices in terms of the furs in exchange for the highly prized European goods. The French from New Orleans and Illinois had a similar motivation: their driving force was to obtain peltry for France rather then to dispose of French manufactures, and they were quite willing to use British goods to buy the fur.

In contrast, the colonial merchants wanted to sell merchandise at any cost and were willing to take any form of payment: peltry, farm products, or bills of exchange on the British treasury provided by the army. Their driving force was to profit by selling a maximum volume of merchandise to find a means to pay for the flood of British merchandise then being purchased by the colonists on the coast. As a result, the colonial merchants were willing to sell at lower prices to increase volume. They were selling a brand (English), trying to capture the Indian trade from the French, whereas the French were selling a product (no matter the source) and finding new consumers in the Missouri Valley, the northern Mississippi, and northwest of Lake Superior.

The intense competition between the French and the colonial merchants continued between 1765 and 1768. In the five years that followed Pontiac's Uprising, commerce on the frontier changed as the French Canadians formed alliances with British merchants to monopolize the fur trade in the upper Great Lakes area, driving out the colonial traders and diverting the fur trade income from New York City and Philadelphia to Quebec and Montreal. The traders from New York and Pennsylvania were handicapped by the restriction to trading with Indians who traveled to the posts at Detroit, Fort Niagara, Fort Pitt, Oswego, and other minor posts. The British army sought to enforce the iron-clad rule restricting trade to the posts to protect the Indians from unscrupulous colonial traders who dealt primarily in rum. As can be expected, the French gained an advantage when they were allowed to continue going to the Indian villages and exchanging goods obtained from British merchants in Montreal and Quebec for the furs gathered by the Indians.

Forced out of the lucrative fur trade north of Lake Superior, the New York traders continued a limited trade at Detroit, Fort Niagara, Michilimackinac, and Oswego. To ensure Indian favor, the Indian Department purchased some goods as gifts from the New Yorkers. The British garrisons at the posts and the French farmers at Detroit were also good customers. The Pennsylvania traders continued to trade with the Indians at Fort Pitt and in villages in western Pennsylvania as well as in the area of present Ohio. The main focus of the trade, though, was the Ohio Valley and Illinois. Baynton and Wharton was the major firm seeking to exploit the Illinois market by supplying the British army, selling goods directly to the Indians at posts located in the French villages between the Ohio River and Lake Michigan, and providing merchandise to French fur traders who were dealing with the tribes along the Mississippi and Missouri Rivers.

By 1769 the British merchants in Canada had allied themselves with the French and stifled the colonial merchants from Albany, who concentrated on the Indians who traveled to Michilimackinac, Detroit, Fort Niagara, and Oswego as well as other posts. For the most part the colonists restricted their activity to the posts for fear of being robbed while the French, who were more friendly to the Indians, circulated in the villages, taking most of the peltry.

In Illinois, Pennsylvania merchants also failed to overcome the French, who held the fur trade firmly in their grasp. The colonials were able to sell to the French traders some British goods when the ships from France arrived too late in New Orleans to transfer their cargoes to the spring convoys of boats rowed up to Illinois. The major markets for the Pennsylvania merchants in Illinois were the army and the Indian Department. When the troops were moved to the coast after 1768 to reduce expenses, this market disappeared along with the purchases of the Indian Department as bribing the Indians to safeguard the troops was no longer necessary.

The French succeeded in expanding their markets both in the north and in Illinois and would continue to do so for nearly twenty years, working in concert with British merchants in Montreal. The British merchants, to the relative exclusion of colonial merchants, sold increasing amounts of merchandise to the French in Canada. British merchants in Florida also illegally increased their market among the French merchants in New Orleans. Unable to compete, the Pennsylvania merchants were bankrupted in Illinois and by 1768 held only a small foothold in the Great Lakes trade. The loss of the frontier market was a devastating blow to the colonial economy and turned a number of merchants from passive observers to active opponents of British rule in the thirteen colonies. Many who had lost fortunes on the frontier would appear in the ranks of the leaders of the Continental Army. The last straw was the misguided effort of the British government to force the colonists to pay for the force that was actually assisting their enemies, the French and their Indian allies, under the guise of protecting the colonists and promoting peace.

During the Seven Years War the British army had provided a major source of sterling by its purchase of goods and services from the colonists, both by the army itself and by the individual soldiers who spent their pay on colonial products. When George III decided to maintain a large army in America, the colonial merchants were pleased, because after the war ended, the British army would remain a major market for goods, many of which were produced in America: rum, flour, and salted beef. However, when the British government sought to pay for these goods with taxes raised in America from the colonial business community rather than bills of exchange payable ultimately by the British landowners, the Americans objected. George III and his ministers were in a difficult position.

Britain had an enormous debt as a result of the Seven Years War. During the war Britain paid for its military effort by the sale of "Consols," government bonds that were readily salable in Europe and in Britain because they were a reliable investment. Sir William Johnson invested his profits from his position as superintendent of the Indian Department in Consols and sold some of them during the late 1760s when his income declined.

The British government met the interest payments and attempted to pay some of the principal by heavy taxation, especially the tax on land, which reached 25% of the total assessed value of property, not the income (a 2% real estate tax on the assessed value is common in the United States). This burden was crushing on the landed gentry who made up most of Parliament. The landowners in Britain demanded tax relief, and, as the power base of the government's support in Parliament, they could not be denied. The only British recourse seemed to be to force the colonists to pay for the army or to withdraw it from America. To submit to the demands of the colonists was unthinkable to the crown, and the army remained while a variety of means were sought to extract money from the colonists to pay for it.

On the other hand, the manufacturers and merchants who were making enormous profits from the trade with America paid no commensurate taxes. Although they had little voice in Parliament, the merchants did seek to ameliorate the policy of transferring the tax burden to America. The worst feature of the proposed taxes in America was that they were to be paid in sterling rather than colonial currency. With the new taxes, the colonials would be forced to find some source of sterling to pay the taxes. This requirement was unnecessary, for the expressed purpose of the taxes was to meet the cost of the army in America. New York and Pennsylvania currency was used to pay the troops in America and was acceptable to the suppliers of rations and other needs. Colonial currency was purchased by the army in New York and Philadelphia with sterling bills. Under the new tax structure, the sterling received by the British government would be converted back to colonial paper money and used to pay for rations and other military needs, returning the sterling to the colonial economy. Had the taxes been payable in colonial currency, the transaction would have been less cumbersome, although the colonists still would have been deprived of the sterling income from the army.

Given the loss of prewar fur exports to French competition in Canada and Illinois and the loss of army contracts, the only significant sources of sterling in the thirteen colonies were sale of tobacco to Britain plus sale of lumber and provisions to the West Indies and southern Europe, not enough to support the acquired taste for British imports. To pay the new taxes, the colonists would have to reduce imports of British goods, a setback both to the British manufacturers and to the quality of life in the colonies as most of the cloth, metal merchandise, and pottery was imported.

Potentially the frontier market was worth £700,000 sterling, compared to imports from Britain to the thirteen colonies in 1765 of nearly £2 million sterling ($400 million). British merchandise accounted for £85,500 sterling of the frontier market, about 18%. The merchandise bought by the army, more than 60% of the total of all the markets, was almost entirely colonial produce, provisions, and liquor. While the army was the major customer on the frontier consuming products from Canada and the thirteen colonies, most of the British manufactured goods were sold to the Indians. When the army reduced its expenditures in America and the anticipated quantities of fur from Canada and Illinois did not materialize, the colonists had less sterling to pay for British imports.

If the colonial merchants had been able to retain their share of the fur trade in the lower Great Lakes (for example, an additional £50,000 sterling) and had obtained a major share of the Illinois furs and deerskin (for example, £75,000 sterling), they might have been willing to pay taxes in colonial currency to support the army. Furthermore, if the army had enforced the trade restrictions on the French, the payment of the taxes would not have been a major issue, as it would have been a cost of doing business. But the double blow of losing the fur trade to the French and the profit from supplying the army was overwhelming.

Ultimately the army, supposedly maintained to protect the colonies, actually was used to control them, providing another factor leading to the Revolution. In the four years from 1765 to 1768 the colonial merchants began to develop new sources of income from the frontier such as land speculation while politically trying to ensure that Britain continued to pay for the army. The colonists eventually failed in both endeavors.

## NOTES

1. *Historical Statistics of the United States: Colonial Times to 1957* (Washington, D. C.: U. S. Department of Commerce, 1960), p. 757.

2. Joseph Dobson to Baynton and Wharton, 5 October 1767, Baynton, Wharton & Morgan Papers, Microfilm, 10 Rolls, Original in Pennsylvania Historical Commission [BWM], Roll 3.

3. Askin Papers in the Burton Historical Collections of the Detroit Public Library.

4. Arthur L. Jensen, *The Maritime Commerce of Colonial Philadelphia* (Madison: The State Historical Society of Wisconsin, 1963), pp. 58–65.

5. Ibid., pp. 132–33.

6. Ibid., p. 133.

7. The population of the thirteen colonies included 1.6 million white inhabitants. Of these one fifth or less were adult males (310,000), and at most a tenth of those (31,000) could afford the expensive castor hats. The life of a hat was perhaps five years so the annual rate of replacement was approximately 6,200 hats.

8. Jensen, pp. 138–39.

9. Walter S. Dunn, Jr., *The New Imperial Economy* (New York: Praeger, 2001), passim.

# 1

# CANADA AND THE NORTHWEST

When Britain acquired Canada in 1760 the source of merchandise for the fur trade shifted from France to Britain. The demand in Canada for merchandise and food inspired colonial merchants to send agents to Quebec and Montreal, expecting to reap enormous profits from trading colonial rum and British merchandise. After four years of success, Pontiac's Uprising brought to a halt the colonial efforts in Canada. When trade resumed in 1765, the colonial merchants were faced with new competition from British merchants, many of them former Scottish army officers. The French chose to buy their merchandise from the Scots, and the colonial merchants were left with a small share of the market.

In 1765 both British and colonial merchants in Canada imported rum, molasses, and salt from the West Indies; tea, gunpowder, and manufactured goods from England; and rum from the thirteen colonies to supply the Canadian market and the expanding market in the Northwest, the area northwest of Lake Superior. Benjamin Roberts, a British officer, estimated in 1770 that goods worth £150,000 sterling ($30,000,000) were sent to Quebec each year from Britain. Half of the merchandise, £75,000 sterling, went to the French market along the St. Lawrence River, and the other half (£75,000) was sent on to Montreal and the west.[1] Theoretically the £75,000 sterling would have returned £150,000 sterling worth of fur to be exported from Canada, but at least £20,000 sterling in merchandise passed through Michilimackinac to Illinois, where it was converted to fur and exported to Europe from New Orleans. The remaining £50,000 sterling was exchanged for £100,000 sterling in fur and returned to Montreal. Other sources indicate that the same amount in fur and deerskin was exported from Canada.

In 1761 the French had estimated the value of fur exported at £135,000 sterling. In 1765 the customs value of fur exports from Canada to Britain was

£39,034 sterling (the true value was closer to £80,000 sterling), much less than the French estimate.[2] Another estimate stated that about 100,000 beaver pelts (worth £39,000 sterling or $7,800,000 in London) were exported annually from Canada.[3] Other furs and deerskin would have doubled the total value to about £80,000 sterling ($16,000,000) annually, a very healthy market.

In 1768 imports to Quebec from Great Britain included 195 tons of wine, 2 tons of tea, 7 tons of gunpowder, and a wide variety of manufactured goods. Usually about 30 tons of gunpowder (value about £9,000 New York, $1,134,000) arrived from England each year.[4] The wine and tea were for the French market while the gunpowder was traded to the Indians.

From the thirteen colonies came 250,000 gallons of rum (value about £22,500 New York, $2,835,000) and 3,000 bushels of salt. From the West Indies came 45,000 gallons of molasses and 150 hundredweight of sugar.[5] The salt was used to preserve beef for army rations and the rum was traded to the Indians.

An estimate of the trade made by the French in 1761 concluded that goods worth £60,400 sterling ($12,080,000) were bartered to the Indians in Canada in the following areas:

| | |
|---|---|
| Niagara | £18,330 |
| Detroit | 14,580 |
| Miami River | 3,330 |
| Ouiatanon | 2,500 |
| Michilimackinac | 10,420 |
| Green Bay and Sioux | 4,170 |
| Lake Nipigon | 1,250 |
| La Pointe | 3,330 |
| St. Joseph | 2,500 |
| Total | £60,400 sterling[6] |

Niagara drew furs from the tribes around Lake Erie and Lake Ontario. Detroit was the center for the tribes south and west of the fort. The Miami River and Ouiatanon served the tribes on the Miami and Wabash Rivers in Illinois. Michilimackinac traded with Indians from upper Lake Michigan and Lake Huron. Green Bay drew trade from the Fox River and the Wisconsin River and also from the Sioux Indians, who used those rivers leading from the Mississippi. St. Joseph on the southeast shore of Lake Michigan drew Indians from the area. La Pointe was on the south shore of Lake Superior and Lake Nipigon was in the area northwest of Lake Superior.

By 1767 the pattern of commerce was shifting to the west. The total value of merchandise in 121 canoes that set out from Michilimackinac between July and September 1767 was £38,964 sterling ($7,792,800).

The canoes went to the north and west. Half of the canoes went to the Mississippi and Green Bay and 32 went to the northwest and Lake Superior.

| Destination | Canoes | Value of Goods |
|---|---|---|
| Lake Superior | 18 | £7,481 |
| Northwest via Lake Superior | 14 | 5,117 |
| Lake Huron | 5 | 1,275 |
| Lake Michigan | 24 | 6,875 |
| Green Bay | 43 | 13,364 |
| Mississippi River | 17 | 4,850 |
| Total | 121 | £38,964[7] |

Only 29 went to the older established areas around Lake Michigan and Lake Huron. The value of goods sent to the west increased from £4,170 sterling in the 1761 estimate to a remarkable £18,214 in 1767, indicating a major movement of merchandise to Illinois. The value of merchandise sent to Lake Superior increased somewhat, from £4,580 in the 1761 estimate to £6,392 in 1767. The Lake Michigan total increased from £2,500 to £5,117. In the 1760s the value of goods at Michilimackinac itself was £18,280 sterling ($3,656,000), compared to only £10,420 sterling in the French estimate.[8]

About 100 canoes left Montreal each year for the west. Governor Guy Carleton estimated the average canoe was worth 7,000 livres ($56,000) in 1754 and increased to 9,000 livres (£360 sterling or $72,000) in 1768.[9] The number of canoes sent by French merchants primarily up the Ottawa River to Michilimackinac rose during the period 1765 to 1768. In 1767, 139 canoes have been identified, but there may have been some duplication as a few canoes were reported in both Montreal and Mackinac.[10] On the basis of these statistics the total value of the goods sent west from Montreal in 100 canoes in an average year was about £36,000 sterling ($7,200,000) and that number had increased to £48,960 ($9,792,000) by 1767. Canada and the Northwest constituted a growing market for British manufactured goods.

The impact of the changes from 1764 to 1768 is revealed in the trading licenses that have been preserved. The licenses for fur trading canoes show an average cargo value of £400 sterling ($80,000). In 1769, 77 licenses were issued to trade in Canada. Detroit was the destination of 22; Michilimackinac was listed on 26; Canada was on 22; and the remainder were for points northwest of Michilimackinac.[11] The total value of merchandise and rum carried by these canoes was about £27,720 sterling ($5,500,000), and that did not include the value of the foodstuffs provided by the farmers in Detroit. The enormous volume of trade at Michilimackinac was estimated at 25 canoes (£8,750 or $1,750,000), equal to the combined trade at Detroit and Niagara.

The expansion of commerce by all parties in the Northwest began as soon as peace was restored in 1764. During the 1760s the area northwest of Michilimackinac was explored and trade opened with new tribes of Indians. A temporary abundance in game in the area south of Detroit was created by the limited amount of hunting and trapping during the Seven Years War and Pontiac's Uprising, but that source soon dwindled. As the demand for fur increased, new sources were needed. The rivers and lakes northwest of Lake Superior led to hunting grounds that had not been exploited. There was competition from the Hudson Bay Company, where Indians of the area took some pelts to various factories of the company, but the number was minimal, considering the potential of the area. The Indians preferred that the traders travel to them; that suited the French traders from Michilimackinac, whose dealings with the tribes were more amicable.

The crucial element in the Northwest was time because of the long cold winters in the 1760s. Lake Superior was almost free of ice by 10 June, but as early as the end of September the onset of winter made paddling canoes very risky. In contrast, Lake Michigan and Lake Huron had a longer season, opening about 20 May and remaining navigable until the end of October. Lake Erie was open even earlier, usually from 15 April, and navigable to the end of November.[12] In the Northwest traders from Montreal went to Michilimackinac in June to meet winterers from the Indian villages, providing them with new merchandise. Other traders paddled to Grand Portage and elsewhere in Lake Superior. In September the French traders would return to Michilimackinac to pay their bills with some of their pelts and then return to Montreal via the Ottawa River route. The winterers were on a different schedule and would pay their debts the following summer, when they arrived for more merchandise. In late August 1769 Benjamin Roberts, then in Michilimackinac, waited for the next ship for Detroit because people who owed him had not yet returned.[13]

All across the frontier the Indians were in drastic need of European goods by 1765, as trade had been cut off for several years. Therefore, in 1765 the merchants at Michilimackinac petitioned the post commander, Captain William Howard, quickly to reopen trade, which in former years had produced £90,000 sterling.[14] In 1762 the British had established posts at Sault Ste. Marie, Kamanestaque, and Chequamegon, but these had been closed by Pontiac's Uprising.[15] In 1765 at Chequamegon Bay (on the south shore of Lake Superior) Alexander Henry found the Indians wearing deerskin trousers again because they had no source of the much more comfortable woolen trousers. Deerskin becomes extremely harsh after being soaked and dried, a common condition for Indians around the Great Lakes, who used canoes constantly. Wearing deerskin was a clear indication of the desperate need for European goods in 1765.

The main port of entry to Canada was Quebec, although ships could navigate the St. Lawrence as far as Montreal, where many ships went directly. In 1768 fifteen ships arrived in Quebec from Great Britain; seven from southern Europe, Africa, and the West Indies; and seventeen from the thirteen colonies. The vessels from Britain averaged 150 tons and were probably full-rigged ships. The smaller ones from the colonies averaged 60 tons and were probably schooners and sloops. The seven from the other areas averaged 100 tons and probably were both ships and schooners.[16]

A similar number of ships returned to southern Europe, Africa, Great Britain, the West Indies, and the thirteen colonies. The shipment of furs to

England from Quebec was accomplished by a few ships before the ice blocked the river. In 1764 eight vessels together (*Ranger, General Murray, Canada, London, Nancy, Little William, Eltham,* and *Royal George*) took about 91,000 beaver, 30,000 martin, 25,000 raccoon, and 15,000 deerskins.[17] These shipments were the majority of the furs and skins exported from Quebec that year.

As soon as the river was free of ice again in the spring, the ships from Britain, New York, and Philadelphia moved up the St. Lawrence River.[18] Ships that arrived before the river was clear waited at Halifax in Nova Scotia and usually traveled up river in a convoy. Before the annual convoy, daring ship captains took a chance and sailed to Quebec, and their goods were sold at higher prices before the market was glutted.[19]

Only a slim profit could be expected by the New York and Philadelphia merchants importing goods from Britain and reshipping to Quebec. Goods sold in Quebec at 45% more than their cost in Philadelphia, but the shipping cost was 30% of the value, reducing the profit margin to 15%. The Philadelphia merchants were still able to profit considerably because included in their shipments was a large quantity of the ever welcome rum, which sold at 3/- ($30) per gallon. Baynton and Wharton sold £5,000 Pennsylvania ($575,000) worth of goods in Quebec and Montreal from 1761 to 1765.[20]

There was a rapid influx of British and colonial merchants into Canada after the French surrendered in 1760. Merchants from Britain, Connecticut, New York, New Jersey, and Pennsylvania tried to profit from selling goods on the frontier. Some Jewish merchants did so as well. The merchants employed discharged officers from both the British army and the provincial militia, who contributed experience in dealing with the Indians. Many were Scottish officers discharged in Canada and encouraged not to return to Britain, where they were in disfavor because of their support of Prince Charles, the Stuart Pretender to the throne.[21] Johnson described the British and colonial traders in Montreal as the dregs of society, former colonial militia officers and men from other parts of the British Empire, all of them cheats.[22] The bad opinion of the British and colonial traders endured as late as 1773. The commandant, Henry Basset, at Detroit described them as the outcasts of all nations and the refuse of mankind.[23]

One must remember the deep seated prejudice of the upper class in England against the Scots in the eighteenth century. The aristocratic English officers disliked the Scots because of their support of the Catholic Prince Charles and the attempt to overthrow George II in 1745. Had Prince Charles succeeded, many of the British who had obtained land as a result of the Protestant Glorious Revolution in 1688 would have suffered.

The Scottish regiments had been formed during the Seven Years War and were sent to America to rid Britain of some of the troublesome Scottish lairds and their followers. Another fortuitous step was to disband the regiments in Canada rather than return them to Britain. The former officers had experience on the frontier, but many lacked business skill and left Canada by 1767.[24]

The British and colonials had several advantages: contacts in England for goods, more capital than the French merchants who supplied the traders taking canoes west, and government favor.[25] The British government policy was influenced by Lord Bute, a Scot, who was George III's closest adviser. The Scottish members of Parliament sought to protect the interests of their countrymen in Canada.[26]

In 1764 there were two hundred British and colonial adults in Quebec and Montreal and four hundred by 1767. By 1766 as many as fifty-six business firms in London were trading in Canada.[27] There were about thirty British and colonials in Montreal in 1765, and the number increased gradually to fifty in 1774.[28]

Competition developed between the British and colonial merchants as an aftermath of Pontiac's Uprising. The French made favorable business connections with British merchants and through them ordered goods directly from Britain at lower prices than the colonials offered. However, the colonial merchants retained the near monopoly on liquor even though the British imported some cheap brandy from England.

The French Canadians used their rivers and lakes to ship merchandise to the frontier and to return the furs. The route to the interior from Quebec by way of the St. Lawrence River was deep enough for seagoing vessels to move west as far as Montreal. The city was the commercial capital of Canada with a population of about 10,000. The investment in the town was substantial, considering the damage from the fire in 1765 estimated at from £88,000 to £300,000 ($17,600,000 to $60,000,000).[29]

Although direct trade with the Indians in Montreal continued in the 1760s, the major functions of Montreal were preparing goods for shipment up country and returning furs east to Quebec for overseas shipment. Most of the goods from Montreal were sent up the Ottawa River. The route began by wagon from Montreal to La Chine. Usually the goods arrived at Montreal in May and were divided into packs and small kegs ready to be taken by the annual flotilla up the Ottawa River. The departure of the flotilla, which included up to one hundred canoes, was a gala day in the life of eighteenth-century Canada and was marked by farewells to some men who would not return for several years.[30]

The French had adopted the Indian means of transport in Canada. Two types of birch bark canoes were in common use, the master canoe and the Northwest canoe. The master canoe, 35 to 40 feet long, 4 to 5 feet wide, and 2½ to 3 feet deep, was used both on the lakes and on the Ottawa River routes.[31] Paddled by up to eight with two passengers, its capacity was 65 packs of from 90 to 100 pounds each for a total of three or four tons. On a trip up the Ottawa River, a canoe also carried 600 pounds of biscuit, 200 pounds of pork, 3 bushels of peas, 2 oilcloths to protect the goods from the weather, a sail and rigging, an axe, a tow line, a kettle, a sponge for bailing, gum, birch bark, and watape to repair the canoe. These provisions would last for ten weeks.[32] In

1768 one master canoe carried 8 men, 20 barrels of "de Boisson" liquor, 400 pounds of gunpowder, 1,400 pounds of ball and shot, and 12 fusils. Another canoe carried 12 men with 110 gallons of rum, 110 gallons of wine, 800 pounds of gunpowder, 1,400 pounds of ball and shot, and 6 fusils.[33]

The rough wear on the master canoes, costing £15 in Montreal, limited their use to a maximum of two years and often only a year. The number of paddlers was apportioned according to the weight carried and the direction, with or against the current. Moving north on the Ottawa River, the canoes carried at least six men; moving south with the current, the number was reduced to four or five.[34] Operating the canoes was hard work. Each night the canoe was completely unloaded and beached. The trip from La Chine to Michilimackinac took 35 to 40 days.[35]

Portages between navigable streams were sometimes made in carts, on horses, or carried by Indian porters as at Niagara and on the Wabash route. For the most part, however, the packs were carried on the backs of the voyageurs, the canoe men. A sling was placed across the forehead to support one pack on the back. Novices carried a single ninety-pound load, but the experienced men carried one or two additional packs placed on top of the first to reduce the number of trips across the portage. Each man would have to carry at least six packs to the next stream, and the old hands did this in two or three trips. The canoe was removed from the water immediately and allowed to dry as long as possible. It was the last item carried across the portage because the drier the canoe the lighter it was to carry.[36]

The wages of the canoe men varied with experience. In 1768 a steersman or *Gouvenail* received for a round trip £8.7/ sterling ($1,670) and a front man or *Avant* received the same. The middlemen were farm boys, called *mangeur de lard* (fat eater, because they were unaccustomed to the spartan diet of the voyageurs), who hired on for one or two years. They received only £5 to £6 sterling ($1,000 to $1,200). The wages for one canoe were about £66 ($13,200) plus provisions and a clothing allowance that included *metasses* (moccasins) and a *Brique* or *Arse Clout*.[37]

The canoes went up the Ottawa River to Lake Nipissing, the French River, and Georgian Bay. From there they went to Michilimackinac or to Lake Superior. The advantage of the Ottawa River route was a shorter and quicker trip than the lake route even though there were forty carrying places between Montreal and Michilimackinac. The portages were necessary to go around rapids as well as to move from one river to another. Another advantage of the Ottawa River route compared to the Great Lakes was avoidance of the storms that periled shipping on the lakes. Also the Ottawa route opened earlier than the lakes. In December 1767 when Sir William Johnson ordered Major Robert Rogers to return to Michilimackinac, Rogers was told to take the Ottawa River route, which was generally open some time before the ice cleared from the Niagara River.[38] When the ice on shallow Lake Erie broke up in the spring, the prevailing westerly wind piled it up at the east end of the lake and jammed the Niagara River. Many days of warm weather were needed to melt the accumulated ice pack.

The Ottawa River route also remained open later in the fall, when the time of arrival in Montreal and Quebec was crucial in order to load peltry on board ships to Europe before the St. Lawrence froze. The Ottawa River was more reliable, an important factor because delay could mean disaster if the furs had be held in Canada until the next spring.[39] During the winter letters from Michilimackinac were carried by canoe as far as the lakes were not frozen and then by riders to New York. The port of New York City did not freeze and ships could enter during the winter.[40]

While the colonial merchants and the Scots gained an ever greater share of the wholesale trade in Montreal, the French retained a tight grip on direct trade with the Indians. The merchandise left Montreal in French hands. A few canoes would be sent over the lakes to Detroit, but after 1764 the competition of the French traders from Illinois and the British and colonial merchants from Albany made Detroit less profitable than the trade from Michilimackinac. After 1764 the British merchants played the role of wholesaler, which was based on their connections in England, while the French controlled the other steps of the trade, which were based on lasting relationships with the small traders who dealt with the Indians.[41]

Some of the goods were carried across Lake Ontario to the lower lakes area. After a wagon trip to La Chine to bypass the rapids, the bales, packs, and barrels of merchandise crossed Lake Ontario to Niagara by schooner or whaleboat. The merchandise was transported around Niagara Falls by using the incline machine built by the British army in 1764 to move packs up the Niagara Escarpment. After reaching the top of the escarpment, the packs were moved by wagon to a dock on the upper Niagara River and loaded on schooners to be carried up the Great Lakes.

In 1767 nearly a fifth of the furs from Michilimackinac were returned to Albany and New York via the Great Lakes. Forty traders sent packs of fur from Michilimackinac; twenty-nine French and British merchants sent their packs to Montreal; and thirteen colonial merchants sent theirs to Albany.[42] The Albany shipments were much smaller: of 124,247 pelts and skins sent from the Michilimackinac area, only 28,643 went to New York.[43] In 1768 a French trader, Chabert, sought to send his furs to Montreal and his deerskin to Albany.[44] There was great flexibility in the use of routes as merchants searched for goods at the lowest price and tried to find the best market for furs.

The existence of the two routes was a headache to the British and colonial merchants in Michilimackinac because at times French traders would purchase goods on credit from an Albany merchant in Michilimackinac in the spring, trade them, and then send the furs to Montreal in the fall via the Ottawa River to be sold without paying the colonial merchant.[45] Baynton and Wharton suffered from the French failure to pay in Quebec and Montreal. Collins and Govet, agents for Baynton and Wharton in Quebec, had managed affairs poorly, and in March 1765 a new agent, Samuel Eldridge, was forced to auction off the remaining goods for £6,652 Pennsylvania ($765,000).[46] The former agents refused to pay the amounts collected for previous orders, and the local French merchants were unwilling to pay their debts; some declared bankruptcy to avoid payment. As a result, Baynton and Wharton received only 15% to 25% of the amount owed them by the French for sums ranging from £100 to £500 Pennsylvania ($57,500). In December 1765, eight months later, Eldridge was still attempting to collect from Collins and Govet and trying to explain the problems to Richard Neave in London, who had supplied much of the merchandise in question.[47] However, despite the problem of collecting from the French, Eldridge ordered more rum from Philadelphia because it was still in demand and very profitable.[48]

This same problem of collecting from the French for merchandise sold on credit by colonial merchants made the Michilimackinac exits to the Mississippi River very troublesome. There were five routes from Michilimackinac: one from Lake Erie via the Miami, Wabash, and Ohio Rivers; two from St. Joseph via the Wabash and the Ohio or via the Kankakee River; one using the Chicago River; and the route from Green Bay using the Fox and Wisconsin Rivers. Using these routes, a considerable amount of fur from the Northwest was diverted to Illinois and New Orleans.[49]

Because of the risks and the many hands through which goods and furs passed before the final sale of the fur in London, the profits were not as great as might be assumed. For example, a bundle of tobacco from Brazil purchased in Lisbon and sent to London would be purchased by the agent of a Montreal merchant. The tobacco was shipped to Montreal, where it was placed in ninety-pound packs. The Montreal merchant would engage voyageurs to take the tobacco and other items to Michilimackinac to be transferred to a Northwest canoe and sent to Grand Portage. From there it would be taken up the smaller rivers into the wilderness to be traded to the Indians for fur. The fur would then follow the path in reverse until it reached the agent in London, who would sell the fur at auction, probably to a European buyer, and exported. At that point credits would begin to flow back to all those who had taken part. As the prices fluctuated greatly throughout the transaction, fortunes could be made, lost, and remade within a few years.

High wages contributed to small margins of profit. The cost of liquor, provisions, canoes, and repacking of the goods unloaded from the ships plus the wages of the voyageurs were half the total investment. In 1780 an estimated £750 sterling was made of the total costs of a venture of a single canoe. The dry goods at Montreal cost £300 sterling plus an additional charge of 50% for a total of £450 sterling. Two hundred gallons of rum and wine cost £50 for a total value of £500 ($100,000) in goods. The cost of taking the canoe from Montreal to Michilimackinac was £160. Taking the canoe to Grand Portage was an additional £90, including wages and provisions for eight canoe men and two clerks who would winter with the Indians and trade the goods for fur. The total investment for the canoe was £750 sterling ($150,000).[50]

The cost of returning the fur to Montreal was another charge. In 1768 the average freight charge to move a ninety-pound pack from Michilimackinac to Montreal by way of the Ottawa River was £1.10 sterling ($300).[51] Though slower, shipping the less valuable deerskin by schooner to Oswego and then on to Albany and New York was much cheaper.

The primary destination of the canoes sent up the Ottawa River was Michilimackinac. After the post was captured by the Indians in 1763, it was reestablished in September 1764 by two companies of the 17th Regiment. In 1765 the garrison was a detachment of the 17th Regiment under the command of Captain William Howard, whose first priority was making peace with the Chippewas, the Ottawas, and other tribes.

In 1765 the Indians were pacified, with the exception of one tribe.[52] Always a problem was the resentment of the Indians encouraged by the French from Illinois. In December 1764 Howard reported that the Chippewa Indians obtained ammunition from the French on the west side of Lake Michigan and also that Indians were intercepting the boats from Detroit to Michilimackinac.[53] In May 1765 Howard sent Baptiste Cadot with a belt to show the Indians at Sault Ste. Marie that the Delaware and Shawnee had made peace with the British.[54] However, in April 1765 the relentless French in Illinois had sent a false message to the Indians at Michilimackinac that the French army had retaken Quebec and driven the English up to Montreal. The same message questioned what the Indians would do to survive after selling all their furs to the British for rum.[55]

Despite the French lies, many Indians traveled to Michilimackinac in the summer of 1765 to sell their furs, along with several hundred winterers, who also made an annual trip to the post after spending the winter in the Indian villages.[56] The Indians had been deprived of merchandise during Pontiac's Uprising and were sorely in need. In June Baptiste Cadot escorted eighty canoes of Indians from Lake Superior, whom he had bribed with gifts of tobacco. More Indians were expected later.[57] By the end of June over 700 Indians were at Michilimackinac, most of them from north of Lake Superior. In a successful exchange, they had a large quantity of fur and the merchants had a good supply of merchandise.[58]

In the following years the Michilimackinac trade changed to a wholesale operation. Merchandise was taken there by canoe from Montreal by a merchant and was sold to Michilimackinac merchants, who in turn outfitted canoes to trade to the west and northwest of Lake Superior. The merchants were mostly French. In 1765 28 traders signed a petition at Michilimackinac protesting the army rules. The signers included 22 Frenchmen, 5 British and colonials, and 1 Jew, Solomon & Company.[59]

Even though outnumbered by the French, the British had more political influence. Among the members of a court of inquiry in Michilimackinac in 1767, nine were British or colonial and only four were French, indicating that the British merchants were the dominant political force. The British and colonial traders, including John Christie, Stephen Groesbeck, John Porteus, Benjamin Frobisher, John Chinn, Alexander Henry, John Oakes, William Maxwell, and John Askin, were often mentioned in the records, and most of them had provided security for French traders who received licenses to take canoes to Michilimackinac. British merchants, including Benjamin Frobisher, Isaac Todd, Alexander Henry, Forrest Oakes, and James Finlay, acted as guarantors for the French traders: that is, they signed the licenses ensuring that the French traders would abide by the British rules.[60]

The British in Michilimackinac had contacts in Britain and a greater supply of capital than the French. In 1767 the French traders outnumbered the British by four to one, but the total British investment was higher than the French. The twelve British and colonial merchants had merchandise valued at a total of £22,000 New York ($2,772,000), compared to a total of only £16,000 New York ($2,016,000) owned by the forty French merchants.[61]

Wintering was the major bone of contention in Michilimackinac. The French custom had been to send men to the villages to spend the winter selling goods for furs as soon as the animals were trapped. The French winterers or *hivernants* formed ties to the Indians and often adopted their way of life, marrying Indian women and spending each winter in the same village.[62] Although the French charged higher prices than the colonial traders who tried to compete in the villages, the French gave presents to their Indian friends to cement their friendship.[63]

When trade was reopened at Michilimackinac in 1765 after the end of Pontiac's Uprising, the French wanted to resume wintering in spite of British army rules to the contrary. Captain William Howard, the commandant at Michilimackinac, immediately was faced with the problem as the French had wintered near Chicago and St. Joseph in 1764 and Edward Chinn, a British trader, had wintered with the Ottawas.[64] In July 1765 British and French merchants petitioned Howard, requesting that wintering be permitted on the basis that if they could not winter legally, others would take over the trade illegally.[65] Despite the prohibition on wintering in 1765, some traders did so anyway, leaving the fort at midnight. When they were caught, their goods were confiscated. In early August 1765, a canoe load of rum, smuggled out of the fort bound for Green Bay, which could buy a great deal of fur, placed the traders involved in great danger.[66]

Captain Howard granted permission in June 1765 for a few French and British traders to winter at the villages in response to the Indians' appeal. The Indians requested that some traders return with them to the north to winter.[67] He allowed Cadot to go to LaPointe on Lake Superior and British traders to go elsewhere.[68] Johnson approved of these exceptions but, still concerned about the Indian attitude, feared that they would rob and murder the British traders.[69]

General Gage believed that wintering should not be allowed because it would enable the French to maintain their hold over the Indians. He also feared that the British traders would be in danger and demand that the British army protect them. Unwilling to permit wintering, Gage believed that eventually the Indians would go to the posts to trade. However, he agreed to allow wintering if Howard considered it essential.[70] In 1766 Gage repeated that wintering was to the advantage of the French in their effort to keep the British out of the fur trade in the upper Great Lakes. The French had close connections with the Indians, spoke their languages, and knew their customs. With this personal knowledge the French had an advantage and would seek to solidify their position and keep the commerce with the Indians under French control.[71]

Johnson continued to oppose wintering because he too thought the French would benefit. He knew that the British traders could not winter because of their fear of being robbed, and therefore the French would take over the entire market. Currently the British merchants were selling to the French, who in turn sold to the Indians, portraying themselves as friends. Naively, Johnson strongly believed that the French could be prevented from wintering and that eventually the cheaper goods at the forts would draw in the Indians.[72]

In March 1766 some Montreal merchants sent Johnson a petition urging that wintering be permitted. The merchants estimated that confining the trade to the posts would be devastating. The volume would be cut in half, reducing it to about thirty canoes (a canoe carried goods worth £375 sterling, $75,000, and thirty canoes would equal £11,250 sterling, $2,250,000). The reduction would also result in the loss of wages by the men who paddled the canoes every summer, estimated at £2,000 sterling ($400,000).[73] Each canoe employed eight farm boys at wages from £5 to £6 sterling each and two experienced men at £9 each for a total of £66. The wages for thirty canoes were nearly £2,000 sterling added to the cost of the goods for a total of £13,250 ($2,650,000).

Rather than reducing the trade, the British were interested in expanding the Michilimackinac market. In early 1766 General Gage ordered Major Robert Rogers, the new commandant, to provide information concerning the Lake Superior area. Rogers quickly developed a scheme to create a new colony south of Lake Superior and sent a personal agent to London to further this scheme in Parliament.[74]

Rogers was not trusted by Gage and Johnson, both of whom believed that he would cause trouble with the Indians. Johnson saw him as weak, vain, and romantic.[75] In June 1766 Gage ordered Johnson to have his interpreters and commissaries watch Rogers and his dealings with the Indians.[76] As anticipated, Rogers began private trading with the Indians.

Rogers gathered a group of questionable allies at Michilimackinac, including Stanley Goddard (a trader who illegally went to Green Bay in 1765 and recruited Indians to fight the colonists for the British during the Revolution), James Tute (a captain of one of the companies who later explored Lake Winnipeg and traded in Illinois), Jonathan Carver (another officer who explored south of Lake Superior), and Atherton (an associate of the Wendell family of merchants from Albany). The group were exploring the water routes from Lake Superior to the

Mississippi River, probably as a route for exporting furs to bypass the rigid controls at Montreal.[77]

The soldiers became involved as well. Because of their profitable trading, the dual duty troops became insolent and refused to perform any work other than guard duty.[78] Johnson was outraged that Rogers should use the troops to further his personal gain.[79] Rogers was also using Indian Department funds illegally to further his scheme and was spending enormous amounts of money to impress the Indians. Among the suppliers at Michilimackinac was Stephen Groesbeck, an Albany trader, who provided security for five canoes licensed to three Frenchmen and two British traders in 1767. In 1766 he had sold £290 New York ($26,334) in presents to Major Robert Rogers, the commander.[80] In February 1767 Groesbeck was owed £429 New York ($54,054) by Major Rogers.[81]

To place some control on Rogers, in January 1767 Sir William Johnson recommended that a commissary be sent to Michilimackinac to manage Indian Department affairs, including distribution of gifts to the Indians.[82] In April 1767 Johnson sent Lieutenant Benjamin Roberts to Michilimackinac to manage Indian affairs as commissary.[83] Roberts arrived in June 1767 with instructions to buy goods from the local merchants to give to the Indians. In April Johnson had received a bill of exchange for £300 sterling ($60,000) from a Montreal merchant for presents ordered by Rogers. Johnson refused to pay and referred the bill to Gage. In May Gage stopped payment on all further expenses incurred by Rogers for gifts to the Indians.[84]

Wintering remained a constant demand by the French. The Montreal merchants petitioned Governor James Murray in April 1767, objecting to the form of the pass given to Isaac Todd, which placed him under the supervision of the Michilimackinac commissary and implied that Todd would not be permitted to winter with the Indians. The merchants presented a long list of complaints, objecting to the commissary; the lack of clear instructions as to how trade was to be conducted; the large quantity of presents in the hands of the commissary, estimated at £40,000 sterling ($8,000,000, a gross exaggeration!) to be given freely to the Indians; the heavy security demanded from each person receiving a license to take a canoe to the west; the forfeiture of this security bond if the commissary claimed that a trader had disobeyed his orders; and, most of all, the confinement of trade to the fort at Michilimackinac.[85]

The French in Quebec favored the limitation of the amount of liquor that each trader might carry west as liquor was the main item of sale by the colonial traders. The French were convinced, on the other hand, that the rule restricting the fur trade to the posts and prohibiting wintering with the Indians would ruin the trade and their livelihood.[86]

In August 1767 both the British and the French merchants at Michilimackinac petitioned Rogers to grant passes to winter with the Indians.[87] The British had finally given in to the demands of the French merchants. In April 1767 Gage had informed Johnson that wintering north of Lake Huron should be permitted because the French would do so with or without permission.[88] In June 1767 Shelburne ordered Johnson to permit free access to the area north of the Ottawa River and the Great Lakes, primarily to open the trade with the tribes located far to the north and west, who would not travel to the post to trade in any event.[89]

Even before the restriction was lifted officially, in August 1767, despite efforts to stop them, about 300 traders and canoe men had taken a large quantity of rum and other merchandise to Grand Portage at the west end of Lake Superior. This number of men would have taken at least thirty canoes with approximately £12,000 sterling ($2,400,000) in merchandise, a major share of the Michilimackinac trade. Few Indians from the northwest continued on to Michilimackinac, and therefore, the British and colonial merchants obtained but a small share of the fur.[90]

In response to the merchants' unyielding demands, Rogers granted passes to winter.[91] The right to winter was restricted to Michilimackinac and supposedly to the shore of Lake Superior.[92] However, some of the traders took advantage of the situation and went on to Illinois, where they sold both the fur they had collected and any remaining trade goods to the Illinois French.[93] The Detroit merchants protested the favoritism granted to the Michilimackinac merchants and demanded that they also be granted passes to winter. Jehu Hay, the Indian Department commissary at Detroit, explained that the exception was limited to wintering north of Michilimackinac and that he could grant no passes to winter in the Detroit area.[94]

Rogers continued to purchase numerous presents for the Indians in June, July, and August 1767 from merchants at Michilimackinac.[95] Major Rogers was lavish in his distribution of gifts in 1767, and the merchants complained that the Indians received their wants free from the army. Rogers told Johnson that the gifts were an effort to make peace with the Sioux and the Chippewa. Warfare between the tribes did reduce the amount of fur available and seriously diminished the trade at Michilimackinac, resulting in a shortage of fur in New York. Johnson did not believe giving presents to prevent Indian warfare was a good policy. He thought that Rogers was spending the money to gain favor with the Michilimackinac merchants as well as to impress the Indians. By September the total of the bills received by Johnson was over £5,000 New York ($630,000).[96]

Roberts, the commissary, tried to stop the expense and was soon at odds with Rogers. Even the merchants began to complain, fearing that Rogers would go off to Illinois, leaving the unpaid bills behind. One of Rogers's officers, Fred Spiesmaker, blamed Roberts, saying that before Roberts arrived, both merchants and Indians were content and that the complaints began with the presence of Roberts.[97]

The scale of financial impact of Rogers's purchases can be realized when compared to the total amount of trade merchandise sent to Michilimackinac each year. Usually about one hundred canoe loads of merchandise valued at £375 sterling each or a total of £37,500 ($7,500,000) left Montreal each year bound for Michilimackinac and Lake Superior.[98] From July to September 1767, 121 canoes left for destinations centering around Michilimackinac with goods valued at £38,964 sterling ($7,792,800). Most of these canoes merely passed through Michilimackinac, but still the total amount of its business was around £20,000 sterling ($4,000,000). In June and July 1767 Rogers spent over £5,000 New York ($630,000) on gifts, one-sixth of the total business at Michilimackinac.[99] The merchandise from British and colonial merchants in Michilimackinac was given to the Indians, who were then less willing to pay the traditional high prices for the merchandise being offered by the French merchants. The gifts did not interfere with the French who went to Lake Superior but must have caused a major economic loss to the French merchants who expected to trade with the Indians who went to Michilimackinac. Needless to say, the gifts antagonized the French, from whom Rogers purchased very little.

By mid-September Rogers was ordered to go to Detroit, where Croghan gave him an order removing him from command at Michilimackinac.[100] Gage had evidence that Rogers intended to cheat the merchants at Michilimackinac by purchasing merchandise with bills he knew would not be paid by Gage and then deserting to the French in Illinois. Rogers was guilty of mismanagement and had disobeyed instructions to curtail expenses. Gage had evidence to support his suspicions, a letter from the Spanish inviting Rogers to join the French.[101]

When Rogers left, the only officers remaining were Captain Fred Spiesmaker and John Christie, who reported to Johnson that all was peaceful in October but that the Indians had been promised that many presents would be awaiting when they traveled to Michilimackinac in the spring of 1768.[102]

Spiesmaker continued to purchase presents for the Indians in 1767 and 1768 for £413 New York ($52,038) from John Wetherhead, a New York merchant who was active in supplying the Indian Department in Detroit and Michilimackinac.[103] These sums are but a small fraction of the total business at Michilimackinac, less than 2% of the £38,000 New York of the total value of the canoes licensed in 1767. The small value of the presents had little if any impact on the total business of the area.

In November 1767 merchants from Michilimackinac were in Detroit pleading for Johnson to pay them for Rogers's purchases.[104] After Rogers was dismissed from his post, the merchants had great difficulty collecting from Sir William Johnson, leading some to bankruptcy.[105] By February 1768 Johnson had received bills totaling £4,852 New York ($611,000) from merchants in Michilimackinac. Gage refused to pay the bills on the grounds that the merchants knew Rogers had orders to cut expenses.[106] Furthermore, paying the bills would encourage merchants everywhere to convince post commanders to make unlimited purchases.[107]

Still to be faced were the Indians, who expected another round of lavish gifts when they arrived in Michilimackinac in the spring of 1768. Rogers had excused his expenditures as being used unsuccessfully to stop a war between the

Sioux and Chippewa. Clearly the Indians saw that they could extract gifts if they promised to stop fighting. Promises and unkept promises resulted in continual warfare.[108]

In August 1768 Phyn and Ellice received a report from Detroit that very little fur or deerskin was available, as the Chippewa and the western Indians were at war and therefore did not take peltry to trade in Michilimackinac.[109] At Michilimackinac the clever Indians requested gifts of rum, tobacco, and ammunition in return for remaining peaceful. Captain Beamsley Glazier, the new post commander in 1768, responded that they should take in fur to exchange for their needs. However, in the end Glazier acquiesced and supplied them with food and some rum.[110]

Gage intended to court martial Rogers for his activities. A French merchant, Joseph Ainse, in May 1768 provided information that Rogers would try to escape. Rogers was placed in irons and sent on a ship to Detroit. Ainse had been hired by Rogers in the spring of 1767 as an interpreter, but Ainse claimed later that the disloyal Rogers wanted him to go to Illinois to invite the French to take Michilimackinac with Rogers's help.[111]

Rogers was taken to trial in Montreal but was confident of acquittal. His self-confidence was rewarded when on 30 October 1768, he was found not guilty even though the British judge was suspicious of his behavior. Rogers was not reinstated in his command at Michilimackinac. Gage was astonished that the trial had become a political matter; presumably the French merchants had urged his conviction and the British merchants had defended him.[112] With the departure of Rogers, expenses at Michilimackinac returned to a more reasonable level.

Michilimackinac was the depot for the great Northwest trade that fanned out to sub-centers, including Green Bay, Grand Portage, and smaller centers at St. Joseph, Milwaukee, and Sault Ste. Marie. Lake Huron was not a significant area: its trade was estimated at only two canoes (about £700 or $140,000) in 1768. Saginaw Bay, which separated the thumb of Michigan from the rest of the peninsula, was also a minor post, estimated at three canoes in 1767.

Lake Michigan was far more important than Lake Huron with major trading points at Green Bay and Milwaukee on the west shore and St. Joseph, Kalamazoo, and LaGrand Riviere on the east shore. The major trading point on the west shore was Green Bay. The British had placed a garrison there prior to Pontiac's Uprising. French traders purchased supplies in Michilimackinac, went to Green Bay, and then used the Fox River route to reach the Mississippi River, where they competed with the traders from Illinois.[113]

In the period 1765 to 1768 Green Bay was the most profitable region on the Great Lakes. In 1765 Captain Howard at Michilimackinac reported that winterers had 50,000 livres ($200,000) in merchandise at Green Bay in February 1765 before the Michilimackinac traders had reached the area.[114] Although the total was estimated at thirty canoes annually, in 1767 43 canoes left Michilimackinac for Green Bay led by 27 French traders and 2 British. The value of merchandise carried was £13,364 ($2,672,800). Of this total, 17 canoes were destined for the Mississippi with merchandise valued at £4,850 ($970,000).[115]

Also on the west shore of Lake Michigan was a trading point at Milwaukee with trade estimated at eight canoes in 1767, merchandise worth about £2,800 ($560,000). There was also activity at Chicago on a route from Lake Michigan to Illinois.

The east shore of Lake Michigan was also active in this period. In the summer of 1767, 24 canoes left Michilimackinac bound for the east shore of Lake Michigan with £6,875 ($1,375,000) in merchandise. Four of the traders were British and the others French, although a third of the traders were secured by British merchants in Michilimackinac, indicating that the British and colonials had a larger investment in the business. Nineteen of the canoes were bound for St. Joseph; three other villages were the destination of one or two canoes.[116]

St. Joseph, located on the east shore of Lake Michigan, was the center of trade on the southeast coast of Lake Michigan. The trade was estimated at eight canoes (about £2,800 or $560,000) in 1767. The competition between the British and colonial traders from Detroit and Michilimackinac and the French from Illinois was intense at St. Joseph. During Pontiac's Uprising, the French had encouraged the Indians to rob and kill the colonial merchants and give their merchandise to the French. After the uprising, the French refused to compensate the colonial merchants, including Fred Hambuck, who requested that the army seize the canoes of the French merchants at Michilimackinac.[117]

After 1765 the French from Illinois continued to compete at St. Joseph. In January 1765 Sergeant LaGrandeure from Illinois was at St. Joseph with ammunition, tobacco, flour, and rum to buy fur from the Indians.[118] In 1767 there were forty French traders at St. Joseph, some from Michilimackinac and some from Illinois. The French traders were sending their agents to winter illegally with the Indians in their villages and obtaining the major share of the fur.[119] In 1767 nineteen canoes were sent to St. Joseph by the French and British merchants at Michilimackinac, 20% of the total. Combined with the large number of canoes sent to Lake Superior, Michilimackinac was getting a poor share. The French from Illinois were taking many of the furs.[120]

The French continued to control the St. Joseph area throughout the period 1765 to 1768 through their influence with the local Pottawatomi Indians, who prevented any colonial or British merchants from trading there. As a result of the French intrigue at St. Joseph, the Pottawatomi were the only tribe still at war with the British in 1769.[121]

While Lake Michigan received most of the canoes during this period, the greatest rate of expansion occurred in the area northwest of Lake Superior. The animals were plentiful because few traders had reached the area and therefore the Indians had no incentive to trap large numbers. The Indians west of Grand Portage were eager to have merchandise previously unavailable, especially guns and clothing, and could easily trap enough beaver to pay for it.

Although most of the traders going to Lake Superior were French, some were British and colonial. In 1767 among the Frenchmen were Baby, Chabouillet, Deriviere, and Chenville. Among the British and colonials were Isaac Todd, McGill, Alexander Henry, and Groesbeck.[122] In 1769 Maurice Blondeau led three canoes from Michilimackinac to Lake Superior with nineteen men, 320 gallons of rum and wine, 800 pounds of powder, 14 hundredweight of buckshot and balls, 24 guns, and miscellaneous cloth and metal wares for a total value of £1,350 ($270,000 and an average of £450 per canoe).[123]

The French were active on the south shore of Lake Superior. In 1767 the trade at La Riviere, LaPointe, and Chequamegon (near present day Ashland, Wisconsin) was estimated at eight canoes (about £4,000, $800,000), a very lucrative trade at much less risk than the northwest. On 7 July 1767 a convoy of fourteen canoes left Michilimackinac bound for Lake Superior under the control of five French traders, two of whom were supplied by English merchants and three by French merchants, with goods valued at £5,117 sterling ($1,013,400). During the next few days five more canoes under four French traders all supplied by French merchants left Michilimackinac bound for Lake Huron with merchandise valued at £1,275 sterling ($255,000).[124] The average value of a canoe varied from £365 ($73,100) for the Lake Superior canoes to £255 sterling ($51,000) for the Lake Huron canoes. The canoes carried 1.5 to 2 tons.[125] Major Rogers estimated the average value of a Northwest canoe's cargo at £450 New York (£283.10 sterling or $56,700) and listed a sample cargo:

18 bales of stroud, blankets, frieze, coats, bed gowns,   coarse   calicoes, linen shirts, leggings, ribbons, beads, vermillion, and garters.
9 kegs of gunpowder
1 keg of flint steels and gun screws
10 kegs of British brandy
4 cases of iron work and cutlery
1 box of silver work and wampum
2 cases of guns
2 bales of brass kettles
2 cases of looking glasses and combs
5 bales of tobacco
10 bags of lead buckshot and ball ammunition[126]

In 1765 Alexander Henry purchased four Northwest canoes and goods worth £1,250 sterling ($250,000), an average per canoe of £312 sterling; hired twelve men at £150 ($30,000); and purchased fifty bushels of corn for provisions for £62.10 ($12,500), a total investment of £1,462.10 sterling ($292,500). Rather than paying cash, he promised to pay for his supplies, equipment, and wages with 11,700 pounds of beaver pelts valued at 2/6d ($25) per pound with a total value of £1,462 sterling.[127]

He led his four canoes into Lake Michigan, sent a clerk to winter at Fond du Lac with one canoe, and established himself at Chequamegon for the winter. The next summer he returned to Montreal and sold most of his furs at a profit for £1,875 ($375,000) with twenty-five packs remaining valued at £450 ($90,000) for a total of £2,325 sterling ($465,000), a profit of a little more than 50%, £862.10 ($172,500), well worth the risk.[128]

Although French explorers had traveled as far west as the Missouri River in the 1730s, the more profitable trade was conducted nearer to Lake Superior. Sault Ste. Marie was on the strait that connected Lake Superior to the other Great Lakes. In 1767 the level of trade there was estimated at two canoes, roughly £900 sterling ($180,000). The post had been established in 1751 by the French to discourage the Indians from Lake Superior from going east to Oswego on Lake Ontario to trade with the New Yorkers. In 1762 the British also established a small post at Sault Ste. Marie.[129] Lake Superior had other small trading posts scattered along its shores. Kaministikwia or Three Rivers, located 30 miles east of Grand Portage near present Fort William, was estimated at three canoes in 1767.[130]

The most significant destination in Lake Superior was Grand Portage, located on the north shore of Lake Superior. The British and colonial merchants sent agents to Grand Portage to manage their affairs. Isaac Todd had a man at Grand Portage in 1767 and Phyn and Ellice employed as their agent John Porteus, who later worked for Isaac Todd.[131]

A comparatively short portage connected Lake Superior to the Pigeon River and Rainy Lake, about 150 miles west of Grand Portage. The French built Fort Pierre on the Rainy Lake in 1731 and in 1765 the first British traders reached the area, although the Indians stole all their goods. The same misfortune occurred the next year. In 1767 the Rainy Lake trade was estimated at six small canoes, perhaps £1,800 sterling ($360,000). After 1767 the Indians allowed the traders from Michilimackinac to leave some of their merchandise to be traded during the winter by agent. The Indians also allowed the canoes to go farther west to Lake Winnipeg.

Before reaching Lake Winnipeg, canoes had to cross the Lake of the Woods, the next major lake west of Rainy Lake. The French built Fort St. Charles on the west shore in 1732.[132] Although it was a large lake, the volume of trade was small in 1767, only two small canoes, about £600 sterling.

After a series of portages and small streams, the Winnipeg River led to Lake Winnipeg. The trade on the Winnipeg River was estimated at three small canoes in 1767, about £900 sterling. To avoid the rapids on the Winnipeg River, the French used the Roseau River leading to the Red River, which flowed north into Lake Winnipeg. The French built Fort Maurepas on the Red River in 1734 and Fort Rouge at the mouth of the river, where it fed into Lake Winnipeg.[133]

In the 1730s the French built Fort LaReine on the south end of Lake Winnipeg, and in 1748 they built Fort Bourbon on the north end of the lake.[134] Fort Dauphin was also located on the west bank at the south end of Lake

Winnipeg and had a volume of trade of three small canoes (£900 sterling) in 1767.

In 1765 after Pontiac's Uprising the French traders returned to Lake Winnipeg.[135] In 1767 the trade at Fort LaReine on Lake Winnipeg was estimated at five small canoes, perhaps £1,500 sterling ($300,000) or more, a substantial business. Other small posts in the area added more than a dozen canoes of business in the 1760s, making the area important in the fur trade.

West of Lake Winnipeg were the Saskatchewan River and the Assiniboine and Blackfeet tribes. The French built Fort LaCorne on the river in 1753, but the Seven Years War and Pontiac's Uprising caused a lull. A French trader, Franceway, reached the area in 1765, but it remained dangerous for British traders. In 1769 Joseph Frobisher was robbed of his merchandise by the Indians. In 1768 James Finlay did winter on the Saskatchewan River, the westward limit of trading activity in the Northwest in the period 1765 to 1768, despite the abundance of fur and the needs of the Indians in the area.[136]

The French traders were beginning to infringe on the territory of the Hudson's Bay Company, which operated a network of "factories" as trading posts. Each year the Indians took their furs to the company factories, providing the company with furs at a minimum risk. Seagoing vessels that sailed into Hudson Bay during the summer months provided merchandise for the northern tribes and left with beaver and other pelts. The Hudson's Bay Company annually exported from 20,000 to 50,000 beaver skins, worth from £5,000 to £12,000 sterling.[137]

The French posts northwest of Lake Superior were closed in 1759, when the British invaded Canada, severing the connection between France and Canada and preventing the fur traders from importing merchandise.[138] However, in 1761, with the reopening of trade after the end of hostilities in Canada and the influx of colonial and British merchants with large quantities of merchandise available to the French, traders once again began to compete with the Hudson's Bay Company. In 1761 the employees of the company complained that the French traders were "as thick as Muskettos" on the rivers flowing south into Lake Superior.[139] The French from the Great Lakes competed with the Hudson's Bay Company by traveling to the hunting grounds and trading for the furs before the Indians made the long voyage north. To combat this development, the company began to establish posts of its own in the interior northwest of Lake Superior.

After a pause during Pontiac's Uprising, the influx of French traders into the Hudson's Bay Company territory resumed. Even though the company had no factories in the area directly west of Lake Superior, the Cree and Assiniboine tribes acted as middlemen, obtaining merchandise from the company factories and then reselling the guns, ammunition, blankets, and other items to the Indians to the west. The French in 1767 were performing in the same way, providing the nearby Indians with merchandise to resell farther west at a rendezvous at Fort LaReine on Lake Winnipeg.[140] In 1767 the Hudson's Bay agents were active in the area northwest of Lake Superior while the French were probing beyond Lake Nipigon. The trade moved west as the supply of animals was exhausted and the competition grew more intense.[141] The French continued to probe company territory, and in 1768 twelve French traders were on the Saskatchewan River.[142] The competition with the Hudson's Bay Company would continue and finally forced the French and British traders from Canada to form the Northwest Company.

However, in the late 1760s the Canadian trade was still for the most part unaffected by the Hudson's Bay Company. The farthest outposts infringing on Hudson's Bay factories were not yet the major source of fur. Although 1767 was a profitable year for the Canadians, in 1769 the trend was reversed. Twenty canoes of Indians from the north traveled to Michilimackinac to trade; that was fortunate because only two canoes of fur had arrived from Green Bay that year.[143]

Although wintering was illegal under the rules issued by Sir William Johnson in his attempt to assist the colonial traders in competing with the French, little could be done to enforce the rules because for the most part the offenders, often with families, continued to live with the Indians and to make an annual trip to acquire more goods at Michilimackinac.[144] Although the hivernants caused a great deal of harm by arousing the Indians to resist the British, they were protected by the Indians and nothing could be done.[145]

Fur continued to be shipped to Montreal via the Ottawa River because the route was faster and the fur could be placed on ships bound for England before the river froze. The competition of the route to New York ended with most of the deerskin moving over the lakes and the furs coming down the Ottawa River.[146] Of forty-two consignments of fur from Mackinac in 1767, only thirteen went to Albany.

The French merchants in Montreal and Quebec complained that they should receive preferential treatment under the rules established by the Indian Department. Johnson in 1767 believed that the Quebec merchants were fearful of the New Yorkers because after 1760 for the first time the New Yorkers had a legal right to trade in Detroit, Michilimackinac, and other posts on the Great Lakes. The New Yorkers were actually at a disadvantage in 1765 because they were forced to obey the rule against wintering, which the French ignored.[147] The prohibition of the import from the French West Indies of molasses needed to distill the old standby rum also hampered colonial efforts in the fur trade. The Quebec merchants still had the best routes in the Ottawa River and the Great Lakes. With the intimate knowledge of the voyageurs at their disposal, the Quebec merchants could not be outdone in trading in the hunting grounds. Only through unchecked use of rum had the New York traders seriously infringed on the trade prior to 1764. After 1764 the New Yorkers did gain in the dressed deer market because of the more economical shipment of heavy cargo by the Great Lakes. The value of deer equaled that of beaver in the New York City exports after 1763.[148]

An argument used by the French was that Canada used British manufactures in trading, whereas the colonial traders primarily used rum.[149] The value of British manufactured goods used in Canada was at least £40,000 sterling plus colonial rum worth an additional £15,000 sterling. This combination should have been bartered for furs worth £110,000 sterling, but less than £60,000 (custom value £30,000) was officially exported from Quebec. Of furs and deerskin worth at least £10,000 sterling sent to New York, most was used to pay for the rum, and the pelts were then exported to Britain. British merchandise worth £20,000 sterling traveled in canoes to the Mississippi Valley by way of Green Bay, the Fox River, and the Wisconsin River. The goods were traded for furs, but instead of returning the fur to Michilimackinac, the French traders sold it to merchants in St. Louis, who exported it from New Orleans.

The major source of sterling for the colonists was supplying the six regiments of British troops that occupied forts on the Atlantic coast and garrisoned Quebec and Montreal. The beef and flour to feed the troops were from French farms along the St. Lawrence River or were shipped from the thirteen colonies. The cost of army rations including transportation was probably about 75% of the £160,000 paid by the British treasury.

Table 1.1 Balance Sheet for Canada
(£ sterling thousands)

Assets In
| | |
|---|---|
| British merchandise | £40 |
| Colonial products | £15 |
| French provisions from Detroit | £10 |
| Rations for upper lakes troops | £30 |
| Rations for the British army in Canada | £90 |
| Total | £185 sterling |

Assets Out
| | |
|---|---|
| Fur and deerskins | |
| Exported from Quebec | £60 |
| Sent to New York | £10 |
| Goods sent to Illinois from Michilimackinac | £20 |
| Bills of exchange from army | £160 |
| Total | £250 sterling |

The Canadian fur trade and rationing of the regiments in Canada constituted about a third of frontier commerce in the late 1760s. The British regulations were either amended or ignored, favoring the French traders and allowing them to conduct business in the Indian villages and forestall trade with the colonials. Having used the Indians to drive most of the colonial traders out of the retail trade, the French formed close business ties with the new English and Scottish merchants, who eventually forced the colonists out of the wholesale Canadian trade as well. The loss of this trade to the French and British Canadians was a severe blow to the New York and Albany merchants. British administration of business in their American colonies, which on the surface was expected to aid and protect the colonies, in fact harmed them and led to further unrest in the thirteen colonies.

## NOTES

1. Benjamin Roberts to Johnson, 13 April 1770, Sir William Johnson, *The Papers of Sir William Johnson*, 14 vols. (Albany: The State University of New York Press, 1921-1965) [JMss], vol. 7, p. 540.

2. Murray G. Lawson, *Fur: A Study in English Mercantilism, 1700-1775* (Toronto: University of Toronto Press, 1943), p. 135.

3. Chart F, Exports of Beaver Skins to England, Walter S. Dunn, Jr., "Western Commerce, 1760-1774," Ph.D. Dis., University of Wisconsin, 1971, p. 250.

4. *Canadian Archives Report*, 1882 (Ottawa, 1882), pp. 50-55, 58-59.

5. *Canadian Archives Report*, 1882, pp. 53-55.

6. Harold A. Innis, *The Fur Trade in Canada* (New Haven, CT: Yale University Press, 1930), p. 100.

7. Charles E. Lart, ed., "Fur Trade Returns, 1767," *Canadian Historical Review*, vol. 3 (1922), p. 356.

8. *Michigan Pioneer and Historical Collections*, 40 vols. (Lansing: Wynkoop, Hallenbeck, Crawford Co., 1874-1929), vol. 9, p. 658.

9. Carleton Report, *Canadian Archives Report*, 1886, p. clxxii.

10. Chart E, Dunn, *Western Commerce*.

11. Douglas Dunham, "The French Element in the American Fur Trade," Ph.D. Dis., University of Michigan, 1950, Microfilm in State Historical Society of Wisconsin, p.118.

12. JMss, vol. 3, p. 502.

13. Benjamin Roberts to Johnson, 29 August 1769, JMss, vol. 7, p. 146.

14. Address of Traders at Michilimackinac to Captain William Howard, 5 July 1765, Robert Rogers Papers, State Historical Society of Wisconsin.

15. Gladwin to Bouquet, 20 July 1762, MPHC, vol. 19, p. 158.

16. *Canadian Archives Report*, 1882, pp. 53-55.

17. Baynton, Wharton & Morgan Papers, Microfilm, 10 Rolls, Original in Pennsylvania Historical Commission [BWM], Roll 10, Frame 579.

18. Arthur G. Bradley, *The Making of Canada* (New York: E. P. Dutton, 1908), p. 26.

19. John Collins to Baynton and Wharton, 23 May 1761, BWM, Roll 2.

20. Samuel Eldridge to Baynton and Wharton, 3 March 1765, BWM, Roll 4; John Collins to Baynton and Wharton, 23 May 1761, BWM, Roll 2.

21. Jack M. Sosin, *The Revolutionary Frontier, 1763-1783* (New York: Holt, Rinehart, & Winston, 1967), p. 30.

22. Johnson's Review of Trade, 22 September 1767, *Illinois State Historical Collections* (Springfield, IL: Trustees of the Illinois State Historical Library, 1903-) [IHC], vol. 16, p. 38; Guy Carleton to the Earl of Shelburne, 25 November 1767, *Canadian Archives Report*, 1888, pp. 42-43.

23. Basset to Haldimand, 29 April 1773, MPHC, vol. 19, p. 297.

24. Carleton to Shelburne, 25 November 1767, Adam Short and Arthur G. Doughty, *Documents Relating to the Constitutional History of Canada 1759-1791*, 2 vols. (Ottawa: J de L.Tache, 1918) [DCHC], vol. 1, p. 284.

25. Wayne E. Stevens, *The Northwest Fur Trade, 1763-1800* (Urbana: University of Illinois, 1928), p. 24; Douglas Dunham, "The French Element in the American Fur Trade," Ph.D. Dis., University of Michigan, 1950, Microfilm in State Historical Society of Wisconsin, pp. 105-7.

26. Clarence W. Alvord, *The Illinois Country 1673-1818* (Springfield: Illinois Centennial Commission, 1920), p. 306.

27. Stevens, *Northwest Fur Trade*, p. 24; Dunham, *French Element*, p. 113.

28. Gustave Lanctot, *Les Canadians Francais et Leurs Voisins du Sud* (Montreal: Bernard Valiquettes, 1941), p. 93.

29. Council Minutes, 10 January 1766, *Pennsylvania Colonial Records*, 10 vols. (Philadelphia: J. Severns, 1851-52), vol. 9, p. 290; John Wells to Johnson, 20 May 1765, JMss, vol. 4, p. 742.

30. Innis, *Fur Trade*, p. 207; Alexander Mackenzie, *Voyages from Montreal through the Continent of North America to the Frozen and Pacific Oceans in 1789 and 1793 with an Account of the Rise and State of the Fur Trade*, 2 vols. (New York: T. Cadell and W. Davies, 1902), vol. 1, pp. il-l.

31. Innis, *Fur Trade*, pp. 213-14, 226; Stevens, *Northwest Fur Trade*, p. 151; John Lees, *Journal of [John Lees] a Quebec Merchant* (Detroit: Society of the Colonial Wars of the State of Michigan, 1911), p. 42.

32. Lees, *Journal*, p. 42; Mackenzie, p. lvi; Innis, *Fur trade*, pp. 209, 226.

33. Wayne E. Stevens, "Abstracts of Indian Trade Licenses in the Canadian Archives, 1767-1776" [Abstracts], 3 typescript vols., 1925).

34. Innis, *Fur Trade*, p. 215; Lees, p. 42-43.

35. Stevens, *Northwest Fur Trade*, p. 152; Innis, *Fur Trade*, p. 207.

36. Stevens, *Northwest Fur Trade*, p. 152; Ida A. Johnson, *The Michigan Fur Trade* (Lansing: Michigan Historical Commission, 1919), pp. 166-67; Mackenzie, vol. 1, lix-lx; Innis, *Fur Trade*, p. 207.

37. Lees, pp. 43-44.

38. Johnson to Gage, 26 December 1767, Edmund B. O'Callaghan, ed., *Documentary History of the State of New York*, 4 vols. (Albany, NY: Weed, Parsons, 1849-1851), vol. 2, p. 520.

39. Innis, *Fur Trade*, p. 213.

40. Thomas Walker to William Edgar, 29 August 1768, William Edgar Manuscripts, 1760-1769, vol. 15, Burton Historical Collection.

41. Johnson to Lords of Trade, 16 November 1765, NYCD, vol. 7, p. 776; Gage to Hillsborough, 15 May 1768, IHC, vol. 16, p. 288.

42. Isaac Todd to William Edgar, 14 July 1768, Edgar Manuscripts, vol. 15, Burton Historical Collection; Phyn and Ellice to Hayman Levy, 23 August 1768, Phyn & Ellis Papers, Microfilm in the Buffalo and Erie County Historical Society [PEBF]; Thomas Walker to William Edgar, 29 August 1768, Edgar Manuscripts, vol. 15.

43. Lart, p. 358.

44. Todd to Edgar, 14 July 1768, Edgar Papers, vol. 15.

45. Todd to Edgar, 18 February 1769, Edgar Papers, vol. 15.

46. Samuel Eldridge to Baynton and Wharton, 3 March 1765, BWM, Roll 4.

47. Samuel Eldridge to Richard Neave, 23 December 1765, BWM, Roll 6.

48. George Allsopp to Baynton and Wharton, 22 December 1765, BWM, Roll 3; George Allsopp to Baynton and Wharton, 20 September 1767, BWM, Roll 3.

49. Frederick J. Turner, "The Character and Influence of the Indian Trade in Wisconsin," *Wisconsin Historical Society Proceedings, 1889* (Madison: Democrat Printing Company, 1889), p. 57; Nelson V. Russell, *The British Regime in Michigan and the Northwest, 1760-1796* (Northfield, MN: Carleton College, 1939), p. 62; MPHC, vol. 10, pp. 222-24.

50. Grant to Haldimand, 24 April 1780, *Canadian Archives Report 1888*, p. 60.

51. Innis, *Fur Trade*, p. 210.

52. Gage to Conway, 23 September 1765, IHC, vol. 11, p. 85.

53. Journal of William Howard, 8 December 1764, JMss, vol. 11, p. 696.

54. William Howard to Johnson, 17 May 1765, JMss, vol. 11, p. 739.

55. Journal of William Howard, 6 April 1765, JMss, vol. 11, pp. 697-98.

56. Louise P. Kellogg, "A Footnote to the Quebec Act," *Canadian Historical Review*, vol. 13 (June, 1932), p. 153.

57. William Howard to Johnson, 24 June 1765, JMss, vol. 11, p. 805.

58. Claus to Johnson, 11 July 1765, JMss, vol. 4, p. 789.

59. Traders at Michilimackinac to Captain Howard, 5 July 1765, JMss, vol. 11, pp. 825-27.

60. Dunham, *French Element*, pp. 117, 119; Innis, *Fur Trade*, p. 206.

61. Dunham, p. 117; Louise P. Kellogg, *The British Regime in Wisconsin and the Northwest* (Madison, WI: State Historical Society, 1935), p. 48; Lanctot, p. 149.

62. Gage Report, 20 March 1762, Adam Short and Arthur G. Doughty, *Documents Relating to the Constitutional History of Canada 1759-1791*, 2 vols. (Ottawa: J de L.Tache, 1918), [DCHC], vol. 1, pp. 93-94.

63. Croghan to Johnson, November 1765, NYCD, vol. 7, p. 788.

64. Journal of William Howard, 16 April 1765, JMss, vol. 11, p. 698.

65. Baby and others to Johnson, 6 July 1765, JMss, vol. 11, pp. 828-29; Johnson to Gage, 9 August 1765, IHC, vol. 11, p. 66.

66. Petition of Merchants and Traders at Michilimackinac, 22 August 1766, Robert Rogers Manuscripts, Minnesota Historical Society.

67. Claus to Johnson, 11 July 1765, JMss, vol. 4, p. 789.

68. Kellogg, *British Regime*, p. 40; William Howard to Johnson, 24 June 1765, JMss, vol. 11, p. 805.

69. Johnson to Traders at Michilimackinac, 29 July 1765, JMss, vol. 4, p. 810; Johnson to Traders at Michilimackinac, 2 July 1765, JMss, vol. 11, pp. 816-17.

70. Gage to Johnson, 18 August 1765, IHC, vol. 11, p. 76; Gage to Johnson, 8 September 1765, JMss, vol. 4, p. 839.

71. Gage to Shelburne, 11 November 1766, Marjorie Reid, "The Quebec Fur Traders and Western Policy, 1763-1774," *Canadian Historical Review*, vol. 6, p. 26.

72. Johnson to William Howard, 29 July 1765, JMss, vol. 4, pp. 781-82; Johnson to Gage, 28 August 1765, JMss, vol. 4, pp. 833-34.

73. Montreal Merchant Petition, 30 March 1766, JMss, vol. 5, pp. 130-33.

74. Kellogg, *British Regime*, pp. 77-78.

75. Johnson to Gage, 22 October 1767, DHNY, vol. 2, p. 513.

76. Gage to Johnson, 3 February 1766, JMss, vol. 5, p. 30; Gage to Johnson, 2 June 1766, IHC, vol. 11, pp. 246-47.

77. Benjamin Roberts to Johnson, 31 September 1767, JMss, vol. 5, p. 711.

78. Benjamin Roberts to Johnson, 31 September 1767, JMss, vol. 5, p. 712; Johnson to Gage, 24 November 1767, DHNY, vol. 2, p. 515.

79. Johnson to Shelburne, December 1767, NYCD, vol. 7, pp. 997–98.

80. JMss, vol. 5, p. 380.

81. Account, 25 May 1767, JMss, vol. 5, p. 553; JMss, vol. 5, p. 488.

82. Johnson to Gage, 15 January 1767, DHNY, vol. 2, p. 485.

83. Louise P. Kellogg, *The British Regime in Wisconsin and the Northwest* (Madison, WI: State Historical Society, 1935), p. 76.

84. Johnson to Gage, 18 April 1767, DHNY, vol. 2, p. 494; Gage to Johnson, 11 May 1767, JMss, vol. 5, p. 549; Johnson to Gage, 11 September 1767, DHNY, vol. 2, p. 502.

85. Merchants to Governor Murray, 2 April 1767, Rogers Manuscripts, State Historical Society of Wisconsin.

86. Carleton to Johnson, 16 March 1768, JMss, vol. 6, pp. 156–57.

87. Petition of Merchants and Traders at Michilimackinac, 22 August 1766, Rogers Manuscripts, Minnesota Historical Society; Benjamin Roberts to Guy Johnson, 20 August 1767, JMss, vol. 5, p. 618.

88. Gage to Johnson, 13 April 1767, JMss, vol. 5, p. 536.

89. Shelburne to Johnson, 20 June 1767, JMss, vol. 5, p. 566.

90. Benjamin Roberts to Johnson, 12 August 1767, JMss, vol. 5, p. 614.

91. Johnson to Gage, 8 April 1768, IHC, vol. 16, p. 239; Kellogg, *British Regime*, p. 44; JMss, 2 September 1766, vol. 5, p. 369; Claus to Johnson, 16 October 1766, Rogers Journal, p. 228.

92. Jackson, Marjory G., "The Beginnings of British Trade at Michilimackinac," *Minnesota History*, vol. 11 (September 1930), p. 257.

93. Johnson Review of Trade, 22 September 1767, IHC, vol. 16, p. 62.

94. Jehu Hay to Traders, 4 September 1767, IHC, vol. 16, p. 7.

95. Memorial of Traders, 24 November 1767, JMss, vol. 5, p. 819.

96. Johnson to Gage, 6 September 1767, DHNY, vol. 2, p. 501; Johnson to Gage, 11 September 1767, DHNY, vol. 2, pp. 501–2; Phyn and Ellice to Hayman Levy, 23 August 1768, PEBF.

97. Fred Spiesmaker to Johnson, 22 September 1767, JMss, vol. 5, p. 697.

98. Carleton to Shelburne, 2 March 1768, *Canadian Archives Report*, 1886, pp. clxx–clxxii.

99. Johnson to Hector Theo, 23 July 1768, JMss, vol. 6, pp. 288–89; The value of goods sold at Michilimackinac in 1761 was estimated at 250,000 livres ($2,082,500), at Lake Superior 80,000 livres, and at Green Bay 100,000 livres. The purchases made by Rogers were therefore nearly a third of the business at Michilimackinac.

100. Gage to Johnson, 21 September 1767, DHNY, vol. 2, pp. 502–3.

101. Kellogg, *British Regime*, p. 84; Gage to Johnson, 25 April 1768, JMss, vol. 6, p. 208; Gage to Johnson, 20 June 1768, JMss, vol 6, p. 259.

102. John Christie to Johnson, 28 October 1767, JMss, vol. 5, pp. 764–65.

103. Wetherhead to Johnson, 2 October 1767, JMss, vol. 5, p. 720; Hugh Wallace to Johnson, 12 September 1768, JMss, vol. 6, p. 365.

104. Memorial of Traders, 24 November 1767, JMss, vol. 5, p. 819.

105. Phillips, p. 609.

106. Gage to Johnson, 3 September 1768, JMss, vol. 6, p. 353.

107. Johnson to Gage, 18 February 1768, JMss, vol. 6, p. 115; Gage to Johnson, 13 March 1768, JMss, vol. 6, p. 146.

108. Guy Johnson to Hillsborough, 20 June 1768, NYCD, vol. 8, p. 77; Johnson to Hillsborough, 17 August 1768, NYCD, vol. 8. p. 94.

109. Phyn and Ellice to Hayman Levy, 23 August 1768, PEBF.

110. Report of B. Glazier, 30 August 1768, JMss, vol. 6, pp. 348–49.

111. Deposition, 30 June 1768, MPHC, vol. 19, p. 233.

112. Daniel Claus to Johnson, 10 August 1768, JMss, vol. 6, pp. 317–20; Kellogg, *British Regime*, p. 87; Gage to Johnson, 5 December 1768, JMss, vol. 6, pp. 511–12.

113. Indian Meeting, Green Bay, 23 May 1762, James Gorrell, "Journal of Proceedings from October 14, 1761 to June 1763," *Wisconsin Historical Collections*, vol. 1, p. 26.

114. Journal of William Howard, 22 February 1765, JMss, vol. 11, p. 697.

115. Lart, pp. 355–56; Reid, p. 27.

116. Lart, pp. 353–54.

117. Hambuck to William Edgar, 23 March 1767, Edgar Papers.

118. Journal of William Howard, 22 January 1765, JMss, vol. 11, p. 697.

119. Hambuck to William Edgar, 23 March 1767, Edgar Papers.

120. Hambuck to Edgar, 23 March 1767, Edgar Papers; Lart, pp. 353–54.

121. Baptiste Cadot to Johnson, 29 June 1769, JMss, vol. 7, pp. 47–48.

122. Lart, p. 352.

123. Innis, p. 191.

124. Lart, p. 352.

125. Innis, pp. 218, 226.

126. Phillips, p. 605.

127. Jackson, p. 245.

128. Innis, p. 168; Jackson, p. 245.

129. Innis, p. 89; Jack M. Sosin, *Whitehall and the Wilderness: The Middle West in British Colonial Policy, 1760–1775* (Lincoln: University of Nebraska Press, 1961), pp. 36–37.

130. Sosin, pp. 36–37.

131. John Porteus to Isaac Todd, 10 October 1770, PEBF; William S. Wallace, "The Pedlars from Quebec," *Canadian Historical Review*, vol. 13 (1932), pp. 394–95; R. H. Fleming, "Phyn, Ellice and Co. of Schenectady," *Contributions to Canadian Economics*, vol. 4 (1932), p. 25.

132. Phillips, p. 493.

133. Phillips, p. 494.

134. Phillips, p. 519.

135. Wallace, p. 389.

136. Wallace, p. 394; Phillips, p. 520.

137. Innis, 495.

138. Wallace, p. 388.

139. Wallace, p. 388.

140. Edwin E. Rich, *Montreal and the Fur Trade* (Montreal: McGill University Press, 1966), p. 25.

141. Wallace, pp. 388–89, 394–95.

142. Lanctot, p. 150.

143. Todd to Edgar, 29 June 1769, Edgar Papers, vol. 15.

144. Carleton to Johnson, 16 March 1768, JMss, vol. 6, p. 158; Gage to Johnson, 6 December 1767, DHNY, vol. 2, p. 516.

145. Gage to Hillsborough, 15 May 1768, IHC, vol. 16, p. 288.

146. Wayne E. Stevens, "Fur Trading Companies," *Mississippi Valley Historical Proceedings* (1916-17), p. 283.

147. Stevens, *Northwest Fur Trade*, p. 32.

148. Virginia D. Harrington, *The New York Merchant on the Eve of the Revolution* (New York: Columbia University Press, 1935), p. 167; Dunham, *French Element*, p. 116; Reid, p. 32.

149. Stevens, *Northwest Fur Trade*, pp. 35-36; Innis, p. 174.

# 2

## THE GREAT LAKES

The major competition for the Canadians arose from New York, which had the prime advantage of an ice-free port immediately accessible from the sea. In contrast, Quebec was on the St. Lawrence River four hundred miles from the sea and closed in the winter.[1] The Hudson Valley route was the most important colonial entry into the fur trade, originating in New York City and serving the Great Lakes area via the Mohawk River. This route was well established as the primary avenue to the tribes in western New York and around Lake Ontario. The Iroquois acted as middlemen, receiving goods from the New Yorkers at posts such as Oswego and Schenectady and bartering the goods for furs to Indians farther west.

New York City was the main port of entry for merchandise destined for the Great Lakes area and also served as the port for exporting furs and other commodities gathered from the frontier. Frontier commerce had a major impact on the commercial climate of New York City. Before the Seven Years War, fur was the only domestic product of the colony that could be exported to England. In 1751 fur valued by customs at £2,169 (London price $868,000) was sent to England, about 20% of all exports from New York City. However, during the war the fur trade was dormant, and after the surrender of Canada in 1759 Montreal and Quebec competed for the London fur market. Though the export of furs out of New York City decreased, deerskin exports increased after 1763 as schooners on the lakes reduced the cost of transportation and made more profitable the export of the heavier though less valuable deerskin through New York.[2]

During the Seven Years War New York City turned to a new avenue of sales and prospered from the business with the British army. From 1760 to 1763 New York City received an economic stimulus from sales to the French farmers in Detroit as well as the colonial settlers in western New York and the British army, all of whom needed enormous quantities of European merchandise, supplies, and food. The farmers paid in provisions that were sold to the army, which paid with bills of exchange on the British treasury.

Another misfortune to the New York trade occurred at the end of the war in 1763, when the reduced demand for military supplies cut the flow of imports into New York. With fewer bills of exchange from the army to pay for colonial supplies, the colonists had fewer resources to pay for imports. The total value of imports dropped from £480,000 sterling in 1760 to less than £300,000 annually during the following three years. Furthermore, colonial exports to England were not enough to balance even the smaller amount of imports. Total exports from New York never exceeded £100,000 sterling between 1760 and 1768.[3] Most of the difference was in sterling earned by selling food and lumber in the West Indies or in bills of exchange from the British army. When military expenses were cut back after 1764, New York was left with a severe trade deficit. New York City experienced a period of economic depression from 1763 to 1770 caused by the loss of the fur trade to Canada and the reduction of military expenses. The fur trade in the lower Great Lakes never regained its prewar status.

The political conflicts with Britain added to New York's burden.[4] In 1765 New York Harbor was closed as a result of the first Non-importation Agreement, part of the Stamp Tax controversy, which continued until the act was repealed on 18 March 1766.[5] In 1768 a second Non-importation Agreement resulted from the Townsend Acts passed on 20 November 1767, again closing down the source of merchandise for the frontier merchants.[6] Given the intense competition from Canada, where trade continued without interruption, the political problems were a major handicap for the New York merchants. In 1769 Daniel Campbell, a merchant in Albany, wrote to the Sons of Liberty, pleading that the goods that had arrived from England in his name had not been ordered by him except for £63 ($12,600) in Indian goods. Campbell stated also that if Indian goods were not permitted to enter, the Canadians would order twice as much, and then the colonial traders on the frontier would purchase their goods in Montreal.[7] Trade at Detroit was at a low ebb in 1768 because of the lack of merchandise.[8]

There are a few statistics available on the value of furs returned from the frontier. In 1764 Colonel Bradstreet, the British Quartermaster in Albany, estimated that 180 small canoes went west each year, each with an average cargo worth about £170 sterling for a total of about £30,600 sterling ($6,120,000).[9] In 1765 Johnson estimated the value of a canoe load of goods at £372 New York (£235 sterling), higher than Bradstreet's estimate. Johnson estimated a lower total value of the goods used annually at Oswego, £20,000 sterling ($4,000,000).

In 1767 only one-fifth of the fur pelts and deerskins from Michilimackinac were sent to New York, including more than 7,000 half-dressed deerskins (roughly scraped on the inside by the Indians) weighing about 10,000 pounds and worth £1,590 New York ($200,000).[10] To estimate the total value of legal fur exports from New York City is difficult, but apparently the amount did not exceed £12,000 sterling at London prices per year. An additional part was sold for local consumption to hatters, glove makers, and tailors in New York and Philadelphia, and some was used to pay for goods smuggled in Dutch ships. Part of the fur from the lower Great Lakes was exported from Quebec to London and used there to pay accounts of New York merchants.

To carry cargoes of merchandise and furs to and from New York City, a variety of transportation modes were employed. Sailing ships on the lakes gave the New Yorkers an advantage over the Canadians. Although some canoes still traveled up the St. Lawrence River in 1765 from Montreal, crossed Lake Ontario, and portaged around Niagara Falls, the presence of schooners on Lake Ontario made importing goods far cheaper by way of New York City and the Hudson River.

The Hudson River was one of the few breaks through the Appalachian Mountain chain separating the coastal area from the interior, but the river also presented navigational problems. Skilled sailors coped with the tricky currents and winds in the Hudson River sloops designed similarly to Dutch seagoing vessels. To move swiftly, the sloops carried immense sails some 90 feet long and 100 feet high. Despite the large sail area, numerous tacks (lateral movements) upstream were necessary against the wind. The sloops were from 65 to 75 feet long and 20 to 25 feet wide with a capacity of 50 to 200 tons. A crew of ten with a good wind sailed eight to ten miles per hour.[11] The sloops operated until the river froze. John Wetherhead reported to Johnson on 23 November 1767 that winter was settling in and that the sloops were making their last trips to Albany.[12] During the winter, sleighs were used to carry goods south from Albany to New York City.

North from Albany, supplies were transported by wagons and canoes via Lake Champlain to Montreal. Before 1760, when the French were in control of the Great Lakes, this route had created a conflict of interest, as the Albany merchants dealt profitably but illegally with the French in Montreal. Beaver was smuggled south on Lake Champlain to Albany in exchange for British goods. The result was that the Albany merchants benefited financially, and the French, who dealt with the tribes in the Great Lakes area, gained greater influence over the western Indians.[13] Both the French and the Albany merchants made considerable profits from this trade, according to John Lees in 1768.[14]

After 1760 the British army replaced the French and the colonists could use any route. Then the prime path for goods from Albany was on the Mohawk River route. The merchandise was carried in one-ton wagons fourteen miles from Albany to Schenectady and then by canoe up the Mohawk River to Fort Stanwix and Oswego. Timing was determined by the weather and was as crucial on the Oswego route as on the Ottawa River route. The canoes left Schenectady for Oswego early in the spring as soon as the ice melted. Merchandise that had not arrived in Albany before that time would remain unsold for an entire year.

Hayman Levy was late with a shipment in 1769. His goods arrived long after the canoes had left for Oswego and could not be sent without an agent in charge. Phyn and Ellice informed Levy that they would try to sell the goods in Albany but that some would have to be returned to New York.[15]

The canoes used on the trip from Schenectady to Oswego were paddled by three men and cost about £5 sterling ($1,000). The Schenectady canoe held about a ton of merchandise, either 12 large rum kegs or 25 packs of miscellaneous goods. During the 1750s, Lewis Evans reported that the Mohawk river bateaux were 25 feet long, 3 feet 3 inches wide, 2 feet deep and carried about 1,500 pounds. Elm was used for these canoes as the birch used on Canadian canoes did not grow in the Albany area. The elm canoes did not have lengthwise members for support, relying completely on the bark, which made a weaker structure but one that was easier to build.[16]

The canoes traveled west on the Mohawk to a one-mile portage that led to Wood Creek and Lake Oneida. After crossing the lake, the canoes proceeded to Oswego on Lake Ontario. From there the lake route to Detroit and other points west was used by either schooners or canoes.[17] During the early 1760s canoes were used on Lake Ontario beyond Oswego to Fort Niagara; however, because of the shortage of trained canoe men and their demands for increased wages, there was more reliance on sailing vessels on the lakes during the late 1760s.[18]

From Oswego merchandise and provisions were usually carried in schooners and sloops to Niagara at less cost than in canoes. The ships were much more cost efficient and safer from Indian attack. However, the sailing ships on the lake route were subject to the wind. An unfavorable wind could delay the departure of the sailing ships for days.[19] On Lakes Erie and Huron Johnson strongly recommended the use of sailing vessels, which could avoid robbery by the Indians, compared to canoes, which went ashore at night and during high wind, tempting mischief by the Indians.[20] Johnson believed that the efficient schooners on the upper lakes were the essential ingredient in maintaining the posts at Detroit and Michilimackinac.[21]

In 1767 General Gage contracted for ships to be maintained on the Great Lakes for military use.[22] After that time, much of the heavy cargo was carried in ships from Oswego to Niagara. The goods were portaged at Niagara and reloaded on sailing vessels at Fort Schlosser or Fort Erie and carried to Detroit and Michilimackinac. In 1767 the Naval Department on the lakes consisted of a sloop on Lake Champlain and schooners on Lake Ontario, Lake Erie, and Lake Huron at an annual cost of £7,602 sterling ($1,520,000).[23] The ships provided supplies for two regiments, one at Niagara and the other at Detroit and Michilimackinac. In addition, the ships carried civilian freight, for which the government was reimbursed, and were an asset to the defense of the lakes, compared to the slower Ohio River boats, which required protection when carrying goods west from Pennsylvania.

Frontier commerce had a significant impact on the economy and politics of New York. New York City was divided politically into two parties, the "court party," which included Cadwallader Colden, the lieutenant governor; Sir William Johnson, the superintendent of the Northern Indian Department; Wade and Welles; and Jacob Frank, who received many of the British contracts to supply rations to the army. The other group, "the popular party," was led by William Livingston, whose family was intensely involved in frontier commerce. The Livingstons were major landholders in New York and leading opponents of the Stamp Act. Other members of this group were John Duncan and James Sterling, both active in frontier commerce.[24] In 1768 Peter R. Livingston sold furs for Michael Gratz and Sampson Simson, both Jewish merchants of Pennsylvania deeply involved in frontier commerce.[25]

The New York merchants maintained contacts with London through family ties. Jacob Frank in New York had a son, Moses, in London. John Sanders of Schenectady, who was active in the fur trade, purchased nearly £18 sterling ($3,400) worth of shalleen, a type of cloth, from Moses in 1767 and complained about the quality and price.[26] Gerard G. Beekman had a younger brother, William, in Liverpool. David VanderHeyden of New York had a brother, Dirck, in London. Henry Cruger in New York had his son, Henry Cruger, Jr., in Bristol. The younger Cruger was Sir William Johnson's principal agent for the purchase of supplies for the Indian Department.[27]

Once north of the city, frontier commerce was controlled by the Dutch merchants in Albany, Schenectady, and along the Mohawk River, who continued in the fur trade under British rule. Names like Staats von Lantvoord were common in the Albany account books. Most of the residents of Albany were Dutch, who had political control of the city and a major role in the commercial sphere. Appointment as an officer in the local militia was an indication of political power. In 1767 all of the captains of the Albany militia had Dutch names and included some of the merchants often mentioned in documents relating to frontier commerce. Included were Abraham C. Cuyler, Hendrick M. Roseboom, John M. Veeder, and Jacobus Van Alen.[28] The Dutch used their political power to stifle business by new non-Dutch merchants in Albany. Any new merchants were taxed heavily by the city of Albany. In 1759 four new merchants were taxed each £100 New York ($12,600), which amounted to a twelfth of all the taxes paid to the city. When they refused to pay, their goods were ruthlessly seized by the city.[29]

The Albany merchants used the Iroquois as middlemen in the Indian trade. Because English goods cost less than the French goods available in Quebec, the Albany merchants offered merchandise to the Iroquois at lower prices. Before 1760 these merchants offered eight pounds of powder for a beaver pelt and a gun for two beaver pelts (about $150). The French Montreal merchants demanded much more, four beaver for eight pounds of powder ($300) and five beaver for a gun ($380).[30]

The leading Albany merchant was Jelles Fonda, who was very active in the fur trade. In 1768 Samuel Stringer had a large quantity of merchandise suitable for the Indian trade and offered all of his stock to Fonda, who had a large quantity of fur and was willing to pay cash for goods.[31] Fonda had served Sir William Johnson as an agent from 1758 to 1760 but was removed by General Amherst in 1760.[32] Fonda was also a land speculator, buying land from the Indians with liquor in 1763 in partnership with Rutherford and Duncan.[33]

Robert Adams was an associate of Fonda in the Indian trade. In 1769 Adams and Fonda purchased provisions and goods to trade with the Iroquois, hiring Bernard Wemp to do the actual trading with the Indians. Both Adams and Fonda were also in farming and in production of potash.[34] The extent of the activity of Robert Adams can be measured by Johnson's order to obtain goods for Indian presents that were scarce as a result of the non-importation agreement. Included were blankets, aurora (a type of cloth), fusees (Indian guns), silver lace for coats and hats, and 45,000 wampum beads.[35] Adams also provided financial services to Johnson and was ordered to pay Jelles Fonda, on Johnson's behalf, £393 New York ($49,518), an amount to be added to Johnson's account with Adams.[36]

A small number of non-Dutch traders were in business in Albany in the late 1760s, including John Macomb, who went bankrupt in 1765 and, tired of trading, asked Johnson for an appointment in the Indian Department.[37] Lachlan McIntosh was a Scotsman in business with Henry Laurens. After emigrating to Georgia in 1736, McIntosh became a merchant in Albany; in 1768 he sent merchandise to Detroit. He evidently did not do well as his canoes were ruined by lying two summers in the sun. McIntosh returned to Georgia, where he later served with the Continental Army.[38]

Schenectady was a commercial center with most of the population engaged in the fur trade working as canoe men, making canoes, packing goods, driving wagons, and laboring in other related occupations.[39] Many of the merchants at Schenectady were Dutch, but the Scots and English were more visible than in Albany. The list of captains in the Schenectady militia includes some of the British merchants in frontier commerce, John Duncan; John Glenn, Jr.; John Sanders; and Daniel Campbell. The remaining seven had Dutch names, including Gerart Lansing and Nicholas Groot, who were merchants.[40]

One of the major merchant partnerships in Schenectady was Phyn and Ellice. They were middlemen buying merchandise in England and selling it to traders on the frontier and to the Indian Department. They sold to merchants in Detroit and Niagara, who in turn sold the goods to traders who dealt directly with the Indians and also directly to small traders in New York.[41] Originally the partnership had included Duncan, but he retired in 1767 and demanded a large share of the capital. Paying his demands placed the remaining partners in financial difficulty for several years as Duncan had made some poor investments, and the creditors demanded payment from the remaining partners.[42]

In 1766 Phyn and Ellice informed Johnson that Indian goods were difficult to obtain. There were no blankets available in New York City, and other goods had to be taken in from Philadelphia and Pensacola. However, the partners had been able to supply ammunition to the Indian Department in Detroit.[43]

In 1767 the partners paid William and Alex Forsyth of Aberdeen, Scotland, £327 sterling ($65,400) with three bills of exchange presumably obtained from sales to the army. The Forsyths were their suppliers, and one of the Forsyth family was married to a relative of Phyn. The partners also sent Forsyth a bill for £600 sterling ($120,000) drawn by Peter Hasenclever, a banker in New York City, on Richard Wells of London, which the partners wanted paid to William and Norman Durward. The Durward firm was one of their suppliers in London, from whom they obtained glass, white lead, black cloth, pewter ink stands, and stockings. Later they also ordered a young black male slave and two female slaves from Durward, their contact with the slave traders[44] The partners also sent a bill for £45 sterling ($9,000) drawn by Captain Archibald Montgomery on James Myruk, probably a London banker, indicating that the partners were selling considerable quantities of merchandise to the officers in the army.[45]

The market for the furs that Phyn and Ellice received in payment for their merchandise was New York City. Their agent there was Hayman Levy. The partners received orders for goods from Detroit merchants, including James Sterling and John Porteus, and forwarded the orders to Levy. Most payments were made in fur. In November 1767 the partners informed Levy that they had thirty packs of fur worth £600 New York ($75,600), which they hoped would be enough to pay off all of their debts.[46] Levy was cautious in his dealings with the partners. He complained of the quality of the fur sent to him and of settlement of the debt owed to Duncan. Levy preferred to be paid in cash rather than fur and complained of the large order for British merchandise that the partners had placed with him because they were slow to pay and canceled orders.[47] In December 1767 the partners had £3,000 New York ($378,000) worth of skins and were willing to redeem themselves by giving the skins to Levy as payment for all their debts.[48] In early 1768, the partners had difficulty even in providing bread for the boatmen and had to borrow money from relatives in Scotland. However, by late 1768, the partners had added the younger brother of Alexander Ellice, Robert, and had moved into a larger building.[49]

Phyn and Ellice also owed Neale, Pigou, and Booth, London merchants represented in New York City by Benjamin Booth, £700 sterling ($140,000) in January 1768.[50] In February the partners informed Neale that they would pay their balance, having sent Hayman Levy £3,000 New York ($378,000). Levy had been instructed to pay Benjamin Booth the £700 sterling in January, but he could not because he had trouble selling the fur. Therefore, the partners sent Neale a partial payment of two sterling bills for a total of £250 sterling ($50,000). One bill for £100 sterling was drawn by Daniel Claus, the Indian Department agent in Canada, on William Baker, the London banker who had the contract to supply money to the British army in America. This bill was evidently for Indian presents to be distributed by Claus. The other bill for £150 sterling was drawn by Captain Brown on George Ross, a London merchant, evidently for personal purchases by the army officer.[51] In March the partners sent Neale & Pigou an additional £300 sterling ($60,000) with a bill drawn by Hayman Levy on Peter Hassenclever, the London merchant banker.[52]

In June 1768 the partners sent Hayman Levy some elk skins and a bale of furs, stating that if Levy did not want to buy them at the set price in New York, he should send the skins and furs to Neale & Pigou.[53] Later in the month the partners complained that they had not received merchandise from Levy and canceled part of the order.[54] Relations deteriorated and in September, the partners complained that Levy was selling their fur in New York City for less than the price in Albany. Therefore, the partners requested that any furs remaining with Levy be returned.[55]

The rift was evidently smoothed over because in November 1768 the partners informed Levy that the bateaux were arriving in Schenectady every day with some beaver, raccoon, and deerskin. The partners were buying all available fur and after holding it until March would give Levy the first opportunity to buy. The partners expected to have £2,000 New York ($252,000) worth to sell.[56]

Phyn and Ellice turned to others for merchandise, providing fur and deerskin in payment. In December the partners sent Peter Livingston eight packs of deerskin and three packs of deer leather worth a total of £192 New York ($24,192). Livingston was instructed to sell at the fixed price. If they were not sold, Livingston was to hold the skins for further instructions. Clearly the partners were not entrusting Livingston with the decisions, usually made by the agents, to sell at the best price available.[57] In November 1768 the partners placed an order for 98 pieces of cloth, 800 blankets, 6 hundredweight of powder, and 35 hundredweight of lead with Benjamin Booth, asking that he order from his friends in London if he did not have the goods on hand. If delivery were made by April 1768, the partners promised to place more orders.[58]

Phyn and Ellice also began to bypass the New York City merchants and to order merchandise directly from Britain. In December 1767 they placed an order with William and Alexander Forsyth in Scotland for 24 dozen blankets; 200 pairs of men's shoes; 100 pairs of women's shoes; 110 pairs of fine men's, women's, and boys' shoes; stockings; and a long list of various cloths. This finer merchandise was obviously destined for the colonists not the Indians.[59]

The most important customer of Phyn and Ellice was the Indian Department. James Phyn married a daughter of a close friend of Sir William Johnson, thereby cementing the Indian Department business. In April 1765 the partners sold Indian goods worth £1,691 New York ($213,000) to Sir William Johnson, a major transaction.[60] The amounts continued to be substantial: in October 1768 the partners sent a bill from Lieutenant Benjamin Roberts at Michilimackinac and other Indian officers for £2,144 New York ($270,000).[61] The partners also sold merchandise to merchants in Detroit, including James Sterling and William Edgar, taking furs and deerskin in payment.[62]

The chief trading point west of Schenectady before 1760 was Oswego with eighty traders. Johnson had a low opinion of these traders, who were from Albany, Schenectady, and along the Mohawk River. He wrote that they were "low Dutch" and ignorant and spent very little money on food, clothing, or anything else. They had no ambition to build the trade but were content to sell the contents of a small canoe (value about £372 New York, $47,000) in the three or four months that they traded at Oswego. The remainder of the year they spent in idleness in their homes, living on the small profit made in the summer.[63] Johnson estimated the total value of merchandise traded annually before 1760 as less than £20,000 sterling.[64] He set the mark-up rate at 50% at Oswego, 70% at Niagara, and 100% at Detroit.[65] Therefore, a small canoe of merchandise should have returned £558 New York ($70,300) in fur and a profit of £186 New York ($23,436), enough to maintain a family.

The most prominent Oswego trader was Henry Van Schaack, who moved to Oswego in 1759 from Albany. Until 1769, he traded with Niagara and Detroit and imported British merchandise over the Hudson River route.[66]

Much of the merchandise sold on the Great Lakes did not stop at Oswego but was sent on to Niagara. If Bradstreet's estimate of 180 canoes each with £170 sterling worth of merchandise was correct, about 80 stopped at Oswego with £13,000 sterling, and 100 canoes continued with about £17,000 sterling ($3,400,000) in merchandise.

Fort Niagara was a focal point in commerce on the lower lakes, guarding the portage around Niagara Falls. Fort Niagara was also a major trading post in the 1760s, located at the mouth of the Niagara River on Lake Ontario with a garrison of more than one hundred men.[67] The army closely supervised trade at the fort with the Indians who arrived at the post in the spring. An area on the beach where the traders might deal with the Indians was established. Soldiers were posted to prevent any disturbance.[68]

The Albany merchants also made considerable profits from selling rations to the Fort Niagara garrison and presents for the Indians to the Indian Department. In May 1768 a single payment of £772 New York ($97,000) was made for sixteen boat loads of provisions.[69] In June 1768 Phyn and Ellice were preparing another large order for the garrison and the Indian Department.[70]

Many Indians traveled to Fort Niagara each summer to trade furs with the dozen or so traders usually there during the 1760s. Edward Cole of New York City and Justice Van Eps of Schenectady went to Niagara in May 1760 to trade with the Indians.[71] In 1761 the British granted Walter Rutherford the exclusive right to trade at Fort Niagara, which was protested by Johnson.[72] All trade was halted by the Indian rebellion in 1763. After Pontiac's Uprising, the Rutherford's monopoly was ended and more traders were given passes to trade at Fort Niagara, including those with both English and Dutch names. In 1765 Henry Van Schaack, Edward Cole, and Daniel Campbell joined in a venture to trade at Fort Niagara.[73] In 1766 passes to trade at Niagara were given to Alexander Fraser, Peter Ryckman, Barret Visscher, Garret Van Veghter,

Ephriam Van Veghter, William Hare, Thomas Visscher, Garret A. Rosseboom, Thomas Williams, Edward Pollard, Harms Vandell, Garret Teller, and Henry Williams.[74]

Most of the Indians who traded at Fort Niagara were Iroquois from western New York. In 1770 a Seneca traded furs for silver arm bands and later about fifty Chippewas went to the fort.[75] Some Indians also arrived from the west side of the Niagara River. The post commander commented on 30 April 1765 that the Indians from north of Lake Ontario had not yet arrived at the fort.[76]

The Indians were often troublesome at Niagara, in part as a result of the liberal quantity of rum provided by the traders to encourage them to trade their fur at low prices. In 1766 the Indians were prohibited from entering the fort. A sentry had threatened a Seneca chief with a bayonet and the Indians were very disturbed. They were permitted to sell venison at the post market and could receive only bread in payment.[77]

The amount of trade conducted at Niagara was estimated at ten canoes worth of goods, valued at approximately £3,750 sterling ($750,000) plus the sizable quantities of presents distributed by the Indian Department. The total was probably £4,700 sterling. The presents were distributed by the commissaries, who purchased the goods from the local merchants. The opinions of the French and New York traders were divided over the role of the commissaries at Niagara. The French petitioned Johnson, claiming that the commissaries were discriminating again them. These charges were challenged by the New York traders, Peter Ryckman, Volkert VanVeghter, William Hare, Alex Fraser, Jacob Nukerck, and Groesbeck.[78]

To the loss of the Niagara merchants, many Indians traded before they reached the post. Edward Pollard's trading post at Little Niagara at the south end of the portage around Niagara Falls intercepted the Indians from the Lake Erie area. In 1768 Phyn and Ellice of Schenectady sent a cargo in three canoes to Edward Pollard worth £591 New York ($75,000) as well as a previous cargo worth £451 New York ($56,800). Pollard had also ordered rum worth £115 New York ($14,500), about 200 gallons, from Macomb.[79] Pollard's aggressive business activities, combined with the competition from Toronto on the north shore of Lake Ontario, brought trade at Fort Niagara to a standstill in June 1766.[80]

The French from Montreal were breaking the rules and trading along the north shore of Lake Ontario, where they intercepted the Indians from the north and bought their fur before they reached Niagara.[81] Toronto was astride the alternate route to the south from Georgian Bay and Michilimackinac. Many Indians preferred the shorter route to Toronto and then crossed Lake Ontario to Niagara or to Oswego, rather than make the many portages from Georgian Bay to Montreal. The level of trade at Toronto was estimated at five canoes (£1,875 sterling, $375,000), one-half the estimate for Niagara. In 1762 Thomas Dunn and John Gray purchased the right for exclusive trade at Toronto for fourteen years at £400 per year and held this right until 1765.[82]

In January 1766 French traders were active at Toronto and elsewhere on the north shore of Lake Ontario.[83] Needless to say, the colonial traders at Niagara complained bitterly because the Indians would trade at Toronto rather than make the hazardous trip across Lake Ontario. In March the traders at Niagara protested this activity, which defied the rule limiting trade to the posts.[84]

In August 1766 James Murray, the governor of Canada, upheld the rights of Dunn and Gray and prohibited other traders from competing with them.[85] Early in 1767 Johnson reported to General Gage that two traders, Joseph Bryan and James Morrison, had been arrested for trading illegally at Toronto and taken back to Niagara in the spring of 1767. Unfortunately the Indian Department commissary at Fort Niagara, Benjamin Roberts, allowed both of the men to proceed farther west without punishment. In June Gage ordered that the two traders from Toronto be punished as a deterrent to others who might be tempted to trade away from the posts.[86]

Regardless of the rules, French traders traveled by canoe from Montreal and dealt with the Indians at various points along the north shore of Lake Ontario. Frontenac's share of the trade on the north shore before 1760 was estimated at two canoes, one-fifth that of Fort Niagara. The main concern of the colonial merchants at Niagara in 1767 was the French, who broke the rules and ruined the colonists' trade. The illegal trade was protested in October by Peter Ryckman, Harmanus Wendell, Alex Fraser, William Hare, William Groesbeck, Jacob Nukerck, and Gerritt Teller.[87] However, all of the efforts to stop the French were unsuccessful. To compete, colonial merchants established a post at Toronto in 1770. Their stock was exhausted by mid-June in 1770 because the Indian demands were so great.[88]

The significance of Fort Niagara was not as a trading post, but as a guard post at the portage around Niagara Falls. Canoes from Lake Ontario were unloaded about nine miles from the fort and carried to a point about eighteen miles south of the fort to a point on the Niagara River where the current was slow enough to allow paddling to Lake Erie. Even then the current was so strong that the canoes had to travel near shore.[89] Nevertheless, a portage this long would have taken too many days for the canoe men to carry their own cargo. Before 1760 the Seneca Indians had conveniently carried all of the packs and the canoes for the French voyageurs. In 1762 the rate was 4/- New York ($25.20) per pack.[90] Under British rule, a road was constructed and some of the packs and canoes were carried by ox carts. The carts and oxen were provided by John Stedman, who had been granted a monopoly for this service despite Johnson's objections.[91] In 1768 Stedman charged the British army a hefty £100 New York ($12,600) to carry military supplies around the falls.

The Indians charged £3 New York ($380) to carry an empty canoe and each pack was 3/10d New York (about $24). The cost of carrying 25 packs and a canoe was £7.7.6 New York ($920). A canoe and its load of about 25 packs were carried in three carts, each of which cost £5 New York or a total of £15 New York ($1,890). Cezar Cormick paid Stedman £47.8 New York ($5,972) in 1761 to portage his goods around the falls.[92] Therefore, even though the cost was twice as much to use Stedman's carts, there was less chance of theft or damage to the goods. The shifty carriers often stole an eight-gallon keg of rum from the cargo.[93] Furthermore, the Indians were not always available when needed, and a trader might have to wait for days to have his goods portaged.

In 1763 John Stedman had received a contract to widen the portage road, but the number of carts was limited.[94] In February 1764 Colonel Bradstreet, commander of an army sent to quell the Indian revolt, had to move his expedition from Lake Ontario to Lake Erie. Not only was the cost of movement by carts prohibitive, but there were not enough carts available. Bradstreet's force had 6,000 barrels of supplies that would have needed 50 ox carts 15 days with 8 barrels on each trip. The boats would require additional carts, and the estimate was three weeks to move the 2,000 men and supplies around the falls. Some improvement was needed to make the transfer feasible.

In the spring of 1764, Lieutenant Benjamin Roberts was ordered to create a machine to raise supplies and canoes up the sheer Niagara Escarpment, which previously had been skirted by the steep nine-mile portage road. Roberts supervised the construction of machines for lifting canoes from the water at the foot of the Niagara Escarpment, the land formation that created the falls farther upstream. The escarpment was about six miles south of Fort Niagara. The machine, a huge windlass, was capable of lifting 45-foot long boats from the river and raising them 90 to 100 feet to the top of the escarpment. Roberts also constructed wharves and other works to facilitate the movement before the arrival of Bradstreet and his army. At the top the canoes and goods were loaded on ox carts and carried seven miles on a level road to Little Niagara beyond the falls.[95]

This method cut the cost and shortened the time to move a canoe load of goods to less than a day, allowing the cart to return to the escarpment in the afternoon to pick up another load. The machine remained in service after Bradstreet's army had departed and was used by the fur traders. The demand for the convenient service was greater than the equipment could fulfill. In 1768 Stedman was still providing carts and carriers at the old rates for the eighteen miles of steep road.

The cost of moving goods from New York to Michilimackinac by way of Lake Ontario and Lake Erie was far lower than that to Michilimackinac from Montreal via the Ottawa River with its numerous portages. Lees estimated the cost at about 12/- sterling ($120) per 90-pound pack from Schenectady to Detroit using the Mohawk River and the lakes.[96] The cost for carrying a hundred-weight from New York to Schenectady was from 1/- to 3/- sterling ($20 to $60), including the trip on a sloop to Albany and carriage from Albany to Schenectady.[97] The total cost of shipping a cargo from New York to Detroit was about 13/- sterling ($140) per pack.

The transportation cost per pack was higher from Montreal to Michilimackinac via the Ottawa River, 30/- Quebec or about 27/- sterling ($270) per pack, compared to 13/- sterling from New York to Detroit.[98] Therefore, even adding 4/- sterling for the cost of the freight from Detroit to Mackinac by schooner, the New York merchant could deliver a pack to Mackinac at 17/- sterling ($170), a much lower price than the 27/- sterling paid by the Montreal merchant.

In 1765 Sir William Johnson estimated the cost of taking a canoe from Schenectady to Detroit (see Table 2.1). The total weight of the cargo was about 3,000 pounds, and the cost of moving a hundredweight from Schenectady to Detroit, including the cost of the canoe and the return trip, was about 57/- sterling ($570). This estimate seems rather high, but the return trip would double the normal cost, and the price of the canoe added materially to the total.[99] Deducting the cost of the reusable canoe, a one-way trip would be £30.12/- New York (£19.6/- sterling, $3,856). The cost per pack was approximately 13/- sterling, a like amount to Lees's estimate. Johnson's estimate was less than Bradstreet's, which included a canoe at £9 New York; wages, £60 New York; and expenses at portages, £13 New York for a total of £82 New York (£51.14/- sterling, $10,332) compared to Johnson's estimate of £61.2/- New York.[100]

Table 2.1  Cost of Moving a Canoe of Goods
From Schenectady to Detroit

| Cargo of dry goods | £300 N.Y. | $37,800 |
|---|---|---|
| 330 gallons of rum | 57.15 | 7,276 |
| 140 kegs for the rum | 14 | 1,764 |
| Cost of canoe | 10 | 1,260 |
| Provisions and liquor for men | 13.16 | 1,739 |
| Expenses at portages | 6 | 756 |
| Wages for three men (6/- per day) x 26 days to Detroit and 20 return | 41.8 | 5,216 |
| Total | £442.19 | $55,811 |

The Oswego canoe cargo included 330 gallons of rum, far more than Bradstreet's estimate of 200 gallons of brandy in a Canadian canoe cargo. The cost of the Canadian brandy was 5/- sterling per gallon ($50) compared to the lower priced New York rum of about 3/6 New York ($22). Johnson expected the goods to be sold at Detroit with a profit of £357.15 ($45,025), as the furs would sell for more than £800, double the value of the goods.[101]

Detroit, the next major post beyond Fort Niagara, had 300 dwellings and about 2,500 persons in 1760. In 1761 Captain Daniel Campbell described the fort as large and in good repair with two bastions facing the river and one facing the land. On each bastion a three-pounder cannon and three small mortars were mounted. The fort was surrounded with palisades all in good repair. Seventy or eighty houses were inside the fort laid out in regular streets. Most of the French lived on sixty farms, each having a narrow frontage on the Detroit River. The farms stretched ten miles on both sides of the river, which was 900 yards wide.[102]

Detroit, the second major garrison on the Great Lakes, was a substantial market for colonial merchants, with a demand for rations, rum, and presents for the army and the Indians. When the Indians laid siege to the fort in May 1763, only 120 men were willing to defend the fort, including a hundred soldiers of the 60th Regiment and about twenty English traders. As a result of the haphazard reinforcements to defend the fort against Pontiac in 1763, the garrison consisted of small companies from three regiments. In early 1765 Lt. Col. John Campbell of the 7th Regiment arrived to take command. In the fall of 1766, he was succeeded by Captain George Turnbull of the 2nd Battalion of the 60th Royal American Regiment.[103]

After the uprising was quashed in 1764, Detroit resumed its role as a center of the fur trade, serving the routes leading south to the Ohio River valley by way of the Maumee River and the Wabash River and also St. Joseph located on the east shore of Lake Michigan. The value of the fur trade at Detroit was estimated at seventeen canoes (about £6,375 sterling, $1,275,000), compared to only £3,187 for Fort Niagara. Most of the goods were sold to traders and winterers who visited the fort in the spring. Few Indians traveled to Detroit compared to Michilimackinac, Fort Pitt, or the posts in Illinois.

As the use of sailing vessels on the lakes increased, Detroit became relevant as a source of provisions for the army and the French traders in the Great Lakes area. The army also purchased a variety of merchandise from the merchants. To repair the fort in 1763, James Sterling sold the army construction tools worth £261 New York ($33,000). In addition, the army purchased £156 New York ($20,000) worth of presents for the Indians in the fourteen months ending November 1763 from Sterling.[104] Sterling was only one of nearly twenty merchants supplying the troops at Detroit. In 1767 Johnson sent Croghan to Detroit with £1,000 sterling ($200,000) to pay for Indian Department expenses, primarily gifts for the Indians.[105]

The French farmers at Detroit were also a market for British and colonial goods. They paid for the merchandise with farm products that were in turn sold by colonial and British merchants to the garrison for bills of exchange or to traders who paid in fur. Corn, peas, and other produce were shipped to Michilimackinac to provide food for the traders traveling to the Northwest.

The French farmers were producing sizable surpluses that were available for sale to the British army and the fur traders. In 1750 a thousand acres cultivated in Detroit by sixty farmers produced about 52 tons of wheat at six bushels per acre. The amount of flour obtained from grinding wheat was nearly equal to the weight of the wheat. In 1766 twenty-seven French farmers (nearly half of the sixty farms in the area) offered to provide rations to the British garrison including 279 hundredweight (16 tons or nearly a third of the harvest) of flour. Each soldier needed a pound of flour per day. The quantity offered was enough to feed 85 troops for a year. The price of £1.13.4 New York ($170) per hundredweight was exorbitant compared to the price of less than 17/- Pennsylvania ($98) per hundredweight in Philadelphia in 1768. The French also engaged to supply 1,340 pounds of pork, which would vary the diet of salt beef. This was a trifling amount, but (according to the French) all that they could spare from their own needs.[106]

The French continued to present obstacles to the British attempts to win over the Indians. In the spring of 1765 there were no presents at Detroit to give the Indians, one of the complaints that led to the uprising. In January 1765 Johnson had ordered that presents were to be given to the Indians only if unavoidable. Strict controls were imposed: when presents were given, the action was to be certified by the commanding officer, two other senior officers, and the commissary of the fort. The prices of the presents purchased from local merchants had to be certified as current, that is, the usual prices charged to others at the fort. The presents were to be delivered by an Indian Department deputy if one were available.[107]

Lacking merchandise to give to the Indians, the Detroit commandant, Lt. Col. John Campbell, hoped that traders would arrive early to sell goods to the Indian Department. Campbell also informed Johnson that the rule limiting trade to the posts would be strictly enforced at Detroit.[108] Campbell met with the Indians and promised that trade would be opened, but goods still had not arrived at Detroit by April. Such disappointments, General Gage feared, would cause the Indians to attack again in the summer.[109]

In June reports indicated that Pontiac would attack Detroit again and the commander was instructed to be on guard. British and colonial traders finally arrived in late June with plenty of goods to meet the Indians' needs.[110] The Indians were anxious to resume trading and to end the fighting with the British. However, the French traders from Illinois continued to stir up trouble to prevent the Indians from going to Detroit where prices were much cheaper than those of the French.[111]

In August George Croghan, the Indian Department agent, arrived in Detroit to confer with the Indians. The Wabash tribe from the area between Illinois and Detroit was anxious for trade to resume. They also requested that traders be sent to their villages; otherwise they would have to obtain their supplies from the French from Illinois. Croghan conferred with Pontiac, who verified that the French had urged him to attack the British and had furnished weapons and other supplies. The Indians remained loyal to the French traders because they had always supplied the tribes in the past.[112]

Fortunately the Indians gave no trouble at Detroit in the fall and winter of 1765 and the colonial traders had a brisk business. However, near St. Joseph two traders were murdered by the Pottawatomis, probably encouraged by the French from Illinois. Even though, as a result, trade with the Pottowatomis was suspended, they were able to sell their fur to the French from Illinois. Colonel Campbell hoped that the British could occupy Illinois and terminate French competition from Illinois. He believed the secret to peaceful relations with the Indians was a plentiful supply of goods at low prices. However, the ever intruding French at Detroit continued to resist British attempts to improve relations with the Indians. The French discouraged visiting Indians from attending a conference to be held at Oswego by Sir William Johnson.[113]

By the summer of 1767 British relations with the Indians had improved. Jehu Hay was appointed the Detroit agent of the Indian Department and was cooperating with the army. He rented for £500 ($100,000) a sumptuous house, formerly the home of the French commander of Detroit, which had been sold to John Stedman, the operator of the Niagara portage carts.[114]

However, Hay did not have enough presents for the Indians. During the summer of 1767 the Indians took in a very considerable number of furs and the trade was much larger than in many previous years. The various tribes were quarreling with one another and some looked to the British for support. Nevertheless, the French continued to encourage the Indians to resist the British and trade only with them. The competition with the Illinois French, however, was reduced, perhaps as the French had increased their business west of the Mississippi River.[115]

The British were making an effort to win over the French in Detroit. In April the commandant, Captain William Turnbull, appointed Philippe Dejean to hold court and settle civil disputes.[116] Dejean was one of three French traders who petitioned Jehu Hay in September 1767 concerning the competition from Illinois. The other petitioners, Baptiste Chapaton, Duperon Baby, and Fleurimont, were leading traders in Detroit along with Isaac Todd, a Jew; Henry VanSchaack, an Albany Dutchman; and four British merchants, Thomas Williams, William Edgar, Richard McNeal, and Samuel Tyms.[117]

The petition reviewed the issue of the Illinois traders and restriction of the Detroit traders to the posts. In a separate letter Henry Van Schaack outlined the position of the Detroit traders. In the past two years the merchants had been unable to pay their bills in England because they had been prevented from going to the Indian villages to sell goods as was customary in other areas, notably Michilimackinac. The French traders from Michilimackinac and Illinois, on the other hand, did winter with the Indians and thereby acquired most of the fur. The Indians too complained to the Detroit merchants that they preferred to have the traders go to their villages so that they did not have to waste their time traveling to Detroit during the hunting season to sell their fur. The Indians were uncomfortable in Detroit, which was too large and had too many people. Even the Detroit merchants were dissatisfied because the competition prevented them from charging prices for merchandise as high as those charged by traders who wintered with the Indians. The Detroit merchants were at a further disadvantage because the Indians obtained goods on credit in Detroit and seldom returned to pay their debts. Therefore, goods had to be bartered for furs rather than given to the Indians on credit. The usual system in the Indian villages was to provide the Indian with supplies to enable him to hunt with the knowledge that he would return to the village and pay for the goods with the fur he collected.[118]

In October 1767 the Detroit merchants complained that Edward Cole, the commissary in Illinois, had granted passes to French traders to winter in the Indian villages up to the Miami River. In addition, French traders from Canada had passes to trade at Illinois posts, but they seldom went there. Instead they traded their goods in the Indian villages along the Miami and Ohio Rivers.[119]

The Illinois commissary reported that French traders were not as active around Detroit and were concentrating on the Illinois River farther west. The only Indian complaints about traveling to Detroit were those of the Miami and Wabash Indians, who were repeating the lies of French renegade traders. After only one year of enforcement of the rule restricting trade to the posts, the trade at Detroit was greater than in many years. Hay still suggested that the merchants refuse to sell goods to anyone who broke the rule by going to the villages and that the merchants help to apprehend anyone violating the rule. As events were transpiring, Hay believed that the merchants would make greater profits at less risk than going to the villages, and furthermore trading only at the posts would make the Indians dependent on the British.[120]

One of the Detroit traders, James Syms, ignored the rule and did winter with the Indians, along with Collin Andrews. In addition, the two men had provided lodging for Indians in the fort at Detroit without permission, a further violation. The Indian agent, Jehu Hay, had them arrested. Another trader who signed the petition, Richard McNeal, requested that the two be sent down to Niagara or Montreal for trial, but the charitable Captain George Turnbull, the post commander, intervened and forgave the offenses.[121]

Hay was proving to be a good customer for the Detroit merchants. In September 1767 he sent to Croghan accounts for expenses for the summer totaling £775 New York ($97,713). He paid the merchants with two bills of exchange given to Henry Van Schaack, who in turn probably credited the other merchants for their share of the business. Hay, concerned that Johnson would consider the amount too large, justified the expense on the basis of the large number of Indians who had traveled to Detroit.[122]

Again in November the Detroit traders asked for free trade and the end of the rule confining trade to the posts. They stated that there was too much brandy at Detroit and it was sold to the Indians at a low price by unscrupulous traders to get their furs. Furthermore, given the amount of liquor available, the Indians did not hunt as vigorously as in the past.

The Detroit merchants presented a petition suggesting that liquor be held in a warehouse in Detroit as in Michilimackinac to control the amount being given to the Indians. Only upstanding merchants with integrity would be permitted to winter with the Indians, and they would be limited to fifteen gallons of brandy for the entire winter. In a village of one hundred Indians (25 adult males, 25 women, and 50 children), this allotment would provide a small amount, less than three quarts for each adult male for the winter. Few villages were larger than one hundred and most were smaller, so the suggested amount was seen as being quite reasonable. The merchants from Quebec and New York were to limit the amount of liquor to one half of the total cargo with the remaining half dry goods. Before Pontiac's Uprising, many of the New York traders arrived with canoes filled with liquor, which was the item of choice to obtain furs at the lowest price.

The Detroit merchants believed that if permitted to winter with the Indians, they could compete with the French traders from Illinois and in fact force the French to go to Detroit to purchase merchandise in order to compete in the villages. The petitioners believed the fear that winterers would be robbed was unjustified because if the Indians wanted to rob the merchants, they could do so easily while the canoes crossed Lake Erie and did not have to wait until the traders reached the villages. The signers of this petition were both French and British, du Chene, Pierre Baron, H. Miller, Isaac Todd, William Edgar, P. Dejean, Jean Baptiste Prudhomme, Antoine Gamelin, Grano, J. Bond, Eustache Gamelin, Louis Campeau, Mier(?), and others (whose names were burned during the fire at the New York State Library that destroyed many of the Johnson manuscripts).[123]

The British and colonial merchants in Detroit prepared another petition to Johnson four days later, again complaining that traders from Illinois were wintering south of Detroit and taking the furs. The petitioners claimed that if they were permitted to winter with the Indians, the Illinois competition would be eliminated. That no French merchants signed this petition suggests that the French merchants in Detroit and the British and colonial merchants disagreed concerning wintering. The signers included Henry VanSchaack, Rinkin and Edgar, Williams and Van Alen, George Meldrum, Hugh Boyle, Peter Pond, Joshua Rand, Henry Williams, Cornelius VanSice, Jacob Lansing, Allan McDougall, John Magill, James Sterling, John Porteus, and Benjamin James.[124] The Albany merchants were well represented in the trade at Detroit. William Edgar, one of the prominent merchants in Detroit, had ties with John Duncan. In 1764 Livingston, Duncan, Rutherford, and Phyn were represented in Detroit by James Sterling and John Porteus. William Edgar had contacts with Robert Callender, one of the partners of Baynton and Wharton in the Illinois scheme.

Despite their claims of unfair competition, the Detroit merchants did very well in 1767. James Sterling claimed to have obtained thousands of packs of fur worth £100,000 sterling ($20,000,000) from the Missouri River valley west of the Mississippi.[125] This sum seems exorbitant and may have referred to an accumulation over the years after the British entered the fur trade at Detroit.

However, it does indicate that the French traders from Illinois were disposing of at least some of their fur in Detroit rather than trying to ship all of it down the Mississippi River to New Orleans.

The following year was not so propitious. In May 1768 General Gage was concerned about the murder of British and colonial traders at the instigation of the French in order to retain control. The commandant at Detroit had been ordered to inform the Indians that no trade would be permitted with any tribe who did not offer the British and colonials the same opportunity to trade as the French.[126] Some of the British and colonial traders took matters into their own hands and ignored the rules to remain in the fort at Detroit. Even though they wintered, they were not punished when they returned. Chabert Joincaire complained to Johnson that he duly had remained in Detroit over the winter of 1767–68 and, having done very poorly in 1768, he requested a pass to winter at Sandusky to recoup some of his losses to pay his debts.[127]

If a Frenchman from Detroit were in such dire straits, the British and colonials really must have been in great difficulty. In December Phyn and Ellice complained that they had received no returns, either bills or furs, from James Sterling, Lyme, John Farrell, and Robinson, all of Detroit. They had received bills of exchange from Henry VanSchaack, presumably obtained from the army in return for supplies.[128] VanSchaack acted as a broker, receiving a large bill of exchange from the army and in turn paying the army accounts with various merchants in Detroit. The implication was that the Detroit British and colonial merchants were continuing to sell to the army, but the fur trade had been usurped by the French.

In the following year, 1769, the non-importation agreements and the strife on the coast made supplying the Detroit merchants with trade goods impossible. Phyn and Ellice informed Alex Macomb in Detroit that they would not be able to fill his order, nor the orders of Porteus, Sterling, and James Cassety. Porteus had ordered four canoe loads of goods, but there was nothing available—no goods, no rum—neither were there men to paddle the canoes.[129] The fur trade at Detroit was at a standstill, and the business with the army and the Indian Department had been curtailed by the lack of merchandise to sell.

In addition to Detroit, a great deal of merchandise was sold at the smaller outposts from 1765 to 1768. The posts were located at strategic points on the rivers leading to Illinois from Detroit and Lake Michigan. One route was down the Detroit River and along the south shore of Lake Erie to Sandusky and up the Sandusky River. The British built a fort at Sandusky in 1761. Unfortunately the garrison was killed and the traders robbed and killed during Pontiac's Uprising and the fort was not restored in 1765. From the Sandusky River a portage took the traders to the Scioto River, which led down to the Ohio River to the Mississippi. This route went through the Mingo and Shawnee villages.

Two routes connected Detroit to Illinois. After paddling up the Maumee River from the Detroit River, a portage connected the Maumee River to the Miami River and thence down to the Ohio. Another nine-mile portage from the

Maumee led to the Wabash and Ohio Rivers passing through the villages of the Miami tribe. The Wabash route was by far the most significant for the Detroit traders. Before 1760 the French had maintained Miami on the portage from the Maumee to the Wabash. Trade was estimated at five canoes per year (£1,875 sterling, $375,000). After 1760 the British maintained the portage road and appointed a manager for the portage. Horse-drawn carts and pack horses were used to carry the packs and canoes at a fixed rate.[130]

In compliance with the maxim that the best place to trade is at a point where one "breaks cargo" (changing from one means of transport to another), Miami was a very active trading post. Croghan described the post at Miami in 1765 as forty or fifty Indian cabins plus nine or ten French houses and referred to the French inhabitants as lazy, indolent refugees from Detroit intent on stirring up the Indians against the British. During the late 1760s there was bitter competition at Miami between the French and the British and colonial traders traveling down from Detroit. French traders from Illinois took goods to Miami, Vincennes, and other villages along the Wabash River.[131] Competing with the French was difficult for the British and colonial traders. In 1765 Mr. Tadot was robbed near Miami by Indians who told him that they would not make peace with the British until the French at Fort Chartres told them to do so.[132]

Fred Hambuck was a petty trader based at Detroit during the 1760s receiving his goods from William Edgar. In 1763 Hambuck sent 35 packs of fur to Edgar to pay part of his debt.[133] Hambuck lost his goods during Pontiac's Uprising, but by 1767 he was again in business at Miami. Competition arose not only from the French but also from Pennsylvania traders who traveled to Miami from Fort Pitt. In May 1767 Hambuck informed Edgar that his liquor had been stolen and the Indians would not repay past debts because traders, Linsley, Eder(?), and James, had arrived with liquor and were offering trade goods at very low prices.[134] Samuel Edie had been active in York County, Pennsylvania, in the early 1760s; Benjamin James was a merchant in Detroit active in the Indian trade in 1766 and 1767; and Samuel Lindsey had been an officer in the Pennsylvania militia from 1759 to 1763.

Later in May 1767 Hambuck planned to send thirty packs of fur (worth at least $75,000) to William Edgar. The Indians were passing through Miami on their way to Detroit, where they expected to get a better price for their fur than at Miami. Hambuck suggested to Edgar that he send three hundred gallons of liquor, which could be sold at a good price to Miami by the end of May.[135]

The traffic must have been very heavy to dispose of that quantity. The Indians seldom purchased more than an eight-gallon keg of rum for a group of perhaps twenty. Three hundred gallons would provide 1,200 Indians with a quart each. A gallon of rum usually was traded for a beaver worth 6/6 New York ($41) or a Spanish dollar ($43) on the frontier, whereas a gallon of rum sold in Schenectady for only 3/6 New York ($23), so Edgar could have made a handsome profit if Hambuck had charged more than one beaver per gallon. Even at one beaver per gallon, three hundred beaver were worth £97.10 New York

($12,300), whereas the rum would have cost only £52.10 New York. The entire load would have been less than a canoe load, and the trip from Detroit to Miami would have taken but a few days with no portage other than at Miami.

Although the profits were great, so was the danger. As an example of the great risk in wintering with the Indians, Hambuck was killed at Miami by the Pottawatomi in 1768. Gage believed that Hambuck was killed under orders from a French trader, Chevalier, who was heavily in debt to the victim.[136] Another trader, Robert Rogers, was murdered near St. Joseph. Rogers had received a license to winter at St. Joseph with Isaac Todd as his security. These incidents point up two facts, the evasion of the rule to confine trading to the posts and the great personal danger in ignoring the rule. Despite the prohibition, the colonial traders were wintering with the full knowledge and cooperation of established merchants such as Isaac Todd and William Edgar. Given the close relationship between the French from Illinois and the Indians, there was little hope for the colonial and British traders from Detroit to carry on a profitable trade even had the army permitted them to winter with the Indians.

The relations with the French at Miami did not improve. In 1767 Johnson complained to Carleton that the French were wintering there. The French task of sustaining Indian friendship was augmented by the negative British attitude shown by their neglect of the Indians, their prejudice against them, and their policy of restricting presents.[137]

Ouiatanon was located on the Wabash River at the present site of Lafayette, Indiana. The post was established in 1720 by the French to serve the Wea Indians.[138] Murray in 1761 estimated the level of trade at Ouiatanon in 1761 as being worth 60,000 livres ($480,000) during the French period. Hutchins estimated the amount of skins at Ouiatanon as worth £8,000 sterling ($1,600,000—more than Detroit) when he passed through.[139] The post was considered one of the most valuable in the west by Johnson, but its trade was served as often with supplies moving up the Wabash from Illinois as those going down from Detroit via the Maumee and across the portage at Miami.[140] In 1765 George Croghan described the post as having a considerable trade because a large quantity of fur was available in the area and doing business there was very profitable for the traders.[141]

In 1761 Lieutenant Edward Jenkins was sent by Captain Campbell from Detroit to occupy Ouiatanon with twenty men and four months provisions.[142] However, the garrison was withdrawn as a result of Pontiac's Uprising and the French regained complete control. In 1765 during his peace making mission George Croghan was captured by Indians and taken there. All of the French at Ouiatanon lived by selling goods to the Indians at very high prices.[143]

Alexander Maisonville was the leading merchant. In 1765 Maisonville had traveled up to Detroit and then went to Fort Pitt. In 1766 Maisonville purchased two canoes of goods worth £2,234 Pennsylvania ($257,000) from Baynton and Wharton, the Philadelphia merchants who were active in Illinois.[144] In July 1767 Edward Cole, the commissary at Fort Chartres, recommended Maisonville to Croghan. Maisonville was well acquainted with the Wabash Indians and had been working for the Indian Department dispensing presents.[145] By March 1767 he had formed an association with Baynton and Wharton and had sent them 125 packs of pelts valued at £1,542 Pennsylvania ($177,000, an average of £12.7 Pennsylvania or $1,416 per pack) in payment for merchandise sent previously. The packs had been sent down the Mississippi River to New Orleans and carried on the sloop *York* to Philadelphia. The transportation cost was 9/- New York ($57) per pack for a total of £52 New York ($7,182). The packs from Maisonville must have been mostly deerskin, as a shipment of 62 packs of mixed deerskin and fur to Phyn and Ellice was valued at £1,302 New York ($164,000 or an average of $2,645 per pack), almost twice the value per pack.[146] Maisonville continued to receive goods from Baynton and Wharton and sent them pelts by way of New Orleans. In 1768 Maisonville was working with Baynton and Wharton purchasing lead from the French and sending out hunting parties to obtain meat for the British army.[147] The only benefit to the colonists and the British of the trade on the Wabash was supplying merchandise to the French, who effectively had cut off any direct contact between the Indians and the colonists.

Vincennes was the next post south of Ouiatanon on the Wabash River just north of the juncture of the Wabash and White Rivers. The territory along the Wabash River was an excellent hunting ground for the Indians. In 1765 Croghan described the post as of great importance in the fur trade because the surrounding country abounded in game.[148] Vincennes was established by the French on the Wabash River in 1727 to control traffic between Lake Michigan and the Mississippi. Vincennes had the benefit of being halfway between Illinois and the Great Lakes, saving the Indians the trouble of going all the way to either Illinois or Detroit.[149]

In 1763 Aubrey described Vincennes as a fort surrounded by a picket (a wall formed by logs with the larger end driven into the ground). The garrison consisted of twenty married French soldiers and some French inhabitants.[150] Although the British sent a garrison to Vincennes in 1761, the French soldiers remained after the British occupation and continued as Indian traders.[151] In 1763 there had been a garrison of twenty British troops, but Pontiac's Uprising ended military occupation.

The settlement had 88 landowners in 1733. By 1763 most of the inhabitants were part Indian and part French and many were illiterate. In 1769 the village priest stated that there were 80 farmers in the village and nearly 800 persons. An estimate of the population in 1769 was much lower, only 50 men able to bear arms, 50 women, and 150 children including slaves. By 1768 half of the inhabitants were newcomers, including French traders from Illinois and British and colonial merchants from Detroit and Fort Pitt.[152] In 1770 Johnson called it a lawless community with vagabond French traders, derelict French soldiers, and hostile Indians, all of whom hated the British and the colonial traders.[153]

The leading merchant was Nicholas, who in 1768 sold fur worth £61.10

($7,072) to George Morgan, a partner of Baynton and Wharton.[154] Among the other French traders were John Baptiste Bosseron, Rassicault, Neauveau, Flamboice, Vadrie, and Moros. Baynton and Wharton established a store in the village in the late 1760s in the care of Williamson, who in 1768 rented a house with a cellar to store furs. The goods provided by Baynton and Wharton were sold both to Indians and to the French. The French paid with either cattle or furs. In July 1768 Baynton and Wharton purchased fur, cattle, and tobacco worth over £2,000 Pennsylvania ($230,000) from the French.[155] In the fall of 1768 Morgan obtained twenty head of cattle for army provisions from Vincennes.[156]

There were also French traders from Detroit in the area. Maisonville reported that Jaconte from Detroit was trading with the Indians in the neighborhood at low prices, a blanket for two beaver (each worth a Spanish dollar, $43, on the frontier), which was the price in Detroit and much less than charged by the French who obtained their supplies from Illinois.[157]

The volume of trade was substantial. In 1765 trade goods were plentiful, and seven canoes were seen in the river with merchandise worth about £2,625 sterling ($525,000). Blankets were selling for three beavers ($130).[158] However, trading was not without risk. In July 1768 a band of Indians returned to Vincennes with nine British and colonial scalps and eight horse loads of fur. They had attacked two groups of traders in the Ohio Valley near Fort Pitt. The British arrested the chiefs, demanding that they deliver the Indians guilty of the crimes.[159]

Cole believed that establishing a military post at Vincennes in 1768 with an Indian Department deputy was essential. A garrison might stop the illegal trade on the Wabash and also limit the French influence on the Indians.[160] Nothing was done, and in 1769 the store at Vincennes that belonged to Rumsey and Brown was looted by Indians.[161]

Estimating the total value of commerce around the lower lakes (see Table 2.2) is extremely difficult because of the competition with the French from Illinois and Canada.

The total assets sent to the Great Lakes area is estimated at £82,600 sterling, including £30,600 in merchandise plus the army rations, which included a substantial amount of rum. The amount of manufactured goods from Britain was probably worth about £20,000 sterling. The value of goods sent to the various posts in the lower lakes is documented by estimates of the number of canoes that traded at that post each year. General Bradstreet made a contemporary estimate that the frontier commerce of New York required £21,000 sterling in merchandise annually. Of the 180 canoes that set out from Schenectady, several sources indicate that 80 remained in Oswego with merchandise worth £13,600, which was traded at a 50% markup for furs and deerskin worth £20,400. The remaining 100 canoes contained £17,000 in merchandise. Using various estimates, these goods were divided among Niagara, Toronto, Detroit, Michilimackinac, and Illinois. The Niagara and Toronto merchandise was traded at a 70% markup. Of the goods sent to Detroit about £1,000 in rum and other heavy goods plus £1,000 in provisions for the voyageurs were sent to Michilimackinac, and about £2,000 sterling in fur and deerskin were sent to New York from Michilimackinac. Merchandise worth about £2,000 was sent south to Ouiatanon, Miami, and Vincennes and traded for furs that were then sent to Illinois.

Table 2.2 Balance Sheet for Great Lakes Area
(£ sterling in thousands)

Assets In
    Merchandise and rum

| | | |
|---|---|---|
| To Oswego | £13.6 | |
| To Niagara | 4.7 | |
| To Toronto | 1.9 | |
| To Detroit | 6.5 | |
| To Michilimackinac | 2.0 | |
| To Illinois | 2.0 | |
| Total merchandise | | £30.6 |
| Rations for three regiments | | £52 |
| Total | | £82.6 |

Assets Out
    Fur and deerskin

| | | |
|---|---|---|
| Oswego | £20.4 | |
| Niagara | 7.6 | |
| Toronto | 3.2 | |
| Detroit | 12.8 | |
| Michilimackinac | 2.0 | |
| Total Fur | | £46 |
| Legal exports | £11 | |
| Domestic market | £ 9 | |
| New Orleans exports | £ 4 | |
| Illegal export | £22 | |
| | | |
| Bills of exchange from army | | £70 |
| Total Assets out | | £116 |

During this period the British army usually had a regiment at Niagara, a regiment divided between Detroit and Michilimackinac, and a regiment in transit in New York City. Regiments on the frontier cost about £30,000 sterling to maintain, so the two frontier regiments would have spent at least £50,000 and the regiment in transit probably purchased about £20,000. The purchases included a pound of flour used to make a pound of bread and a pound of meat for each man per day. In addition some peas and other provisions were purchased. Each man received a gill of rum per day, and most soldiers used their pay to purchase more. The officers had more expensive tastes, wine and brandy. The army also required tools and material to maintain the forts and barracks. All of these expenses were paid with sterling bills of exchange. The cost for the three regiments was comparatively low because of the ease of transportation to the two regiments on the frontier and the third regiment scattered about New York. The cost of the rations was estimated at 75% of the return.

The return in fur and deerskin was less than two to one because of the lower price exacted from the Indians at Niagara and Oswego. Still a substantial amount of fur was unaccounted for and presumably exported illegally. The total value of fur and deerskin sent to New York City was more than £40,000 sterling, but only £11,000 in London value was legally exported. The local market could not possibly have absorbed £30,000 sterling in fur and deerskin. If half the value were in beaver at 4/- sterling per beaver, 75,000 beaver skins would have been used to make 75,000 hats, far more than could have been sold. A reasonable conclusion is that the more than £20,000 sterling in fur and deerskin was used illegally to pay for Dutch imports smuggled into the bays and coves around New York City and Boston. The alternative conclusion is that the New York and Albany merchants invested over £30,000 sterling in merchandise and received in return fur and deerskin worth only £11,000, plus at most £9,000 sterling for the local market.

Fur was one of the few colonial commodities in demand in Europe. Beaver was a valuable commodity, selling in Europe for nearly 8/- sterling per pound ($80), and a ton of beaver worth £800 sterling easily could be added illegally to the cargo of a ship loaded with legal lumber and provisions heading for Lisbon or the West Indies. During the period 1765 to 1768 about 480 ships left American ports annually and about one-third left Boston, New York, and Philadelphia. Nearly half of these ships were bound for southern Europe and the West Indies, so there were potentially 75 ships each year that could have carried smuggled furs. The total weight of £20,000 sterling worth of fur and deerskin was only about fifty tons.

The successful frontier trade in the lower Great Lakes region therefore produced three sources to pay for luxury imports that had become part of the American life-style by the middle of the eighteenth century: £70,000 in sterling bills of exchange from the army, £11,000 in legally exported fur and deerskin, and about £22,000 sterling in illegally exported fur. Together these sources formed a valuable addition to New York's ability to pay for luxuries.

When the British army reduced its expenditures, the colonist's ability to pay for imports was also reduced. When the Royal Navy increased its vigilance and the tax on tea from India was reduced, smuggling became a far less lucrative business after 1768. Both factors had a negative impact on the colonists' life-style and further stirred the climate of hostility toward Britain.

NOTES

1. John Watts to Isaac Barre, 28 February 1762, Virginia D. Harrington, *The New York Merchant on the Eve of the Revolution* (New York: Columbia University Press, 1935), p. 310.
2. Harrington, p. 167.
3. Harold A. Innis, "Interrelations between the Fur Trade of Canada and the United States," *Mississippi Valley Historical Review*, vol. 20 (December 1933), p. 322; Askin Papers in the Burton Historical Collections of the Detroit Public Library, vol. B4, 10 May 1761; Harrington, p. 167; Chart J, New York, Pennsylvania, Quebec, and Hudson's Bay Co. Exports and Imports to and from England, Walter S. Dunn, Jr., "Western Commerce, 1760–1774," Ph.D. Dis., University of Wisconsin, 1971, p. 255.
4. Harrington, p. 316.
5. Governor Moore to Secretary Conway, 21 December 1765, Edmund B. O'Callaghan and Fernold Berthold, eds., *Documents Relating to the Colonial History of the State of New York*, 15 vols. (Albany: Weed, Parsons, 1853–1887) [NYCD], vol. 7, p. 802; R. H. Fleming, "Phyn, Ellice and Co. of Schenectady," *Contributions to Canadian Economics*, vol. 4 (1932), p. 12.
6. Fleming, p. 17.
7. Daniel Campbell to Sons of Liberty, 14 November 1769, Sir William Johnson, *The Papers of Sir William Johnson*, 14 vols. (Albany: The State University of New York Press, 1921–1965) [JMss], vol. 7, p. 251.
8. Phyn and Ellice to Hayman Levy, 9 May 1768, Phyn & Ellis Papers, Microfilm in the Buffalo and Erie County Historical Society [PEBF].
9. John Bradstreet, "Statement on Indian Affairs, 1764," printed in Franklin B. Hough, *Diary of the Siege of Detroit...* (Albany: J. Munsell, 1860), p. 144.
10. Harrington, pp. 235–36.
11. "The Hudson River Sloop," published by Hudson River Sloop Restoration, Inc.
12. Wetherhead to Johnson, 23 November 1767, JMss, vol. 5, p. 816.
13. Harrington, p. 233.
14. Harold A. Innis, *The Fur Trade in Canada* (New Haven, CT: Yale University Press, 1930), p. 177.
15. Phyn and Ellice to Hayman Levy, 20 May 1769, PEBF.
16. John Lees, *Journal of [John Lees] a Quebec Merchant* (Detroit: Society of the Colonial Wars of the State of Michigan, 1911), p. 43; Edward Pierce Hamilton, *The French and Indian War* (Garden City, NY: Doubleday, 1962), pp. 4, 6, 38.
17. Wayne E. Stevens, *The Northwest Fur Trade, 1763–1800* (Urbana: University of Illinois, 1928), pp. 16, 18–19.
18. Innis, *Fur Trade*, pp. 219–20.
19. Innis, *Fur Trade*, p. 213; Stevens, p. 151.
20. Johnson to Lords of Trade, 20 January 1764, NYCD, vol. 7, p. 600.
21. Johnson to Eyre, 29 January 1764, Bradstreet, p. 231.
22. Contract, 2 September 1767, *Canadian Archives Report 1885* (Ottawa: [Canadian Archives], 1885), p. 167.
23. January 1766, General Thomas Gage Papers [Gage Papers] in Clements Library, Ann Arbor, Michigan.

24. Harrington, p. 40; Arthur L. Jensen, *The Maritime Commerce of Colonial Philadelphia* (Madison: The State Historical Society of Wisconsin, 1963), p. 336; Colden to Henry Conway, 13 December 1765, Colden Papers, *New York Historical Society Collections*, 1877, p. 67.

25. Peter R. Livingston to Michael Gratz, 27 February 1768, William V. Byars, ed., *B[ernard] and M. Gratz* (Jefferson City, MO: The Hugh Stevens Printing Co., 1916), p. 84.

26. John Sanders to Moses Frank, 21 May 1767, John Sanders Letter Book, New York Historical Society.

27. Harrington, pp. 185–86.

28. Return of 1st Albany Militia Battalion, 18 May 1767, JMss, vol. 5, p. 556.

29. William Corey to Johnson, 23 August 1759, JMss, vol. 3, p. 129.

30. Helen G. Broshar, "The First Push Westward of the Albany Traders," *Mississippi Valley Historical Review*, vol. 7, p. 229.

31. Samuel Stringer to Jelles Fonda, 6 June 1768, Miscellaneous Manuscripts File 1768 in the State Historical Society of Wisconsin.

32. 8 November 1760, JMss, vol. 3, p. 278.

33. 10 March 1763, JMss, vol. 4, pp. 50–61.

34. Jelles Fonda to Johnson, 14 July 1769, JMss, vol. 7, p. 59.

35. Robert Adams to Johnson, 7 August 1768, JMss, vol. 6, pp. 311–12.

36. 30 October 1769, JMss, vol. 7, p. 236.

37. John Macomb to Johnson, 14 April 1765, JMss, vol. 11, pp. 690–91; John Macomb to Johnson, 23 February 1765, JMss, vol. 11, pp. 598–99.

38. Phyn and Ellice to Lachlan McIntosh, 6 December 1768, PEBF.

39. Lees, p. 15.

40. Return of the 2nd (Schenectady) Battalion of Militia, May 1767, JMss, vol. 5, pp. 556–57.

41. Fleming, pp. 11–13.

42. Ibid., pp. 11–12.

43. James Phyn to Johnson, 26 February 1766, JMss, vol. 5, p. 41.

44. 8 July 1769, PEBF.

45. Phyn and Ellice to William and Alexander Forsyth, 25 December 1767, PEBF.

46. Phyn and Ellice to Hayman Levy, 30 November 1767, PEBF.

47. Phyn and Ellice to Hayman Levy, 30 January 1768, PEBF.

48. Phyn and Ellis to Hayman Levy, 16 December 1767, PEBF.

49. Fleming, pp. 12–14.

50. Phyn and Ellice to Hayman Levy, 11 January 1768, PEBF.

51. Phyn and Ellice to Neale & Pigou, 27 February 1768, PEBF.

52. Phyn and Ellice to Neale & Pigou, 7 March 1768, PEBF.

53. Phyn and Ellice to Hayman Levy, 2 June 1768, PEBF.

54. Phyn and Ellice to Hayman Levy, 21 June 1768, PEBF.

55. Phyn and Ellice to Hayman Levy, 19 September 1768, PEBF.

56. Phyn and Ellice to Hayman Levy, 3 November 1768, PEBF.

57. Phyn and Ellice to Peter V. Livingston, 12 December 1768, PEBF.

58. Phyn and Ellice to Benjamin Booth, 19 November 1768, PEBF.

59. Phyn and Ellice to William and Alexander Forsyth, 25 December 1767, PEBF.

60. Account of Duncan and Phyn, 5 April 1765, JMss, vol. 11, p. 671.

61. Phyn and Ellice to Johnson, 8 October 1768, PEBF.

62. Phyn and Ellice to John Duncan, 16 February 1768, PEBF; Phyn and Ellice to Hayman Levy, 16 December 1767, PEBF.

63. Johnson's Review of the Trade, 22 September 1767, NYCD, vol. 7, p. 953; Johnson to Lords of Trade, 8 October 1764, JMss, vol. 4, p. 556.

64. Johnson to Lords of Trade, 8 October 1764, JMss, vol. 4, p. 557.

65. Johnson to Colden, 9 June 1764, JMss, vol. 4, p. 443.

66. Lees, p. 15; Johnson to the Lords of Trade, 8 October 1768, *Illinois Historical Collections*, vol. 10, p. 336; Frederick W. Barnes, "The Fur Traders of Early Oswego," *Proceedings of the New York Historical Association*, vol. 13 (1914), p. 134.

67. Bradstreet, p. 149.

68. Johnson to Colonel Vaughn, 17 January 1765, JMss, vol. 4, p. 638; Orders to Govern Indian Trade, 1 April 1766, JMss, vol. 5, p. 143.

69. Phyn and Ellice to Henry White, 28 May 1768, PEBF.

70. Phyn and Ellice to Hayman Levy, 1 June 1768, PEBF.

71. Johnson to Haldimand, 3 May 1760, JMss, vol. 3, p. 234.

72. Johnson to Amherst, 29 July 1761, JMss, vol. 3, p. 514.

73. Articles of Agreement, 26 April 1765, JMss, vol. 4, pp. 725–26.

74. Niagara Merchant's Petition to John Clarke, 3 April 1766, JMss, vol. 5, p. 144.

75. Brown to Gage, 8 June 1770, JMss, vol. 7, pp. 715–17.

76. Lt. Col. John Vaughn to Johnson, 30 April 1765, JMss, vol. 11, p. 711.

77. Norman McLeod to Johnson, 4 January 1769, JMss, vol. 6, p. 566.

78. Peter Ryckman to Johnson, 22 October 1767, JMss, vol. 5, p. 742.

79. Phyn and Ellice to Edward Pollard, 5 December 1768, PEBF.

80. Benjamin Roberts to Johnson, 10 June 1766, JMss, vol. 5, p. 244.

81. Peter Ryckman to Johnson, 29 October 1767, JMss, vol. 5, pp. 765–66.

82. Phillips, p. 550.

83. DeCouange to Johnson, January 1766, JMss, vol. 5, p. 1.

84. Petition of Niagara Traders to Johnson, 27 March 1766, JMss, vol. 5, p. 118.

85. James Murray Papers, 9 August 1766, copy in the State Historical Society of Wisconsin.

86. Gage to Johnson, 28 June 1767, JMss, vol. 5, p. 573.

87. Niagara Traders to Johnson, 29 October 1767, JMss, vol. 5. p. 765; Norman McLeod to Johnson, 5 November 1767, JMss, vol. 5, p. 277; Captain Hugh Arnot to Johnson, 31 December 1765, JMss, vol. 4, p. 889.

88. Wade and Keyser to Johnson, JMss, vol. 7, p. 756.

89. Thomas Hutchins, *A Topographical Description of Virginia, Pennsylvania, Maryland, and North Carolina Reprinted from the Original Edition of 1778* (Cleveland: The Burrows Bros. Co., 1904), pp. 116–17.

90. Askin Papers, B4, 1 June 1761 and 16 July 1762.

91. Johnson to Lords of Trade, 30 August 1764, IHC, vol. 10, p. 306.

92. Cezar Cormick to John Askin, 1 June 1761, Askin Papers, B4.

93. Innis, pp. 177–78.

94. Innis, p. 177.

95. Memorial of Lieutenant Benjamin Roberts to Hillsborough, Minnesota Historical Society; Lees, p. 26; Bradstreet to Amherst, 20 February 1764, Bradstreet, p. 245.

96. Lees, p. 43.

97. "Carriage Costs," William Henry Papers, Historical Society of Pennsylvania.

98. Innis, p. 210.

99. Schedule of Prices by Johnson, c. 1765, IHC, vol. 10, p. 403.

100. Bradstreet, p. 144.

101. Schedule of Prices by Johnson, c. 1765, IHC, vol. 10, p. 403.

102. Clarence M. Burton, *The City of Detroit, Michigan, 1701-1922* (Detroit: J. S. Clarke, 1922), 2 vols., vol. 1, p. 118.

103. Burton, pp. 121-22.

104. Amherst Papers, vol. 7, pp. 53-54, Clements Library.

105. Johnson to Gage, 6 September 1767, DHNY, vol. 2, p. 501.

106. Ernest J. LaJunesse, *The Windsor Border Region* (Toronto: University of Toronto Press, 1960), pp. 80-81.

107. Orders for the Regulation of Trade, 16 January 1765, IHC, vol. 10, p. 400.

108. John Campbell to Johnson, 20 February 1765, JMss, vol. 11, p. 589.

109. Gage to Johnson, 21 April 1765, JMss, vol. 4, pp. 722-23.

110. John Campbell to Johnson, 3 June 1765, JMss, vol. 11, pp. 764-66; Dr. Shuckburgh to Johnson, 14 July 1765, IHC, vol. 10, p. 521.

111. Richard Shuckburgh to Johnson, 14 July 1765, JMss, vol. 11, pp. 853-54.

112. Croghan Journal, 30 August 1765, Rueben C. Thwaites, *Early Western Travels, 1748-1846*, 2 vols. (Cleveland: A. H. Clark, 1904-1907), vol. 1, p. 159; Croghan to Johnson, November 1765, IHC, vol. 11, p. 53.

113. John Campbell to Johnson, 24 February 1766, IHC, vol. 11, p. 157; John Campbell to Johnson, 10 April 1766, JMss, vol. 5, p. 159; Johnson to Gage, 23 August 1766, JMss, vol. 5, p. 362.

114. Jehu Hay to George Croghan, 13-17 August 1767, JMss, vol. 5, pp. 619-20.

115. Gage to Shelburne, 24 August 1767, IHC, vol. 11, pp. 595-96.

116. Burton, p. 123.

117. Detroit Traders to Jehu Hay, 4 September 1767, JMss, vol. 5, p. 656.

118. Henry Van Schaack to Jehu Hay, 4 September 1767, IHC, vol. 16, p. 3.

119. Norman McLeod to Johnson, 8 October 1767, IHC, vol. 16, p. 83; Norman McLeod to Johnson, 8 October 1767, JMss, vol. 5, pp. 723-24.

120. Jehu Hay to the Detroit Traders, 4 September 1767, IHC, vol. 16, pp. 6-7.

121. George Turnbull to Johnson, 14 October 1767, JMss, vol. 5, p. 726.

122. Jehu Hay to Croghan, 25 September 1767, JMss, vol. 5, p. 703.

123. Detroit Traders' Petition to Johnson, 22 November 1767, JMss, vol. 5, pp. 809-15.

124. Detroit Traders' Memorial, 26 November 1767, JMss, vol. 5, p. 830.

125. James Sterling to Major Henry Basset, 22 December 1767, Colonial Office 5, 154, p. 35c in Phillips, p. 593.

126. Gage to Hillsborough, 15 May 1768, IHC, vol. 16, p. 288.

127. Chabert Joincaire to Johnson, 1 October 1768, JMss, vol. 6, pp. 430-31.

128. Phyn and Ellice to Edward Pollard, 5 December 1768, PEBF.

129. Phyn and Ellice to Alex Macomb, 26 August 1769, PEBF.

130. Phillips, p. 591; Gage to Shelburne, 11 November 1766, CO 5/84, f. 521 in Reid, p. 27; Amherst to Bouquet, 13 March 1763, *Michigan Pioneer and Historical Collections*, vol. 19, p. 180; Hutchins, p. 101.

131. VanSchaack to Hay, 4 September 1767, IHC, vol. 16, pp. 3-4.

132. Court of Inquiry, 6 April 1765, JMss, vol. 4, pp. 673-76.

133. Fred Hambuck to William Edgar, 13 May 1763, William Edgar Manuscripts.

134. Hambuck to William Edgar, 8 May 1767, Edgar Manuscripts.

135. Hambuck to William Edgar, 8 May 1767, Edgar Manuscripts.

136. Gage to Hillsborough, IHC, vol. 16, p. 287.

137. Johnson to Carleton, 27 January 1767, JMs, vol. 5, p. 479.

138. Dunham, p. 37.

139. Hutchins, p. 101.

140. Phillips, p. 591.

141. Croghan's Journal, June 23, 1765, Thwaites, vol. 1, p. 145.

142. Lieutenant Edward Jenkins to Bouquet, November 4, 1761, *Canadian Archives*, 1889, p. 194.

143. Croghan to Johnson, 12 July 1768, JMss, vol. 11, pp. 836–41.

144. Baynton and Wharton Journal B, 17 July 1766, Baynton, Wharton & Morgan Papers, Microfilm, 10 Rolls, Original in Pennsylvania Historical Commission F8.

145. Cole to Croghan, 3 July 1767, IHC, vol. 11, pp. 580–81.

146. Baynton and Wharton to Clarkson, Jennings, and Long, 19 March 1767, BWM, Roll 3; Baynton and Wharton Journal C, 24 September 1767, BWM, Roll 9.

147. Morgan to Baynton and Wharton, 20 July 1768, IHC, vol. 16, p. 360.

148. Aubrey's Account of Illinois, 1763, IHC, vol. 10, p. 3; Phillips, p. 591; Croghan's Journal, 15 June 1765, Thwaites, vol. 1, p. 142.

149. Croghan's Journal, 15 June 1765, Thwaites, vol. 1, p. 145.

150. Aubrey's Account of Illinois, 1763, IHC, vol. 10, p. 3.

151. Phillips, pp. 591–92.

152. Reid, p. 30.

153. Gage to Hillsborough, 14 March 1770, CO 5, 88, p. 152 in Phillips, p. 592.

154. Haldimand Papers Calendar, *Canadian Archives 1885*, p. 203; Morgan to Williamson, 14 July 1768, IHC, vol. 16, p. 351.

155. Morgan to Williamson, 8 July 1768, IHC, vol. 16, pp. 345–46.

156. Charles B. Lasselle, "The Old Indian Traders of Indiana," *Indiana Quarterly Magazine of History*, vol. 2 (March, 1906), p. 4; Morgan to Williamson, 8 July 1768, IHC, vol. 16, p. 344.

157. Matthew Clarkson Diary, 26 November 1766, IHC, vol. 11, p. 359.

158. Capucin to Baptiste Campeau, 7 June 1765, JMss, vol. 4, p. 765.

159. Captain Forbes to Gage, 28 July 1768, IHC, vol. 16, p. 367.

160. Cole to Johnson, 18 April 1768, IHC, vol. 16, p. 255.

161. John Finley to Rumsey and Brown, 1 November 1769, BWM, Roll 6.

# 3

# Pennsylvania and the Ohio Valley

Philadelphia was one of the largest cities in the British Empire and the economic center of the thirteen colonies. During the 1760s, the value of imports from Britain to Philadelphia was nearly £400,000 in all but two years, while exports to England remained generally between £25,000 and £40,000 per year. In Britain crop failures from 1766 to 1772 expanded the market for Pennsylvania flour and wheat. In addition, about £11,000 Pennsylvania ($1,265,000) of iron was shipped to England. Less than £4,000 sterling worth of fur and deerskin was legally exported to Britain, but as much as £15,000 sterling was illegally sent to Europe. The major exports were flour and wheat worth about £300,000 sterling ($60,000,000) sent to the West Indies and southern Europe.[1] In accordance with the imperial policy to limit the development of industry in the colonies to ensure dependence on the mother country, only raw materials were sent to Britain.

In return for the exports Pennsylvania merchants received Madeira wine and salt from Portugal worth about £30,000 sterling. The remainder were paid for with bills of exchange the Portuguese received for wine sold in Britain. The trade with Portugal was favorable to Pennsylvania, and the trade with the West Indies was nearly balanced. The West Indies sent molasses, which was distilled into rum in Philadelphia. Merchants in the West Indies also paid for some of the imports of provisions and lumber with English bills of exchange received for sugar shipped to Britain. The bills were used by Pennsylvania merchants to pay for part of their imports from Britain.[2] James and Drinker, one of the most prominent merchant houses in Philadelphia dealing in the West Indies trade, used the credits obtained from that trade to import from Britain in 1760.[3]

The British acquisition of Canada in 1759 opened a new market for the Philadelphia merchants for the sale of rum and British manufactured goods to the French, who in turn traded with the Indians. In 1766 Baynton and Wharton through their agent, George Alsopp, were selling rum at 1/11 Pennsylvania ($11) per gallon in Quebec. Alsopp also paid Hide and Hamilton of Manchester, England (probably manufacturers of metal goods that had been sent to Quebec), £200 sterling ($40,000) on behalf of Baynton and Wharton. Alsopp expected to be repaid by Baynton and Wharton from the proceeds of a shipment of wine from Philadelphia.[4]

The British army was a major customer in the 1760s. The Seven Years War had created prosperity in Philadelphia as the British army made large purchases of provisions and rum. After the fighting ended and the regiments were sent to the West Indies, a depression set in. In November 1760 Daniel Clark, who had been selling beef to the British army at Fort Pitt, was forced to cancel large orders in England except merchandise for the Indians.[5]

The Forbes Road and the Ohio River were the keys to all the markets west of Fort Pitt: the Ohio Valley, Detroit, and Illinois. Merchandise moved by wagon from Philadelphia to Carlisle and then by pack horse to Fort Pitt. From there pack horses carried merchandise to the Indian villages north of the Ohio River. Boats were used on the Ohio, but the route was very dangerous because of the hostile tribes. During the spring floods floating down the Ohio to the Mississippi was simple at a speed of six to seven miles per hour. The return trip was formidable and necessitated a double crew of rowers. Pennsylvania traders also went north on the Allegheny River and up French Creek to Lake Erie and Detroit.[6]

Two roads led from Carlisle to Fort Pitt, Braddock's Road via Fort Cumberland in Virginia and Forbes Road via Bedford, the one more used in the late 1760s. The prosperity on the Pennsylvania frontier was fostered by the construction of these two roads to Fort Pitt. Goods were transported by farm wagons pulled by a team of horses carrying about 2,000 pounds, although fitting the heavy barrels and odd-shaped packages on the wagons often reduced the load. The weight of a load on wagons was limited to twenty hundredweight (2,240 pounds) by a Pennsylvania act of March 17, 1757, concerning the hire of carriages.[7] The Conestoga or Dutch wagon pulled by oxen or horses carried more, over two tons. The wagons could haul the more bulky objects at a cheaper rate than pack horses but required a road rather than a dirt trail. Road maintenance was a problem in the mid-1760s. Often the Forbes Road to Fort Pitt was usable by wagons only as far as Carlisle, at the foothills of the mountains.

Carlisle, located about a hundred miles west of Philadelphia, was a center of frontier trade. Westward the Forbes Road to Fort Pitt was often too rough for wagons. Therefore, merchandise went by wagon to Carlisle, where it was repacked in bundles of about one hundred pounds. Liquor was transferred from large barrels to eight-gallon kegs. A pack horse in Pennsylvania was able to carry as much as 200 pounds, including forage for the horse, which meant that the actual payload was smaller.[8] The horses moved in brigades of thirty or more with a driver for every six or seven horses.[9] Pack horses could be purchased for £14 Pennsylvania ($1,610) each in the Lancaster area.[10] In 1765 Croghan reported that the Indians arrived with several horse loads of furs, an indication that the Indians were stealing horses and adopting the horse as a means of transportation.[11]

Weather restricted movement in Pennsylvania as well as on the lakes. The winter of 1764–65 was bitter and the road from Philadelphia to Fort Pitt was closed by snow. In February 1765 Croghan crossed the mountains to Fort Pitt in the first pack train after the snow had closed the Forbes Road for weeks.[12]

Because of the mountains the 300-mile wagon trip from Carlisle to Fort Pitt took twenty days at only ten miles per day, compared to the twenty miles per day traveled by a horse-drawn wagon on level roads.[13] In comparison, the 560 miles from Niagara to Fort Pitt was a sixteen-day trip by way of Lake Erie, a portage to Fort LeBoeuf, and rivers flowing into the Ohio.[14]

The cost of carrying a hundredweight of goods (112 pounds compared to a Canadian "pack" of about 90 pounds) by wagon and pack horse from Philadelphia to Fort Pitt was £2 Pennsylvania ($230). The return cost was only £1 Pennsylvania ($115) because much of the road eastward sloped downward from the mountains. There was little demand for cargo space going east as the furs were less bulky than the merchandise going west. In 1766 David Robb and William Boyd were paid only 6/- Pennsylvania ($34.50) per hundredweight to carry fur by wagon from Carlisle to Philadelphia.[15] The rate from Fort Pitt to Carlisle was probably about 14/- Pennsylvania ($80.50) per hundredweight. The road from Carlisle to Philadelphia was a bit more than one hundred miles; the road to Fort Pitt from Carlisle was much longer, nearly two hundred miles.

In 1766 Baynton and Wharton paid Ephraim Blaine, a well-known wagon master, £130 Pennsylvania ($15,000) for transporting goods to and from Fort Pitt. The rate was £3 Pennsylvania ($345) for each horse load, about 180 pounds, from Carlisle to Fort Pitt, whereas the rate to return the easier to handle fur from Fort Pitt to Carlisle was only £1 Pennsylvania ($115) per hundredweight. At the same time William Finlay took a wagon carrying 21 hundredweight all the way from Philadelphia to Fort Pitt for £43 Pennsylvania ($4,945 or $235 per hundredweight), less than the Blaine's charge for moving merchandise by pack horse the shorter distance from Carlisle to Fort Pitt. Robert McCord received £32 ($3,680) Pennsylvania for shipping 16 hundredweight ($230 per hundredweight) on a wagon from Philadelphia to Fort Pitt, a means far cheaper than use of pack horses from Carlisle to Fort Pitt.[16] Beside the cheaper rate, other advantages of taking the wagon all the way was that the merchandise would not have to be repacked at Carlisle and larger units could be carried, for example, hogsheads of sugar and coffee.[17]

In 1768 a wagon carried two hogsheads of rum (63 gallons each), a hogshead of sugar (63 gallons, 600 pounds), and two bales of french matchcoating (a heavy woolen used to make coats) to Carlisle, where all of the goods were repacked in small kegs and bundles to be loaded on pack horses.[18] Twelve and one-half horses were needed to carry the contents of one wagon.

Rope was in great demand because eleven yards were needed to tie down a single horse load.[19] The containers had to be designed specifically to fit on the racks placed on the pack horse back. Joseph Rigby in Carlisle complained that the half barrels of sugar and coffee were too large and cut into the sides of the horses: the barrels had to be made flatter in the bilge (curved side of the barrel), and the hoops had to be flatter as well.[20] The trip was subject to the hazards of theft and carelessness. In 1766 a shipment of cloth was ruined by the wagon drivers who forded a river, soaking the contents of the wagons.[21]

The quantities carried were enormous. In 1764 a convoy left Fort Loudon with 410 horses loaded with forage and 132 with flour escorted by fifty men. Another convoy of 800 horses arrived in Fort Pitt on 10 April 1764.[22] Captain Robert Callender played a prominent role in movements on the road, transferring goods and provisions from wagons to pack horses at Fort Loudon. In 1765 Baynton and Wharton paid Callender £431 Pennsylvania ($49,565) for transporting merchandise from Philadelphia to Carlisle.[23] Croghan's cargo of presents for the Indians in 1765 required 65 pack horses. John Jennings was paid £62 for carrying two wagon loads to Fort Pitt in November 1765, thirty hundredweight at 41/- Pennsylvania.[24] In 1766 fifteen horse loads of flour arrived at Fort Pitt for Baynton and Wharton, about 3,000 pounds, enough to feed a hundred soldiers for a month.[25] In March 1766 Baynton and Wharton had a contract with Edward Morton of Cumberland County to have twenty wagons with horses on hand to carry goods from Philadelphia to Fort Pitt for Baynton and Wharton exclusively. Morton was to make three trips in 1766 at a rate of £2 Pennsylvania per hundredweight to Fort Pitt and £1 Pennsylvania from Fort Pitt to Philadelphia.[26] In February 1767 Baynton and Wharton paid Edward Morton £2,267 Pennsylvania ($260,700) for carrying 69 wagon loads of goods with a total weight of 1,057 hundredweight from Philadelphia to Fort Pitt, so Morton more than fulfilled the contract.[27] In September 1766 Baynton and Morgan engaged Stephen Duncan and Daniel Duncan to provide wagons to carry merchandise from Philadelphia to Carlisle and 200 pack horses to carry the cargo to Fort Pitt from Carlisle.[28] This contract alone was sufficient to move eighteen tons compared to three tons carried by a master canoe from Montreal to Michilimackinac.

The Forbes Road was a busy thoroughfare, as shown by M. Clarkson's diary in 1766. He left Philadelphia on horseback with a servant on 6 August 1766 and passed a wagon loaded with pork for the garrison at Fort Pitt and four wagons of fur and deerskin on their way to Philadelphia. The wagons carried a minimum of four tons of pelts worth at least £1,200 sterling, if all deerskin, and probably twice as much if combined with fur. After 35 miles, Clarkson stopped for the night. On the second day he reached Lancaster, having passed six wagons of pelts (worth at least £1,800 sterling) on the way to Philadelphia and three wagons of pork headed for Fort Pitt for Baynton and Wharton. After traveling a little more than a hundred miles in four days he reached Carlisle and remained there for three days. He traded horses in Carlisle and set off for

Shippensburg, passing thirty head of cattle being driven to Fort Pitt for Baynton and Wharton. On the eighth day he passed sixteen horse loads of pelts (worth at least £480 sterling) headed for Philadelphia for Baynton and Morgan and 32 horse loads of flour for the garrison at Fort Pitt. After covering 34 miles through the hills, he reached Fort Loudon. The next day he arrived in Bedford, passing three wagons loaded with fifteen barrels of pork for Fort Pitt. He rested a day in Bedford and then met Indians on the road. He reached Fort Pitt on the thirteenth day in less time than a wagon. Whereas Clarkson rode as much as 35 miles in a day, a loaded wagon averaged only 10 miles.[29] The value of the deerskin and fur that he passed was at least £3,480 sterling and very likely £6,000 sterling or more. The total value of legal exports of fur and deerskin from Philadelphia annually was only £4,000 sterling.

The destination of most of the west bound traffic was Fort Pitt. In 1763 the fort had a garrison of 330 soldiers, 104 women, and 106 children plus some traders. Most of the women were attached to the army and received army rations. Many were wives of the soldiers and did laundry and other tasks in return for their rations.[30]

Fort Pitt on the Ohio River was the kingpin in the route to Illinois. From Fort Pitt in 1765, Colonel Bouquet had launched his campaign to pacify the Indians in Ohio. In August 1765 the expedition of one hundred men of the 42nd Regiment to occupy Illinois was sent from Fort Pitt.[31] Fort Pitt was a thriving community by 1766. Baynton and Wharton were building boats for their convoy for Illinois and had carpenters, boat men, and interpreters on their payroll. The Indian Department had two assistant Indian agents, an interpreter, and a doctor.[32] In addition to rations, the army was a steady market for rum for the merchants at Fort Pitt who sold it to the soldiers for 8/- Pennsylvania ($46) for a gallon compared to the much lower cost of 3/- New York ($18.90) on the coast.[33]

Many of the traders at Fort Pitt were former Pennsylvania militia officers, including Robert Callender, John Clark, Hugh Crawford, Fred Hambuck, Alexander McKee, William Patterson, John Prentice, Thomas Smallman, and at least fifteen others. Many of the Philadelphia merchants employed these former officers and others to act as their agents at Fort Pitt. Among those who had established trading stores at Fort Pitt in 1766 were Joseph Spear, John Gibson, Daniel Elliott, Alexander Lowery, and John Boggs.[34] John Hart was the agent for Field, Callender & Company in 1765.[35] Some of the traders at Fort Pitt were of poor character and traded rum freely to the Indians at the expense of the established traders, who had supplied the Indians on credit and were not paid.[36] The number of licensed traders in Pennsylvania was remarkably low. Only eighteen were licensed in 1765 and as few as ten in the following four years.[37]

Among the traders receiving licenses were William Trent, Joseph Simon, David Franks, and Levi Levy. Trent was a partner of Simon, Franks, and Levy, all Philadelphia Jews. The partners placed Trent in charge of the operations at

Fort Pitt in 1763 until 1769. Fort Pitt was the depot for the Pennsylvania traders and Trent sent agents throughout the area west of Fort Pitt.[38]

George Croghan had been in the fur trade in the 1750s and had become an Indian agent under the supervision of Sir William Johnson, head of the northern sector of the Indian Department. Croghan had business relations with William Trent and Baynton and Wharton.

Baynton and Wharton was a leading Quaker merchant house in Philadelphia with an extensive trade with Europe and the West Indies. Many of the merchants in Philadelphia were Quakers, who were part of a network of fellow Quakers throughout the colonies and in Britain. For example, John Reynell of Philadelphia was a close business associate of William Redwood, a Quaker merchant in Newport, Rhode Island.[39] Baynton and Wharton, the major competitor to Simon, Franks, and Levy, supplied large quantities of goods to the Indian Department.[40] Their competition would continue until the late 1760s, when Baynton and Wharton and their new partner Morgan went bankrupt as a result of the failure of their Illinois venture.

Although commerce with the Indians was prohibited in 1764 as a result of Pontiac's Uprising, in June 1765 General Gage ordered Governor Penn to open the trade as soon as possible as the Indians had made peace and trade was open in other areas.[41] Gage again ordered Penn to open the trade two weeks later as he had a report that the French were intensifying their activity in Illinois. The French had sent up the Mississippi two convoys of goods that would be used to draw the trade to Illinois. Governor Penn finally opened the trade to those who obtained licenses, and the wagons and pack horses streamed to Fort Pitt on the way west.[42]

The frontier had become a major market in the mid-eighteenth century. Pennsylvania merchants developed an extensive trade in the Ohio Valley with the Shawnee and the Delaware Indians.[43] The trade was substantial even before 1764; by 1762 the Pennsylvania Indian Commission sold nearly £22,000 Pennsylvania ($2,530,000) in merchandise to the Indians.[44] Philadelphia businessmen financed small traders who went to the Indian towns with a small stock of merchandise and rum worth about £400 sterling and returned with deerskins and pelts.[45]

The Treaty of Paris, which transferred all of the land east of the Mississippi River from France to Britain, opened a new market for the Pennsylvania traders. At Fort Pitt in 1764 Colonel Bouquet was preparing to occupy Illinois. Because Pennsylvania could not provide enough troops to protect any mission to Illinois, the permission and cooperation of the Indians were needed. Bouquet thought that Croghan was the best man to negotiate with the Delaware and Shawnee.[46] Croghan returned to Philadelphia in January after conferring with General Gage in New York and receiving his authorization to deal with the Indians to open the fur trade at Fort Pitt, Detroit, Michilimackinac, and Illinois. To pacify the Indians, Gage authorized Croghan to purchase presents for them worth £2,000 sterling ($400,000).[47] By mid-January Croghan had already received £439

Pennsylvania ($50,485) to pay bills to Philadelphia merchants.[48] In Canada General James Murray had declared the trade with the Indians open on 31 January 1765: therefore, time was of the essence if the Pennsylvania merchants were to get a share of the fur.

Baynton and Wharton had been planning in 1764 to expand their market to Illinois. The enthusiasm of the Philadelphia merchants to begin selling merchandise to the Indians was not shared by the people who lived on the frontier and had suffered from numerous attacks in 1764 as part of the uprising. Indian attacks on Pennsylvania traders continued in 1765. In June 1765 the Seneca Indians killed a trader near Fort Pitt. William Dice and another colonist had been killed by three Indians earlier near Redstone.[49]

The frontiersmen were especially concerned about the sale of guns, ammunition, and knives to the Indians. One of the most salable items was the "Indian gun," a small-caliber, smooth bore fowling piece or fusil that was lightweight and easy to carry compared to the heavy weight of the military musket. The fusil had enough power to wound a deer, enabling the Indian to finish it off with a knife, and also could be used in warfare.

In January 1765 the British were faced with a dilemma. The settlers objected to providing arms to the Indians, who only months ago had been killing families on the frontier. On the other hand, if the British and colonial merchants did not supply the Indians with needed guns, knives, and ammunition, the Indians would turn to the French from Illinois, who would instigate even more trouble to maintain Indian alliances and promote hostility toward the British.[50] At Fort Pitt in February 1765 Croghan conferred with the Shawnee, who promised to release white captives. However, Croghan deferred giving presents until the Indians had complied with the terms of the agreement. Croghan had £1,200 sterling worth of presents and £2,000 in cash to purchase more.[51]

In June 1765 Gage had urged Governor Penn to open the Indian trade officially despite the objections of the fearful settlers on the frontier. The Indians had met all terms of the agreements negotiated by Croghan in February. If goods were unavailable at Fort Pitt, Gage said the Indians would deal with the French in Illinois. By the end of June, Penn reopened trade, but in retaliation the frontiersmen were still threatening to attack the convoys.

Johnson had promised the Delaware Indians that trade would be reopened as a condition of peace on the frontier, and he was also making the same promise to the Chippewas and the Shawnee. He was concerned that the unhappy frontiersmen would continue to obstruct the movement of merchandise unless the army provided an escort.[52] Baynton and Wharton asked the British army to provide escorts. When the first escorted convoys went forward, shots were exchanged by the soldiers and the settlers.[53] The damage had been done. The settlers were at odds and the Indians did not trust the Pennsylvania merchants to supply them at Fort Pitt and went to Detroit with their fur, leaving Baynton and Wharton with unsold merchandise at Fort Pitt.[54]

Although the frontier trade would eventually prove disastrous to Baynton

and Wharton, the stakes were high at the time and might have paid off in
enormous profits. In January 1765 Baynton and Wharton recorded a net profit
of only £9,861 from 18 October 1763 to 31 January 1765. The records showed
an inventory of goods on hand at £6,445 Pennsylvania ($741,000).[55] During
this period, 1763 and 1764, Pontiac's Uprising had caused major losses to all
frontier traders, and the small profit that the partners made probably resulted
from their exports of flour and trade with southern Europe and the West Indies.
In 1765 the partners had a deficit of £3,940 Pennsylvania ($453,100) most of
it in the first half of the year. Only October and December were profitable (see
Table 3.1). By June 1765 Baynton and Wharton owed their supplier in England,
Richard Neave, £26,080 Pennsylvania ($2,999,200), equal to about six months
receipts for Baynton and Wharton.[56] Already in February 1765 Samuel
Wharton was trying to obtain bills of exchange from the Indian Department in
advance of providing the presents.[57]

Table 3.1 Baynton and Wharton Cash Received and Paid[58]
(in Pennsylvania Currency)

| Month | Cash Received | Cash Paid |
|---|---|---|
| March 1765 | £2,900 | £3,557 |
| May 1765 | £4,200 | £4,500 (est.) |
| June 1765 | £5,617 | £6,049 |
| July 1765 | £2,981 | £3,561 |
| August 1765 | £1,880 | £3,079 |
| September 1765 | £4,366 | £6,137 |
| October 1765 | £10,723 | £6,307 |
| November 1765 | £1,533 | £6,564 |
| December 1765 | £6,385 | £4,771 |
| Total | £40,585 | £44,525 |

The total cash flow out for Baynton and Wharton was £40,585 Pennsylvania
($4,770,000), a considerable sum. The deficit for nine months was £3,940
Pennsylvania and for the full year probably £5,250 Pennsylvania ($603,750),
about equal to the cash flow of a single month and less than the profit of the
previous year.

The Pennsylvania Indian Commission did not do even that well, recording
a profit of only £694 Pennsylvania on a gross of £14,000 ($1,610,000) for the

period 1760 to 1765. The commission's total profit was £9,014 Pennsylvania ($1,036,000) for all of their business to date.[59] Baynton and Wharton was a major customer of the Indian Commission. In early 1765 the firm purchased a large quantity of Indian goods worth £4,350 from them to be delivered to Fort Pitt for the Illinois venture. This one transaction was equal to half of the total profit of the commission.[60]

Both the Commission and Baynton and Wharton operated stores at Fort Augusta north of Fort Pitt. The partners' store was run by Thomas McKee. In May 1765 the store had an inventory of £1,752 Pennsylvania ($200,000), so it was a comparatively small venture equal to three canoes of merchandise in Canada.[61]

Pennsylvania traders were active in the Detroit market as well in 1765. A Pennsylvania merchant, Edmund Moran, was trying to collect debts of previous years from merchants in Detroit.[62] Baynton and Wharton paid some of their debt to Neave with a shipment of fur from Detroit owned by Robert Callender worth £3,000 Pennsylvania ($345,000). A similar amount of fur owned by Thomas Smallman, a relative of Croghan and involved in the Illinois venture, was shipped from Detroit to Neave by way of Montreal.[63]

These shipments of fur were an attempt to pay down the huge debt owed to Neave for orders of merchandise for the Illinois venture. To outline the magnitude of the merchandise gathered by Baynton and Wharton for the Illinois market, the total value ($2,185,000) was equal to the cargo of 29 canoes outfitted for trade in the Great Lakes. Thirty-nine canoes were licensed to go to Michilimackinac in 1765, and a total of 66 canoes, including Michilimackinac, were licensed for the entire year. The Baynton and Wharton Illinois venture was nearly half the value of the entire Canadian fur trade and three-fourths the value of the trade at Michilimackinac.

The partners in the Illinois venture were becoming dubious of success. In August 1765 Baynton and Wharton paid Samuel Eldridge £1,891 Pennsylvania for his one-tenth share of the venture. Eldridge and Baynton and Wharton were at odds over the failure of Eldridge to collect accounts in Quebec in 1764, which had cost the firm an enormous loss.[64] The sum paid Eldridge was equal to half the cash flow for a month for the firm, a considerable strain.

The huge purchases made for the Illinois venture and the inability to get the goods to Illinois to sell left Baynton and Wharton in a financial quandary in 1766. In January 1766 the partnership received £2,416, including £243 from the sale of fur. They paid out £2,344, a slightly favorable balance, but the volume of transactions was low, considering the immense investment in the Illinois venture.[65] In February the volume was even less, only £2,286 received and £2,399 paid out, mostly for merchandise. The consortium with Croghan, Callender, and Field was dissolved when Baynton and Wharton bought out the shares of the others and John Baynton retained his original share personally.[66] The amount paid to the other shareholders is unknown. The firm claimed a profit of £5,637 Pennsylvania ($648,000) for the twelve months ending 28

February 1766, but this amount seems possible only if the inventory of goods for Illinois is included as a valid asset.[67] Baynton and Wharton told Henry White, their agent in New York, that they had merchandise worth £40,000 Pennsylvania ($4,600,000) at several trading posts in the Indian country and in transit.[68]

Other Pennsylvania merchants were having difficulty on the frontier. In 1766 the army at Fort Pitt restricted trade to the fort and issued an order that any goods offered for sale to the Indians other than at the fort were subject to seizure by anyone, in the same manner as an abandoned ship.[69] However, these efforts to control trading off the post were futile. Because few Indians would go to the fort, the merchants in desperation sent men to the Indian villages to trade illegally. In 1767 some merchants at Fort Pitt protested that traders were in the Indian villages. The merchants demanded that the army force them to return to Fort Pitt in the spring of 1768.[70] Their plea was of no avail, for in January 1768 John Gibson and Daniel Elliott left Fort Pitt to trade with the Indians in the Delaware towns.[71]

Small trading posts were set up along the rivers west of Fort Pitt. A store established on the Scioto River in 1765 intercepted the Indians on the way to Fort Pitt and caused the Delaware Indians to complain about this favoritism granted to the Shawnee Indians.[72] In 1766 Baynton and Wharton received a license from Pennsylvania to set up another store in the Shawnee territory.[73]

Many of the financial problems of Baynton and Wharton revolved around George Croghan, who was striving to collect from the British army for his large purchases of gifts with Indian Department funds. Gage was insisting on details of each expenditure and even then was delaying payment. In May 1766 Croghan protested that Gage had not paid Baynton and Wharton for Croghan's purchases from them. The liberal terms of the agreement with Baynton and Wharton had been immediate payment in exchange for reasonable prices.[74] Croghan submitted an account in June 1766 that totaled £2,176 Pennsylvania ($250,240), most of which had been purchased from Baynton and Wharton (£937). Additional amounts were purchased from Alexander McKee and Joseph Simon. A sizable sum was owed for items taken from the army's stores at Fort Pitt, presumably gunpowder and lead balls. The payroll for the six men at Fort Pitt and Detroit—Richard Butler and Theophilus, gunsmiths; St. Martin and La Bute, interpreters; and Thomas McKee and Alexander Potts, agents—was another sizable item in the account. The gunsmiths repaired the damaged guns taken in by the Indians.[75]

Croghan gave Baynton and Wharton a draft for £2,321 New York, the equivalent of the Pennsylvania total, which the partners sent by special messenger to Johnson Hall in upper New York with instructions to wait for payment as cash was needed immediately.[76] Johnson made the payment in the form of a bill of exchange, but he questioned the amount and demanded vouchers and receipts for the expenditures from Baynton and Wharton. The partners insisted that Croghan had been given all the documents needed at Fort

Pitt in June.[77] Evidently Johnson was becoming very suspicious of the dealings between Croghan and Baynton and Wharton.

The bill of exchange Johnson gave to Baynton and Wharton was refused by Gage. The money was needed by Baynton and Wharton as they had no returns from the goods sent to Illinois and could not sell bills of exchange from Johnson. Philadelphia merchants refused to accept bills of exchange drawn by Johnson because the British treasury had refused bills in 1765.[78]

The financial problems of Baynton and Wharton continued. By August 1766 they had practically ceased their old business of fitting out ships and sending cargoes to London, Boston, Newfoundland, and other ports because of the long lag between investing the money in such ventures and receiving payment.[79] On the other hand, the partners continued to invest more money in frontier commerce. In February the partners had 140 horse loads (nearly thirteen tons) of goods on the road to Fort Pitt, including matchcoating, stroud, guns, powder, shirts, half thicks, rum, and knives.[80] Another example is purchase of French and English blankets worth £318 Pennsylvania ($36,570) from Henry White on 1 July 1766.[81] In April they sent goods valued at £926 by wagon to Fort Pitt.[82]

There was a steady run of charges ranging from £20 to £150 for transporting goods to and from the frontier from March to May 1766. In May they paid Mease and Miller £202 Pennsylvania ($23,230) for transporting goods to and from Fort Pitt.[83] In September Baynton and Wharton purchased from Franks and Inglis provisions worth £397 ($45,600) that were delivered to Fort Pitt.[84]

Baynton and Wharton joined with Thomas McKee to establish a store at Fort Pitt in 1766 to sell to the British garrison and buy fur that the Indians might take to the fort. For this purpose about £1,200 Pennsylvania worth of merchandise originally intended to go to Illinois was left at Fort Pitt.[85] Baynton and Wharton contributed £798 Pennsylvania in goods from the Augusta store and £919 Pennsylvania from their stock at Fort Pitt for a total investment in the new store of £1,717 Pennsylvania ($197,000).[86] In June John Irwin was given charge and instructed to clear out the store and to check the gunpowder, clothing, and other items for possible damage. Any fur that Joseph Spear should send down from Detroit to Irwin was to be sent to Philadelphia in Edward Morton's wagons.[87]

The partners were receiving substantial quantities of fur at Fort Pitt. In May King Beaver, a Delaware chief, had forty horse loads (at least 7,200 pounds worth $216,000) of fur to pay off his debt and to buy additional goods.[88] In September Baynton and Wharton sold beaver and raccoon worth £156 Pennsylvania ($18,000) from Fort Pitt to Andrew Tybout in Philadelphia.[89] The sale of these small lots likely means that they were being used to pay for smuggled goods, as fur was readily salable in Europe. Baynton and Wharton's affairs at Fort Pitt were being managed exceptionally well. Joseph Dobson had sent fourteen horse loads of fur obtained locally, had sixty more horse loads with Alexander Lowry to be sent to Philadelphia, and would collect another five horse loads from John Hart for a total of 79 horse loads or about seven tons of fur and deerskin.[90]

The partners' store at Fort Augusta was not doing well in 1766. Some of the stock was sent to Fort Pitt during the summer. In September beaver and raccoon from Fort Augusta worth only £62 were sold to Andrew Tybout.[91] George Croghan continued to be their major customer. By November they had sent Indian goods worth £1,683 ($193,545) to the trading store Croghan was operating on the Scioto River in the Shawnee territory.[92] This store intercepted Indians with furs on the way to Fort Pitt and effectively reduced the volume of trade enjoyed by the other merchants in Fort Pitt.

In September the partners pleaded with John Irwin, then their agent in Illinois, to send a thousand pounds of fur as soon as possible up the Ohio River to Fort Pitt. Peltry could be converted to cash immediately in Philadelphia, and the partners were in desperate need.[93] In 1766 Henry White, their agent in New York, made a payment of £4,000 sterling to Richard Neave, Baynton and Wharton's supplier in England. The payment was made with a draft from General Gage and a personal bill. In October Baynton and Wharton sent White £3,000 Pennsylvania, so most of the payment apparently was from White's personal account. In October Baynton and Wharton paid out £7,076 Pennsylvania ($813,740); hence the drain on the firm's resources to pay for the Illinois venture was never ending.[94]

At the end of November 1766, the firm owed Richard Neave £7,573 sterling ($1,515,000) compared to £15,000 sterling in June 1765; they had cut their debt in half in only eighteen months, primarily with the £4,000 sterling payment in September 1766. Where the partners acquired this large sum is unclear, possibly from the sale of small lots of furs in Philadelphia. The partners continued to draw bills of exchange on Neave, which Baynton and Wharton sold for Pennsylvania currency to pay their bills in Philadelphia. Such action merely delayed payment to Neave, who would have to be paid eventually, and created bad relations between Neave and the partners.[95] In November Moses Mordecai was paid £16 Pennsylvania for his efforts in selling £3,200 sterling ($640,000) in bills of exchange.[96] This enormous sum increased the debt to Neave to almost £9,000 sterling ($1,800,000). The bills were probably drawn on Richard Neave in London without his knowledge. In December the partners paid out only £3,097 Pennsylvania ($356,000) as they had little cash to meet their debts.[97]

In January and February of 1767 the downward spiral of the finances of Baynton and Wharton continued. They were able to pay for transporting goods to Fort Pitt and to pay their agents, but there was little other business. The account of sales to the British army and Indian Department at Fort Pitt for the period June 1766 to March 1767 was only £222 Pennsylvania ($25,530), a trivial sum, considering that the store had been stocked with merchandise worth £1,200 Pennsylvania in 1766. Most of the sales were for gifts to groups of up to four Indians. Because the spring was the best time to sell on the frontier, the total sales had increased to £450 Pennsylvania by 30 May 1767, but still the volume was very low.[98]

One of the problems with sales at Fort Pitt was that the merchants ignored the rules restricting them to the posts and went directly to the Indian villages to buy deerskin. They used pack horses to carry the merchandise and returned loaded with deer hides. The process was slow and the profits were very small, but the practice hurt Baynton and Wharton.[99] General Gage blamed Governor Penn for failing to enforce the rules—if the rules were not enforced, what was the use of having them.[100]

Baynton and Wharton did not fit out any new ships in 1767 and took in only minor receipts from a few previous voyages in 1766. There was no income from the flour or bread trade, once a major part of their business. They were meeting their obligations by selling sterling bills of exchange drawn on Richard Neave in London to James and Drinker, Jonathan Zane, and others, to obtain Pennsylvania currency.[101] Baynton and Wharton did have considerable assets. They listed the following at the end of January:

| | |
|---|---|
| Skins expected from Nuttle | £800 Pennsylvania |
| Skins expected from Gatter | £2,000 |
| Skins expected from Egdon | £2,600 |
| Skins sold at Philadelphia | £3,000 |
| Drafts on Sir William Johnson | £2,300 |
| Drafts on George Morgan | £4,000 |
| Bills from Finney | £1,300 |
| Bills from Messrs ? and March | £1,000 |
| Skins collected in town | £3,000 |
| Skins at Shawnee Town | £4,000 |
| Maisonville | £5,000 |
| Draft on Maisonville | £4,000 |
| Skins collected by Maisonville | £5,000 |
| Skins from Pittsburgh | £2,000 |
| | |
| Total | £40,000 Pennsylvania ($4,600,000)[102] |

This estimate of their worth was optimistic as most of the assets could not be readily converted to cash. The demand for cash was crucial. A noteworthy fact is that £14,000 of the assets was tied up with a French merchant, Alexander Maisonville in Ouiatanon on the Wabash River. Unlike most Frenchmen, Maisonville had a favorable attitude to the British and had bribed the Indians in 1763 not to kill the British soldiers in Ouiatanon, where in 1766 he was the leading merchant. In February 1766 Maisonville and Richard Winston, a British merchant at St. Joseph, ordered a major shipment of Indian goods from John Jennings, Baynton and Wharton's agent at Fort Pitt. The order included 2,000 French matchcoats, 2,000 gallons of Philadelphia rum, 30 gross of scalping knives, and 2,000 pounds of gunpowder.[103] This order would have supplied two thousand adult Indians, a large percentage of all of the Indians living along the Wabash River. Croghan recommended Maisonville to Samuel Wharton, and negotiations were under way to send him a shipment worth £1,600 Pennsylvania ($184,000) in May 1766.[104] By April 1766 the arrangement had been completed and Baynton and Wharton sent two boat loads of merchandise to Maisonville.[105] In September 1767 Baynton and Wharton received from him 125 packs of fur worth £1,542 Pennsylvania. The fur had been sent down the Mississippi River to New Orleans and shipped to Philadelphia on the sloop *York*.[106]

In February 1767 Baynton and Wharton drew bills on Richard Neave for £3,470 sterling ($694,000), which they expected to pay by shipments of fur and deerskins.[107] However, they had little actual cash to make payments. In the second half of January they were able to pay out only £2,407 Pennsylvania.[108] In February their future brightened when they received a payment of £1,700 sterling ($340,000) from the British government in payment for presents purchased by Croghan in Illinois in 1766.[109] Instead of sending this bill to Richard Neave to apply against their debt, the partners sold the bill for cash. In March George Morgan returned from Illinois with a draft from Edward Cole, the Indian Department agent there, for £1,468 New York ($185,000), which Baynton and Wharton sent immediately to Sir William Johnson for payment pleading that they had no money to meet their obligations.[110] Later in the month they received two sterling bills from General Gage, which they sold to Moses Mordecai for £859 Pennsylvania, again selling sterling bills for ready cash rather than paying their debt to Neave.[111]

In May 1767 Thomas Lawrence sold for Baynton and Wharton in New York City sterling bills of exchange that had been sent from Illinois, but the total was only £832 Pennsylvania ($95,680), a trifling sum, considering their investment in Illinois.[112] In June a draft drawn on Sir William Johnson for Indian Department expenditures arrived from Illinois by express, presumably by horseback. Baynton and Wharton sent the draft to Johnson, pleading for immediate payment of the £3,721 New York ($470,000), as they had received no other remittances from Illinois.[113] Johnson was slow to pay because of his concern about the validity of their accounts and was investigating each one.

Throughout the year they continued to receive small amounts of fur and deerskin from the frontier. In January they sold pelts worth £285 ($33,000) to Thomas Francis, Jacob Horn, Robert Towers, and Godfrey Deal.[114] Francis was a former Pennsylvania militia officer who was trying to obtain a position as an agent in the Indian Department. He was a minor trader who purchased only £20 worth. The others have not appeared in the records. Possibly these small purchases were made by merchants to pay for smuggled Dutch goods because shipping such small lots to England for sale would have been impractical. The partners were selling the furs to others in Philadelphia for immediate cash rather than sending them to London to pay their debt to Richard Neave. In

June the partners sold skins worth £229 Pennsylvania ($26,300) received from Joseph Spear and applied the amount to his account.[115] In September they sold another lot of skins received from Spears worth £257 Pennsylvania ($30,000).[116] A larger lot of skins arrived from Detroit and was sold for £1,044 Pennsylvania in the same month.[117] In November the partners paid Ralph Nailer £109 Pennsylvania for carrying 3,641 pounds of skins from Shawnee Town to Carlisle and an additional £730 Pennsylvania for carrying goods from Philadelphia to Fort Pitt.[118] The skins would have sold for about £546 Pennsylvania. In September the partners paid Daniel Duncan £543 Pennsylvania ($62,500) for carrying goods from Philadelphia to Fort Pitt.[119] The fees for carrying goods west indicated that major shipments were still being made to Fort Pitt.

Baynton and Wharton were continuing to buy merchandise and invest more money in the Illinois venture in an attempt to obtain revenue. In June 1767 they purchased 1,102 pairs of shoes from seven shoe makers in Philadelphia at from 6/- to 9/- a pair, about £400 Pennsylvania total—an indication of an attempt to sell to the French in Illinois.[120] Another shipment confirmed the same story. In October 1767 Joseph Hollingshead, one of the best agents working for the partners, set out with three boats from Fort Pitt manned by 25 boat men and 20 riflemen to hunt buffalo to supply rations to the British army in Illinois. In a third transaction John Campbell, their agent in Fort Pitt, recommended that the next shipment to Illinois include silver work for the Indians, 5,000 pounds of coffee, 5,000 pounds of sugar, 1,000 pounds of chocolate, 15 barrels of muscovado (unrefined) sugar, a chest of bohea (Chinese) tea, 100 pounds of green tea, 1,500 pairs of men's stockings, and English cheese.[121] Other than the silver, these goods were for sale to either the garrison or the French. The army had become the major customer for Baynton and Wharton in Illinois.

The merchants in Philadelphia were becoming reluctant to take orders from Baynton and Wharton. In May 1767 Joseph Simon, competing with Baynton and Wharton for the Illinois trade, advised Bernard Gratz to try to collect immediately the money from a bill drawn on Baynton and Wharton by George Croghan: "I hope you will dun them for the money due. I should not like to risk with their bills."[122]

Baynton and Wharton tried to collect outstanding debts. In August 1767 Croghan gave them a note for £459 Pennsylvania, presumably for Indian Department purchases.[123] In November James and Drinker paid Baynton and Wharton £1,540 ($177,000) and John Morris paid them £291. The partners received a loan of £400 from Reese Meredith, and Thomas Wharton loaned the firm £250.[124] The partners simply had insufficient capital to meet their obligations while awaiting the sale of merchandise in Fort Pitt, Illinois, and their other stores.

Further disaster befell the firm in July. A band of Chippewa Indians robbed two canoes of merchandise belonging to Baynton and Wharton and killed eleven men. The value of the merchandise was £3,000 Pennsylvania ($345,000).[125]

In August Samuel Wharton went to New York City to plead for payment of £2,000 Pennsylvania from General Gage but Gage, refused to see him.[126] In September Baynton and Wharton stopped payment because no money was arriving from Illinois. The merchants who were not paid appointed a group of trustees to look into the finances of the firm. The trustees found that the firm had a surplus of from £30,000 to £60,000 Pennsylvania if all of their merchandise were sold and amounts owed them were collected. However, the trustees commented that the partners had overextended themselves. The trustees gave them three years to settle their affairs; in the meantime they continued to do business.[127]

By March 1768 Baynton and Wharton were apparently weathering the crisis. Croghan purchased £1,200 Pennsylvania from the partners at Fort Pitt for Indian Department gifts to the Indians, and Sir William Johnson had recommended that Croghan purchase more.[128] The partners were very active in the frontier business; their journal for March and April is filled with entries for transport of goods to Fort Pitt, for wages, and for purchase of merchandise. In April they paid £1,578 Pennsylvania ($181,000) to various accounts.[129]

Also in April 1768 John Campbell, the Baynton and Wharton agent at Fort Pitt, sent out a hunting expedition down the Ohio River to obtain meat for sale to the army in Illinois. Campbell had difficulty finding men and finally recruited eighteen white men and three black men to serve under the direction of Captain Andrew(?) Robertson. Campbell hired a butcher, Frederick Dunfield, who knew how to cure and pack meat.[130]

Business was improving at Fort Pitt in 1768 and a considerable amount of deerskin was being collected. In January Robert McCulley was sent to the Shawnee Towns on the Scioto River with a stock of merchandise belonging to Baynton and Wharton and probably sold all of the goods. Twelve horse loads of deerskin had arrived from the Shawnee Towns in the past few months (valued at £360 sterling).[131] In July Joseph Spear, a close associate and former partner in the Illinois venture, sent six wagon loads of deerskin (at least six tons worth £1,800 sterling, $360,000) from Carlisle to Philadelphia.[132] These amounts are significant when one considers that the total annual legal export of fur and deerskin from Philadelphia was only £4,000 sterling.

Baynton and Wharton must have had brisk sales at their Fort Pitt store in the first half of 1768. In March Samuel Wharton thanked Johnson for telling Croghan to purchase £1,200 Pennsylvania worth of Indian goods at Fort Pitt from Baynton and Wharton.[133] In April the store was without liquor, silver, shirts, guns, powder, and lead. Croghan needed to buy goods for an Indian treaty and would have to go elsewhere.[134] In May Croghan transferred goods worth £243 Pennsylvania at Fort Pitt back to Baynton and Wharton to be sold to Pennsylvania for Indian presents. The partner's store did not have sufficient stock to fill the order and Croghan provided the needed items.[135]

The partners were slow to replace their stock. In the three months ending 20 July 1768, Baynton and Wharton purchased merchandise worth £1,892

Pennsylvania ($217,000), a comparatively small amount.[136] The goods were probably purchased for Illinois as Joseph Dobson, the partner's agent at Carlisle, was moving merchandise from Carlisle to Fort Pitt in July in time to have it sent to Illinois along with a military convoy.[137]

The business in Illinois continued to be active. In November 1768 Robert Callender, a former partner in the Illinois venture, left Carlisle on his way to Fort Chartres in Illinois with 2,000 gallons of rum on 100 horses and 40 horse loads of dry goods.[138] The dry goods would have weighed about 7,200 pounds and the rum about 16,000 pounds for a total of approximately 12 tons, roughly the amount carried by four canoes in the Canadian trade. Therefore, this was a major shipment, worth up to £1,600 sterling ($320,000). A week later Joseph Spear, another former partner in the Illinois venture, left Carlisle with sixty horse loads of rum and Indian goods bound for Fort Pitt. Included in this shipment were ten hogsheads of rum (630 gallons, about thirty horse loads).[139] The total shipment was over five tons and equal to two canoe loads in Canada with a value of about £800 sterling ($160,000). The timing of the shipments was significant. The road to Fort Pitt was often closed by snow in December and the Ohio River was frozen until the following spring. Therefore, these large shipments were made in anticipation of an expansion of trade in Illinois in 1769.

By mid-1769 Baynton and Wharton claimed to have recouped all of their losses and made a profit. For the period 28 February 1766 to 24 September 1769 the firm claimed a net profit of £20,544 Pennsylvania ($2,363,000) including £10,000 Pennsylvania in profits from Illinois.[140] If the account is accurate, the firm had a sudden turn for the better in 1768. However in a downturn the partners lost the army ration business to David Franks and withdrew from the Illinois market selling their stock of goods to Franks at a discount which would have accounted for the improved cash flow.

The partners did well to abandon the Illinois market. In 1768 Fort Pitt was threatened with the loss of the army garrison. Gage believed its cost was not worthy of maintaining the garrison and considered it the most difficult to guard in the event of trouble with the Indians. The only function of the post was to maintain communication with Illinois which was also to lose its garrison.[141] The garrison was withdrawn and moved to the east coast leaving the Illinois market in the hands of the French.

In anticipation of a healthy business with the army, a large amount of capital had been invested in the western market by Philadelphia merchants. The following table presents the overall picture. Most of the figures are estimates based on scraps of information gleaned from the four-year period. The values of the fur and deerskin are those received in the London market.

The estimates in Table 3.1 are based on fragmentary evidence, including orders by Baynton and Wharton for merchandise for the Fort Pitt and Fort Augusta stores. Payments as high as £25 sterling to carry a wagon load of about a ton of goods to Fort Pitt were common. A rough estimate of the value of a ton of miscellaneous trade goods is £125 sterling. Twelve pack horses could carry a ton and a single convoy of 410 horses carrying 34 tons left Fort Loudon in 1764. The value of this shipment alone was about £4,250 sterling. The shipment may have included rations for the army, but it does confirm that the total value of goods sent to the Pennsylvania frontier probably exceeded the £33,000 sterling in Table 3.1. The value of the army rations is calculated at 75% of the return.

Table 3.1 Pennsylvania Balance Sheet
(in £000 sterling)

| Assets Invested | | |
|---|---|---|
| Merchandise primarily from Britain | | £7 |
| Colonial produce | | |
| Rations for army at Fort Pitt | | £23 |
| Rum for army and frontier trade | | £3 |
| Total | | £33 |
| Assets Received | | |
| Fur and deerskin exports | (legal exports, £4; smuggled, £15) | |
| from the Ohio Valley | £6 | |
| from Detroit | £5 | |
| from Fort Augusta | £3 | |
| from New Orleans | £5 | |
| Total | | £19 |
| English Bills of exchange from the army | | £30 |
| Total | | £49 |

Trade goods were normally exchanged for double their value in fur and deerskin, which would have been about £17,000 sterling in fur for the merchandise and part of the rum sent to the frontier. Baynton and Wharton asked two associates to send £6,000 Pennsylvania (£3,450 sterling) from Detroit in 1765 so the £5,000 sterling estimated as arriving from Detroit is probably low. The inventory of the Fort Augusta store would indicate a trade of at least £3,000 sterling. Maisonville, one of the Baynton and Wharton agents, had fur and deerskin worth £5,000 Pennsylvania (£2,875) to ship to Philadelphia in 1767, and Morgan was sending more from Fort Chartres, so the £5,000 sterling is reasonable. In 1767 Baynton and Wharton had fur and deerskin worth £9,400 Pennsylvania (£5,404 sterling) in the hands of agents on the Pennsylvania frontier, hence the estimate of £6,000 sterling in Table 3.1 is probably conservative.

In the early 1760s legal exports of fur from Philadelphia were valued by customs at about £20,000 sterling (London value £40,000 sterling) so the estimate is probably low. Available records show only about £4,000 sterling worth of fur and deerskin at London prices was exported legally in the late 1760s; therefore, at least a large share of the remaining £16,000 sterling must have been smuggled. The local market was very limited. Hat makers and glove makers in America are seldom mentioned in the financial correspondence, in contrast to other trades.

The fur and deerskin had a ready market in Europe and were probably smuggled out on Dutch and colonial ships plying the trade between southern Europe and Philadelphia. About fifty schooners and sloops loaded with an average of sixty tons of bread and flour from Philadelphia sailed to Lisbon and returned with small cargoes of wine and salt. The ships could load illegal European goods in Lisbon or the West Indies and unload them before entering the port at Philadelphia. Many ships arrived either empty or with small cargoes. One ship had unloaded so much before entering the port that the captain had difficulty managing the ship. A long list of the Dutch goods available at St. Eustatius imported by William West was in the Baynton and Wharton financial records.[142]

With ships of the Royal Navy the British began to enforce the laws against smuggling in 1768 after years of salutary neglect. In the years that followed, the Philadelphia merchants suffered from the loss of this lucrative source of income.

One can assume that the limited success of the Pennsylvania merchants in the Ohio trade had an important effect on the development of the west. The trade from Fort Pitt fell into the hands of the Gratz Brothers of Philadelphia, who financed the Croghan group of Thomas Smallman, Alexander McKee, and Alexander Ross in 1771. The unsuccessful merchants turned to land jobbing schemes and new colonies to make up their losses. The "suffering traders," representing those who had lost goods during Pontiac's Uprising, were the same men who made up the Illinois Land Company. Many of those who lost money in frontier commerce in the late 1760s blamed the British government for its failure to contain French competition from Illinois and its parsimonious policy concerning presents to the Indians which would have purchased their loyalty and prevented a great deal of conflict.

## NOTES

1. *Historical Statistics of the United States: Colonial Times to 1957* (Washington, DC: U.S. Department of Commerce, 1960), p. 757.

2. Arthur L. Jensen, *The Maritime Commerce of Colonial Philadelphia* (Madison: The State Historical Society of Wisconsin, 1963), pp. 68, 90-91.

3. Jensen, p. 48.

4. George Allsopp to Baynton and Wharton, 24 June 1766, Baynton, Wharton & Morgan Papers, Microfilm, 10 Rolls, Original in Pennsylvania Historical Commission [BWM], Roll 3.

5. Jensen, p. 119; Clark to Bouquet, 24 August 1759, *Canadian Archives Report 1889* (Ottawa: Canadian Archives, 1889), p. 316.

6. Ernst A. Cruikshank, "Early Traders and Trade Routes in Ontario and the West, 1760-1783," *Transactions of the Royal Canadian Institute,* vol. 3, p. 257.

7. George Shumway, Edward Durell, and Howard C. Frey, *Conestoga Wagon, 1750-1850* (York, PA: George Shumway, 1966), p. 49.

8. Edward Pierce Hamilton, *The French and Indian War* (Garden City, NY: Doubleday, 1962), p. 3.

9. Vernor W. Crane, *The Southern Frontier, 1670–1732* (Philadelphia: Drake University Press, 1929), p. 127.

10. Bouquet to Stanwix, 20 May 1759, *Canadian Archives Report*, 1889, p. 37.

11. Croghan Journal, 21 April 1765, *Pennsylvania Colonial Records*, 10 vols. (Philadelphia: J. Severns & Co., 1851–52), vol. 9, p. 253.

12. Nicholas B. Wainwright, *George Croghan, Wilderness Diplomat* (Chapel Hill: University of North Carolina Press, 1959), p. 215.

13. Hamilton, pp. 18–19.

14. Captain Lee's Journal, 1759, *Canadian Archives*, 1889, pp. 149–51.

15. Baynton and Wharton Journal B, 20 May 1766, BWM, Roll 8.

16. Baynton and Wharton Journal B, 4 August 1766, BWM, Roll 8.

17. Baynton and Wharton Journal B, 7 October 1766, BWM, Roll 8.

18. Joseph Dobson to Baynton and Wharton, 20 August 1768, BWM, Roll 3.

19. Stephen Duncan to Baynton and Wharton, 9 October 1766, BWM, Roll 3.

20. Joseph Rigby to Baynton and Wharton, 28 May 1768, BWM, Roll 5.

21. Morgan to Baynton and Morgan, 22 April 1766, *Illinois State Historical Collections* (Springfield: Trustees of the Illinois State Historical Library, 1903–) [IHC], vol. 11, p. 217.

22. Callender to Bouquet, March 27, 1764, *Canadian Archives*, 1889, pp. 250–52.

23. Baynton and Wharton Journal A, May 1765, BWM, Roll 8.

24. Baynton and Wharton Journal B, 15 May 1766, BWM, Roll 8.

25. M. Clarkson Diary, 25 August 1766, IHC, vol. 11, p. 355.

26. Contract for Hauling Merchandise, 21 March 1766, IHC, vol. 11, pp. 192–93.

27. Baynton and Wharton, Journal B, 20 February 1767, BWM, Roll 8.

28. Contract for Hauling Goods, 2 September 1766, IHC, vol. 11, pp. 368–69.

29. M. Clarkson Diary, 6-18 August 1766, IHC, vol. 11, pp. 349–52.

30. *Canadian Archives*, 1889, p. 231.

31. Gage to Johnson, 8 July 1765, Sir William Johnson, *The Papers of Sir William Johnson*, 14 vols. (Albany: The State University of New York Press, 1921–1965) [JMss], vol. 11, p. 833; Eddingstone to _____, 17 October 1765, IHC, vol. 11, p. 105.

32. M. Clarkson Diary, 19 August to 16 September 1766, IHC, vol. 11, pp. 353–59; Account of Alexander McKee, 24 March 1766, JMss, vol. 5, pp. 100–2.

33. John Campbell to Baynton and Wharton, 21 January 1768, BWM, Roll 3.

34. Joseph Spear to Johnson, 4 October 1766, JMss, vol. 5, pp. 384–85.

35. Baynton and Wharton Journal A, May 1765, BWM, Roll 8.

36. Charles A. Hanna, *The Wilderness Trail*, 14 vols. (New York: G. P. Putnam's, 1911), vol. 2, p. 302.

37. Traders Licenses Dispensed in the Secretary's Office, 1762–1768, John B. Linn and Dr. William H. Egle, eds., *Pennsylvania Archives*, 2nd Series, 19 vols. (Harrisburg, PA: Joseph Severns, 1874–1893), [PA], 2nd Series, vol. 2, p. 621.

38. A. T. Volwiler, ed., "William Trent's Journal at Fort Pitt, 1763," *Mississippi Valley Historical Review*, vol. 11, pp. 390–92; George A. Cribbs, *The Frontier Policy of Pennsylvania* (Pittsburgh: [no publisher], 1919), p. 24.

39. Jensen, p. 70.

40. N. Franklin, "Pennsylvania-Virginia Rivalry," *Mississippi Valley Historical Review*, vol. 20, p. 474.

41. Gage to Penn, 2 June 1765, IHC, vol. 10, p. 516.

42. Gage to Penn, 16 June 1765, IHC, vol. 10, p. 516; Franklin, MVHR, vol. 20, p. 476; Marjorie Reid, "The Quebec Fur Traders and Western Policy, 1763–1774," *Canadian Historical Review*, vol. 6, p. 21.

43. Charles H. McIlwain, *Wraxall's Abridgement of the New York Indian Records, 1678–1751* (Cambridge, MA: Harvard University Press, 1914), p. xxl.

44. Invoice Book of Skins, Pennsylvania Indian Commission, Gratz Collection, Historical Society of Pennsylvania.

45. Paul C. Phillips, *The Fur Trade*, 2 vols. (Norman: University of Oklahoma Press, 1961) vol. 1, pp. 401, 505–506.

46. Bouquet to Gage, 5 January 1765, IHC, vol. 10, p. 397.

47. Wainwright, p. 213; Croghan to Johnson, 1 January 1765, JMss, vol. 11, pp. 519–20.

48. Baynton and Wharton Journal A, 18 January 1765, BWM, Roll 8.

49. Alexander McKee to Johnson, 18 June 1765, JMss, vol. 11, pp. 796–97.

50. Gage to Governor Penn, 16 June 1765, *Pennsylvania Colonial Records*, vol 9, p. 268.

51. Croghan Journal, 9 May 1765, *Pennsylvania Colonial Records*, vol. 9, pp. 257–58; Randolph C. Downes, *Council Fires on the Upper Ohio* (Pittsburgh: University of Pittsburgh Press, 1940), p. 127.

52. Johnson to Governor Penn, 7 June 1765, PA, 1st series, vol. 4, p. 227.

53. Gage to Penn, 2 June 1765, IHC, vol. 10, p. 516; Gage to Penn, 16 June 1765, IHC, vol. 10, pp. 518–19; Gage to Johnson, 30 June 1765, JMss, vol. 4, p. 780.

54. Baynton and Wharton to Johnson, 7 July 1765, JMss, vol. 4, p. 787.

55. Baynton and Wharton, Journal A, 31 January 1765, BWM, Roll 8.

56. Baynton and Wharton, Journal A, June 1765, BWM, Roll 8.

57. Samuel Wharton to J Baynton, 15 February 1765, BWM, Roll 5.

58. Baynton and Wharton, Journal A, March, July, August, September, October, November, and December 1765, BWM, Roll 8.

59. Invoice Book of Skins, Pennsylvania Indian Commission, September 1765, Gratz Collection, Historical Society of Pennsylvania.

60. Baynton and Wharton Journal A, August 1765, BWM, Roll 8.

61. Baynton and Wharton Journal A, May 1765, BWM, Roll 8.

62. Edmund Moran to Captain Shelby, 31 August 1765, Edmund Moran Papers, State Historical Society of Wisconsin.

63. Baynton and Wharton to Richard Neave, 6 February 1765, BWM, Roll 5.

64. Baynton and Wharton, Journal A, 2 August 1765, BWM, Roll 7.

65. Baynton and Wharton, Journal A, January 1766, BWM, Roll 8.

66. Baynton and Wharton, Journal B, 28 February 1766, BWM, Roll 8.

67. Baynton and Wharton, Journal B, 28 February 1766, BWM, Roll 8.

68. Baynton and Wharton to Henry White, 16 February 1766, BWM, Roll 1.

69. Alex Mackay to the People West of the Mountain, 22 June 1766, PA, 1st Series, vol. 4, pp. 251–52.

70. John Campbell to Baynton and Wharton, 11 November 1767, BWM, Roll 3.

71. John Campbell to Baynton and Wharton, 21 January 1768, BWM, Roll 3.

72. Alexander McKee to Johnson, 25 September 1766, JMss, vol. 5, p. 383.

73. Baynton and Wharton to Gage, 10 August 1766, JMss, vol. 5, p. 344.

74. Croghan to Gage, 1 May 1766, IHC, vol. 11, pp. 222–23.

75. Croghan's Account against the Crown, 12 June 1766, IHC, vol. 11, p. 258.

76. Baynton and Wharton, 5 July 1766, IHC, vol. 11, pp. 330–31.

77. Baynton and Wharton to Johnson, 28 December 1766, IHC, vol. 11, pp. 464–66.

78. Croghan to Gage, 1 May 1766, IHC, vol. 11, p. 223.

79. Baynton and Wharton, Journal B, July and August 1766, BWM, Roll 8.

80. Baynton and Wharton to Dobson, 11 February 1766, BWM, Roll 1.

81. Baynton and Wharton, Journal B, 1 July 1766, BWM, Roll 8.

82. Baynton and Wharton, Journal B, 16 April 1766, BWM, Roll 8.

83. Baynton and Wharton, Journal B, 24 May 1766, BWM, Roll 8.

84. Baynton and Wharton, Journal B, 4 September 1766, BWM, Roll 8.

85. Samuel Wharton to John Baynton, 30 May 1766, BWM, Roll 2.

86. Baynton and Wharton, Journal B, 17 July 1766, BWM, Roll 8.

87. Instructions to John Irwin, 27 June 1766, BWM, Roll 5; Baynton and Wharton to John Irwin, 31 July 1766, IHC, vol. 11, p. 347.

88. Samuel Wharton to John Baynton, 30 May 1766, BWM, Roll 2.

89. Baynton and Wharton, Journal B, 2 September 1766, BWM, Roll 8.

90. Dobson to Baynton and Wharton, 9 March 1766, IHC, vol. 11, pp. 166–67.

91. Baynton and Wharton, Journal B, 2 September 1766, BWM, Roll 8.

92. Baynton and Wharton, Journal B, 29 November 1766, BWM, Roll 8.

93. Baynton and Wharton to John Irwin, 21 September 1766, IHC, vol. 11, pp. 385–86.

94. Baynton and Wharton, Journal B, 28 October 1766, BWM, Roll 8.

95. Baynton and Wharton, Journal B, 29 November 1766, Roll 8.

96. Baynton and Wharton, Journal B, 18 November 1766, BWM, Roll 8.

97. Baynton and Wharton, Journal B, 29 December 1766, BWM, Roll 8.

98. Thomas McKee to Baynton and Wharton, Ledger A2, BWM, Roll 10.

99. Review of the Trade by Johnson, 22 September 1767, Edmund B. O'Callaghan and Fernold Berthold, eds., *Documents Relating to the Colonial History of the State of New York*, 15 vols. (Albany, NY: Weed, Parsons, 1853–1887) [NYCD], vol. 7, p. 953; Petition of Traders to Croghan, 18 December 1767, JMss, vol. 6, p. 19.

100. Gage to Johnson, 28 June 1767, JMss, vol. 5, p. 573.

101. Baynton and Wharton, Journal B, January and February 1767, BWM, Roll 8.

102. Baynton and Wharton to Trent, 30 January 1767, BWM, Roll 5.

103. John Jennings to Baynton and Wharton, 25 February 1766, BWM, Roll 6.

104. Samuel Wharton to John Wharton, 30 May 1766, BWM, Roll 2.

105. Baynton and Wharton, Journal B, 16 April 1767, BWM, Roll 8.

106. Baynton and Wharton, Journal C, 24 September 1767, BWM, Roll 9.

107. Baynton and Wharton, Journal B, 20 February 1767, BWM, Roll 8.

108. Baynton and Wharton, Journal B, 4 February 1767, BWM, Roll 8.

109. Baynton and Wharton, Journal B, 6 February 1767, BWM, Roll 8.

110. Baynton and Wharton to Johnson, 16 March 1767, IHC, vol. 11, p. 519.

111. Baynton and Wharton, Journal B, 31 March 1767, BWM, Roll 8.

112. Baynton and Wharton, Journal B, 7 May 1767, BWM, Roll 8.

113. Baynton and Wharton to Johnson, 21 June 1767, IHC, vol. 11, p. 580.

114. Baynton and Wharton, Journal B, 26 January 1767, BWM, Roll 8.

115. Baynton and Wharton, Journal C, 28 June 1767, BWM, Roll 9.

116. Baynton and Wharton, Journal C, 24 September 1767, BWM, Roll 9.

117. Baynton and Wharton, Journal C, 25 September 1767, BWM, Roll 9.

118. Baynton and Wharton, Journal C, 4 November 1767, BWM, Roll 9.

119. Baynton and Wharton, Journal C, 19 September 1767, BWM, Roll 9.

120. Baynton and Wharton Memo Book, #684, 25 June 1767, BWM, Roll 10.

121. John Campbell to Baynton and Wharton, 18 October 1767, BWM, Roll 3.

122. Joseph Simon to Bernard Gratz, 10 May 1767, IHC, vol. 11, p. 570.

123. Baynton and Wharton, Journal C, 27 August 1767, BWM, Roll 9.

124. Baynton and Wharton, Journal C, 10 November 1767, BWM, Roll 9.

125. Alexander McKee to Croghan, 20 September 1767, JMss, vol. 5, p. 686.

126. Samuel Wharton to John Baynton, 21 August 1767, BWM, Roll 5.

127. Galloway to William Franklin, 6 September 1767, IHC, vol. 16, p. 8; Croghan to Johnson, 25 September 1767, IHC, vol. 16, p. 67.

128. Johnson to Samuel Wharton, 5 March 1768, JMss, vol. 6, pp. 141–42.

129. Baynton and Wharton, Journal C, March and April 1768, BWM, Roll 9.

130. John Campbell to Baynton and Wharton, 8 April 1768, BWM, Roll 3.

131. John Campbell to Baynton and Wharton, 9 January 1768, BWM, Roll 3.

132. Joseph Dobson to Baynton and Wharton, 5 July 1768, BWM, Roll 3.

133. Samuel Wharton to Johnson, 23 March 1768, JMss, vol. 6, pp. 168–69.

134. John Campbell to Baynton and Wharton, 8 April 1768, BWM, Roll 3.

135. Receipt of John Campbell, 6 May 1768, BWM, Roll 3.

136. Baynton and Wharton, Journal C, 20 July 1768, BWM, Roll 9.

137. Joseph Dobson to Baynton and Wharton, 5 July 1768, BWM, Roll 3.

138. Joseph Dobson to Baynton and Wharton, 26 November 1768, BWM, Roll 3.

139. Joseph Dobson to Baynton and Wharton, 26 November 1768, BWM, Roll 3.

140. Baynton and Wharton, Journal C, 24 September 1769, BWM, Roll 9.

141. Gage to Hillsborough, 16 June 1768, IHC, vol. 16, pp. 318–19.

142. St. Eustatius, no date, frames 803–04, BWM Roll 6.

# 4

## ILLINOIS

In the 1760s, the term "Illinois" referred to the area east of the Mississippi River roughly corresponding to the modern state of Illinois. The potential of this market served by the Ohio, Missouri, and Mississippi Rivers was far greater than that of the other two trading areas, Canada and New York. The Illinois climate was more hospitable and the Indian population greater than either north or south. North of the Great Lakes in the Hudson Bay area the climate was so severe that survival was difficult and the density of Native Americans was low. South of the Ohio River the warmer climate was not favorable to animals with heavy coats and deerskin was the primary pelt gathered. The moderate climate of the Great Lakes and the upper Mississippi and Missouri Valleys including Illinois offered a bountiful harvest of fur and livable conditions for the Indians as well as excellent transportation.

The Indians formed an expanding market for a wide range of dry goods and liquor. Those west of the Mississippi were as eager to have European goods as those to the north who had more experience with French traders. However, the colonists failed in their attempt to wrest the trade from the French who remained in control of the Illinois trade throughout the period between 1760 and 1774. The colonial merchants had to settle for the French farmers and the British army as markets.

The two major mercantile firms competing in Illinois were Baynton and Wharton of Philadelphia and Maxent, LaClede, and Company, the French firm that founded St. Louis. These two companies and their business associates competed for the furs from the Indians as well as sterling bills of exchange from the British army, the two most significant assets that could be used to pay for imports to the area. Some farm products did find a market in New Orleans to feed the people there, to provision visiting ships, and to export to France and other countries, but the farm produce was bulky and difficult to preserve in the warm New Orleans climate.

The French merchants controlled the direct trade with the Indians and obtained the fur in exchange for French merchandise carried up from New Orleans plus some goods that the French purchased from Pennsylvania merchants. Baynton and Wharton imported cheaper British dry goods and colonial liquor, but the French were reluctant to exchange an appreciable amount of fur for this colonial merchandise. Instead Baynton and Wharton were forced to sell their goods to the farmers for farm produce, which was in turn sold to the army for rations. The French farmers were eager to take the dry goods and liquor from Baynton and Wharton but were reluctant to accept English bills of exchange for their produce. Baynton and Wharton were happy to receive bills of exchange because the bills could be used to pay debts in England. George Morgan, Baynton and Wharton's agent in Illinois, used some of the fur he was able to obtain to pay for the merchandise from New Orleans, but most of the fur was sent to Philadelphia.[1]

As long as the British army remained in Illinois, the Pennsylvania merchants could profit from the three-sided trade among the army, the French farmers, and them. However, Baynton and Wharton were not able to make a serious inroad on the fur trade. In 1766 General Gage reported that the British did not control the fur trade in Illinois and neighboring area even though the territory was part of the British Empire. The French were the major hindrance that prevented the colonists and the British from expanding the Illinois market. Despite the lower cost of British merchandise and the difficulty of moving French merchandise upstream, the French in Illinois continued to deal with New Orleans merchants. Fur from Illinois, the Great Lakes, the Missouri Valley, and the upper Mississippi continued to move to St. Louis and from there to New Orleans, where much of it was exported to France.

The colonial merchants had hoped futilely that the acquisition of Illinois and the right to transport goods down the Mississippi River for export to Europe would be a major benefit of the Treaty of Paris. The persistent French determined otherwise because they and later the Spaniards retained control of New Orleans, the only navigable outlet for the trade moving down the Mississippi and entering the Gulf of Mexico.

In 1766 a British officer described New Orleans as only a small town with few good houses, but with people who were healthy and prosperous. In 1769 New Orleans had 1,902 free persons (including 31 blacks and 68 of mixed blood), 1,225 slaves, and 60 "domesticated" Indians. The main business of the town was trading furs and deerskin from Illinois.[2]

Under the French the commerce of the Mississippi River had continually flowed down to New Orleans from Illinois. Skins and hides as well as flour, bacon, corn, ham, corned pork, corned beef, beeswax, cotton, tallow, leather, tobacco, lead, copper, buffalo hides, wool, venison, poultry, bear grease, and oil were sent to New Orleans. In 1765 the merchants of New Orleans imported 15,000 barrels of flour, 2,000 barrels of pork, and 1,200 barrels of beef from various locations.[3] Bartholomew MacNamara, a British merchant in New Orleans, offered to pay Morgan cash or merchandise in Illinois, Philadelphia, or New York City for flour and asked for as many barrels of flour as Morgan could send him.[4]

Indigo, rice, and tobacco from plantations around New Orleans and Illinois went to Europe and lumber went to the West Indies.[5] In January 1767, 100,000 pounds of indigo, 300 tons of cotton, plus tobacco, rice, and sugar were exported from New Orleans.[6] In 1767 British merchants in New Orleans exported flour and pork from Illinois to the French and Spanish West Indies. The British sent 3,000 barrels of flour and pork to Spanish Cuba that year, and the governor wanted a make a contract for 8,000 barrels.[7]

To supplement their business the British merchants in New Orleans also imported large numbers of slaves, selling 300 to the French plantation owners in 1767.[8] The slaves were also sent north to Illinois. In 1768 slaves were selling in Illinois for £360 Pennsylvania ($41,400) compared to the lower New Orleans price of £200 Pennsylvania. Slaves were a valuable commodity. Three hundred slaves were worth £34,500 sterling ($12,300.000) in New Orleans, compared to the total value of the Canadian fur trade of less than £100,000 sterling. Slaves were in such demand that the French farmers in Illinois were eager to sell for them flour, cattle, and salt beef to Morgan and the French merchants. The provisions received for the slaves were in turn sold to the British army.[9]

Even Baynton and Wharton resorted to purchasing goods in New Orleans in 1767 and 1768. In 1767 MacNamara in New Orleans had ordered a cask of wine and cloth for George Morgan.[10] Wine was a major import from New Orleans. In 1768 Morgan ordered four hogsheads and six cases of bottled wine and paid with army bills of exchange. In June 1768 Morgan paid MacNamara for a gross of knives and two hogsheads of wine that were sent up the Mississippi.[11]

Nevertheless, in New Orleans fur was the major business and the most valuable export. Shelburne believed that one-half of all the Indian trade in North America, including Lake Michigan, Green Bay, St. Joseph, Illinois, the upper Mississippi, the Ohio Valley, and lesser rivers flowing into the Mississippi, could be exported to Britain from New Orleans if it were not deliberately diverted to France.[12] The value of the furs that could be obtained in Illinois and the regions served by the French traders was immense, enough to make any firm that was successful in exploiting this market a dominant force in the world fur trade.

In 1765 an official estimate of the fur exported from New Orleans was 700,000 skins (worth approximately £100,000 sterling, $20,000,000), including both deerskin and fur.[13] The Spaniards reported in 1766 that the fur trade had been flourishing in the past two years and estimated that nearly 1 million pelts had been sent from New Orleans to France.[14] The term "pelts" could have included deerskins and miscellaneous low-value fur such as raccoon and muskrat. A beaver pelt weighed about a pound and sold for one Spanish dollar in Montreal in 1761. Assuming one-half of the pelts were beaver, they would have had a value of 500,000 Spanish dollars (£107,500 sterling or $21,500,000), and the others added at least another £50,000 sterling ($10,000,000. The Spanish estimate of 1 million pelts worth about £150,000 sterling may have been an exaggeration.

A 1767 estimate of the exports of New Orleans included 8,000 packs of beaver and deerskin worth an average of 80 Spanish dollars (a Spanish dollar was worth $43 and a pack $3,440. Eight thousand packs were worth $27,520,000 or £137,600 sterling). The value of the furs sent to France was estimated by George Croghan in 1767 at £80,000 sterling ($16,000,000) in that year.[15] This estimate was forwarded to Shelburne by Gage, who thought it might be high.[16]

In 1767 Baynton and Wharton estimated the value of peltry sent annually to France from New Orleans to be £100,000 sterling ($20,000,000).[17] In 1769 the commander of the British troops in Illinois estimated that the total potential value of furs available from Illinois was £53,900 sterling and that a total of 3,300 packs could be gathered, each worth an average of 70 Spanish dollars (a total of 231,000 Spanish dollars or nearly $10,000,000). The pelts would arrive from the Mississippi River valley (500 packs); from the Missouri River valley (1,000 packs); from Illinois (500 packs); from the Peoria, Kaskaskia area (400 packs); and from the Wabash River valley (900 packs). As Wilkins commented, the trade was worth the trouble.[18]

One-third of the peltry was estimated to be from the Missouri Valley, which the French considered the vital new market for their goods. By 1766 400 leagues (about 1,200 miles) of the Missouri had been explored by the French voyageurs, which, given the twists and turns of the river, was probably somewhere in present day South Dakota.[19] The St. Louis governor, Kerlerec, estimated the value of the Missouri trade at 8,000 French livres, only $80,000 at a rate of $10 per livre compared to the Wilkins estimate of 1,000 packs worth $3,290,000. The "French" livre must have had a much higher value, perhaps $40, than the Illinois paper livre.[20] Maxent, Laclede, & Company, the firm that had established St. Louis, concentrated on obtaining fur from the Missouri rather than sending their traders east across the Mississippi into British territory.[21]

The range of estimates of trade from £53,900 sterling to £150,000 tends to confirm that the total trade from both sides of the Mississippi River was worth at least £75,000 sterling and probably £100,000 sterling, approximately equal in value to the total Canadian fur trade. Each year about 100 canoes left Montreal carrying merchandise with a total value of £37,500 sterling ($7,500,000) and returned with at least double that value in fur, £75,000 sterling. Haldimand received an estimate made in 1763 that dry goods worth £40,000 sterling ($8,000,000) were sent up the Mississippi River annually, about equal to all of the goods carried in 100 canoes from Montreal.[22]

One undeniable controlling factor to successful trade was transportation. Moving fur directly back to Philadelphia would have been very costly for colonial merchants first upstream on the Ohio River and then overland 300 miles to Philadelphia or against the current up the Illinois River to the Great Lakes. Instead the enterprising colonial merchants sent their furs down the Mississippi River to New Orleans, as did the French; there some were sold at high prices to French merchants who shipped them to France.[23] Fur was sold at 10d sterling ($8.33) more per pound in the lucrative New Orleans market than in any other.[24] A pack of eighty pounds of beaver sold for $67 more in New Orleans than on the east coast, and the transportation cost was less.

Despite the ready market for fur in New Orleans, some of the fur did reach Philadelphia and New York because it could be used to pay debts in England. Baynton and Wharton shipped their fur by way of New Orleans and from there to Philadelphia or New York. In October 1766 Baynton and Wharton hired Captain Dobson to take his ship from New Orleans to New York City, but because Morgan was unable to send the fur to New Orleans before Dobson left on 20 October 1766, shipment was delayed until the following spring.[25] In 1767 Baynton and Wharton needed money and in desperation demanded that their agents in Illinois send as much fur as possible to New Orleans to be placed on the first ship to either New York City, Philadelphia, or London.[26]

Some of the fur went to New York City. In September 1767 Peter R. Livingston billed Baynton and Wharton for transporting 217 packs of furs shipped from New Orleans to New York City at a cost of £91 Pennsylvania ($10,465 or $48 per pack).[27] Another shipment arrived on the sloop *York* and was sold to Richard McWilliams in New York for £2,105 New York ($265,230). The shipment included 5,000 raccoons at 2/6, 300 otters at 15/-, 2,400 pounds of beaver at 6/6, 2,000 pounds of deerskins at 3/6, and 250 bear at 10/-.[28] A cargo of 125 packs from Alexander Maisonville, the French merchant at Ouiatanon who was an associate of Baynton and Wharton, sold for £1,302 Pennsylvania.[29]

In November 1768 Morgan packed all of his peltry on a boat to New Orleans. He was planning to go to Vincennes to pick up any additional furs to be sent to New Orleans in another boat in time to board a ship for Philadelphia.[30] Baynton and Wharton were in dire need of salable merchandise at the time, and their furs did reach Philadelphia.

Some peltry reached Philadelphia via the Mississippi route in later years also. For example, in 1771 Baynton and Wharton took down the Mississippi three boat loads of peltry, including 375 packs weighing from 100 to 160 pounds each. The price of beaver in London was 5/- sterling per skin and a skin weighed from 1½ to 2 pounds, so a high estimate of the value of a pack would be £25 sterling. The dressed leather packs were worth only about £6 sterling each. Assuming the packs to be half leather and half fur, the Baynton and Wharton shipment was worth about £5,800 sterling ($1,160,000), but its sale was a great disappointment to the firm. The shipment was auctioned in small lots in Philadelphia for only about £3,000 sterling ($600,000), and little was exported to Britain for the higher price.[31]

Not all of Baynton and Wharton's fur was sent to Philadelphia or New York. In 1767 Morgan sent Mr. Young to New Orleans with a few packs of fur to sell or ship and implied that they could be sold to French merchants in New Orleans and presumably sent to France.[32] In 1768 Morgan informed his partners that he wanted to send some furs down to New Orleans but feared that Messrs C.(?) and J.(?), presumably French merchants, would seize the fur when it reached New Orleans as part payment for bills owed them by Baynton and Wharton.[33]

Geography dictated the most economical path for the commerce that included several illegal transactions.[34] General Gage was convinced that none of the fur from Illinois would reach England because of the high price of fur in New Orleans and the ready means to export it to France.[35] Captain Forbes at Fort Chartres reported that the fur went to New Orleans and then to France. In an attempt to force the colonial and French merchants who had obtained their fur in British territory to send the pelts to Britain, Captain Forbes ordered that a bond of £200 be posted to guarantee that the furs were landed at a British port, to be proved by a certificate from a British officer at the receiving port.[36] However, this order was almost impossible to enforce.

The Spanish possession of New Orleans provided an easy avenue for the illegal export of furs to France and the import of French and Dutch merchandise to compete with British and colonial products shipped down the Ohio River. Once goods were in New Orleans, legally determining whether the pelts had arrived from British territory or Spanish territory west of the Mississippi was impossible, so the British were powerless to stop the illegal export to France.[37] Foreign ships awaiting cargoes were regular visitors to New Orleans. In 1768 there were six ships from New York in the harbor of New Orleans, two from France, three from Holland, and others from Carolina and Pensacola, Florida.[38]

Illegal trade also took the form of smuggling fur and deerskin into New Orleans from West Florida in violation of British navigation laws. The threat of smuggling led the Spanish to prohibit British merchant ships from trading on the Mississippi River.[39] However, a large contraband trade was developed about 1763 between West Florida and New Orleans. The trade was illegal because the furs and deerskin were enumerated articles that had been unlawfully taken from British territory by unlicensed French traders and sent down to Mobile and Pensacola.

Traders from Florida pushed north into Illinois using the smaller rivers emptying into the Gulf of Mexico, but the natural route back was the Mississippi River. On the other hand, the French traders from the Mississippi River likewise were intruding into Florida and the area west of South Carolina. The French traders from New Orleans crossed into Georgia and Florida east of the Mississippi River and traded the French merchandise for deerskin, which they took back to New Orleans. To maintain their hold on the trade, the French encouraged the Indians to remain hostile to the British.[40] Officially the French governor prohibited French traders from going east of the Mississippi and sent an officer to order the traders to return to New Orleans. The French governor ordered that any traders inciting the Indians against the British be arrested and sent to Pensacola in chains for punishment.[41] The British tried to counteract French influence on the tribes by distributing £4,000 to £5,000 sterling ($1,000,000) worth of presents for the Indians.

Another part of the illegal trade was the sale of British and colonial goods to the French merchants in New Orleans for subsequent trade with the Indians. The principal merchants from New Orleans purchased the goods from British merchants in Mobile and Pensacola with cash (usually Spanish dollars) and then sold the merchandise for fur, which was shipped to France.[42]

In 1767 British ships were at Mobile and Pensacola loaded with Indian goods to be sold to the French and Spaniards in return for furs. A ship visited Pensacola and Mobile annually with 200 tons of Indian goods, presumably to be sold for deerskins obtained in Florida. Actually most of the goods were used in the contraband trade with New Orleans.[43] In 1769 ten ships sailed directly from Britain to Pensacola with merchandise. Most of the cargoes were destined for the contraband trade with New Orleans.[44]

In 1765 the commander of the British troops, who had been ordered to go up the Mississippi to occupy Illinois, purchased a cargo of deerskin in Mobile with a bill of exchange drawn on General Gage. His intent was to use the deerskin as currency in New Orleans to buy supplies, as British bills of exchange sold at a very poor rate of exchange there. This dealing violated the law prohibiting the export of deerskin to other than British ports, but the governor permitted the transaction on the payment of a duty of £178 sterling ($35,600).[45]

Trade goods also went to Florida from New York City and Philadelphia. When Baynton and Wharton learned of the army proposal to go up the Mississippi in February 1764, the firm joined with Daniel Clark and Jeremiah Warder in a venture sending goods worth £1,500 Pennsylvania to Mobile for shipment to Illinois.[46] In 1766 Cornelius Mereford left Mobile for New Orleans with a cargo of British or colonial merchandise with the intent to sell it to French merchants. Bernard Gratz had a quantity of gin and butter in Mobile, which was sold by his agent.[47] Some merchandise went directly to New Orleans. In 1767 Baynton and Wharton sent merchandise worth £384 Pennsylvania ($44,160) to New Orleans on board the sloop *Superb* to their agent Bartholomew MacNamara.[48] In 1768 a Mr. Bradford sent a schooner to Philadelphia from New Orleans.[49]

In spite of the fact that legal trade was flourishing, various plans were devised to stop the illegal trade in furs. The most ambitious entailed building of a post at Point Iberville and deepening of the river to provide access to the sea from the Mississippi through British soil. The clearing of the canal was attempted and failed twice.[50]

The illegal trade is impossible to estimate accurately but may well have exceeded the legal trade. The Illinois French sent most of their peltry to New Orleans to pay for merchandise for the Indians, wines, and other luxuries. Furs had the best purchasing power because the New Orleans merchants would not accept British bills of exchange, and farm products were bulky and expensive to ship. Although some of the pelts were shipped to New York, Philadelphia, or London, most of the fur remained in French hands and was exported to France. Therefore, the British never controlled a major share of the furs obtained by French traders in Illinois, and the real economic value to the merchants was the sale to the French of British manufactured goods and slaves for produce, which was sold to the army for bills of exchange.

The Philadelphia merchants' attempt to garner the trade on the Mississippi was threatened by the illegal export of fur. Baynton and Wharton received less than 5% of the Illinois trade in 1768.[51] Even if goods were sent to Illinois from Pennsylvania, the furs were sent down the Mississippi to take advantage of the better market. The Pennsylvania merchants themselves finally began to ship their furs to New Orleans, declaring their intent to ship to England, but fulfillment of this promise was difficult to enforce.

The French merchants in New Orleans continued to supply French merchandise to the traders in Illinois. There were more French-made goods in Illinois than British-made. Continued economic control by French traders deprived the other colonies of the majority of fur and deerskin from the area.[52]

Commerce was dictated by the available means of transportation. The high cost of movement could reduce profit margins substantially. Furs were exported from New Orleans in sailing ships. In 1769 Captain Harris was instructed to take his sloop to New Orleans to load peltry owned by Baynton and Wharton. Harris was told that the furs normally left Fort Chartres between 20 and 25 June and arrived within eighteen days in New Orleans. Harris was instructed to ship the furs out of New Orleans quickly to prevent worm damage.[53] The ocean voyage to Philadelphia was not always smooth. In September 1769 Morgan was near Charleston twenty-five days after leaving New Orleans. There had been many storms with little effect on the ship but damage to the cargo.[54] Sea travel in the eighteenth century was hazardous.

Most of the merchandise moved to Illinois by way of inland river routes. There were many avenues of approach to Illinois: up the Mississippi River from New Orleans, via the Fox and Wisconsin Rivers to the Mississippi from Green Bay, down the Illinois River from Lake Michigan, down the Ohio River from Fort Pitt, down the Wabash River from Lake Michigan, up the Maumee from Lake Erie and then down the Wabash, and other lesser routes.

Movement on these rivers was accomplished by a wide variety of boats. Three types of birch bark canoes were used on the Ohio and other rivers: the two-place canoe, twelve to fourteen feet long, capable of carrying 300 to 400 pounds; the four-place canoe, twenty feet long and capable of carrying 1,000 to 2,000 pounds; and the master canoe, thirty-six feet long, four feet wide, and two and one-half feet deep, carried fourteen persons and a ton of freight.[55]

The most dependable vessel on the Ohio River was the flatboat, or bateau (a term also used for canoe on the Great Lakes). The flatboat, originally used in America on the Delaware River, was very adaptable to the shallow waters of the Ohio. With a head and stern sloping a bit fore and aft, it was generally 40 to 50 feet long, 6 to 7 feet wide, and from 2 feet 9 inches to 3 feet deep. Fully loaded it would draw only 20 to 22 inches of water.[56] The boats built by Baynton and Wharton in 1766 were oblong with flat bottoms, 40 feet long, 12 feet wide, and 4 feet deep.[57] Bouquet in 1764 described 23 bateaux built on Amherst's order to embark 400 men. The boats were 34 feet long and carried 20 men and 15 barrels of provisions. In 1765 Baynton and Wharton built 65 boats in a yard at Fort Pitt for the Illinois trade.[58]

In 1767 the cost of building a boat was estimated at £35 sterling ($7,000). The wages of the crew of five men were £2.10.0 sterling per month ($2,500) for a total of £50 sterling for a trip to Illinois, fifty days out and sixty back. Provisions and rum added about £30 sterling. The total cost of sending a boat to Kaskaskia was £115 sterling ($23,000).[59] Another estimate of the cost was £55 Pennsylvania ($6,325) to build a boat plus £4 Pennsylvania ($2,300) per month for a crew of five men.[60]

The boats were generally used for only one trip down the Ohio River. To return the boat to Fort Pitt was impractical because rowing against the current required fifteen men, whose wages ($13,800) would have exceeded the cost of a new boat. However, boats did row up river.[61] In the summer of 1767 after a military convoy reached Illinois, some of the boats were sent down the Mississippi to Mobile and others were rowed back to Fort Pitt.[62]

The heavy boats could not be used during part of the summer when the river was too low and not navigable. In the spring and fall as late as October the river was high enough to be used by the large boats.[63] Otherwise during the hot summer months only small canoes could move on the shallow water.[64] During the winter the rivers north of the Ohio froze sooner, which worked to the advantage of the Illinois traders, as any fur remaining when the rivers froze was diverted to Illinois. The northern rivers thawed later, giving the Illinois traders another advantage: that of being first in the Indian villages in the spring.[65]

A boat could carry approximately five tons. The river portion of the trip cost 23/- sterling per hundredweight, but the cost of the overland part of the trip raised the rate per hundredweight of goods from Philadelphia to Illinois to about 47/- sterling ($470), compared to less than 28/- sterling ($280) per hundredweight from New York City to Detroit.[66] As a result, in Illinois the price of goods to the Indians and the French traders set by colonial merchants was higher than in Detroit. In addition, the length of the trip to Illinois usually allowed only one convoy from Fort Pitt per year.

Despite the high cost, using the Ohio River was still far cheaper than taking the alternate route to Illinois with its tortuous trip up the Mississippi from New Orleans. The upriver trip from New Orleans was accomplished with considerable effort. The boat was often hauled with a rope from shore or poled as well as rowed.[67] The French estimated the trip at 400 leagues, or 1,200 miles (the league varied but was usually about 3 miles). After the voyage of from 70 to 90 days, the men were weary by the time they reached Illinois. In 1767 the British estimated that the distance was 1,540 miles and that boats could be rowed upstream at 22 miles per day for a total of 70 days.[68] The most common vessel used on the Mississippi was the galley bateau, rowed by 14 to 20 men and carrying 40 tons of goods. Pirogues made of large hollowed out logs were also used on the Mississippi because there were no portages and the heavy weight was inconsequential.

The trip down the Mississippi was not always easy either. During the summer the bateau went quickly down river. The trip took only twelve days when the current was running. Morgan made the trip in the summer of 1768 in fourteen days.[69] In November and December 1766 boats traveled 25 days to reach New Orleans from Illinois.[70] During the winter ice had to be considered. In 1767 the ice in the Mississippi River did not break up until 20 February.[71] In the winter of 1767–68 a trip lasted 46 days as the river was choked with ice.[72] The January 1768 winter, when the river froze as far as New Orleans, was the most bitter in memory.

The Mississippi route was not only difficult but dangerous. Because of the slow progress of the boats upstream, bands of marauding Indians paced the boats on land and repeatedly attacked from concealed positions ashore. As a result, the boats were forced to travel in convoys with armed protection, which added to the cost of the trip, and all merchants had to leave New Orleans simultaneously. The first convoy of boats left New Orleans in late winter or early spring. The second convoy started in August in mild weather but was more trying because the water was low and the current swifter.[73]

Trade with the Indians and farming were the main occupations of the Illinois inhabitants. The arrival of merchandise from either New Orleans or Fort Pitt was a major event and a determining factor in the economic welfare of the communities. The timing and the quantity of deliveries determined the availability and price offered to the consumers. The arrival of the first convoy from New Orleans was a crucial event for the Illinois merchants as the traders and Indians entered early in June. In May 1765 an enormous quantity of goods reached Illinois in April in the first convoy, which had left New Orleans in February. The second convoy arrived on 19 May. The cargoes of French merchandise relieved a shortage of goods in Illinois and encouraged the Indians to continue opposing the British. Because of the lack of ammunition, before the convoys arrived the Indians had been on the verge of making peace.[74] Another convoy of 14 boats and 2 pirogues arriving in June included two boat loads of British merchandise in French boats. Not daring to travel themselves because of the Indian threat, the British sold the goods to the French in New Orleans.[75] In 1765 Hugh Crawford reported that on his way down river he had passed a convoy (probably the one that reached Illinois in June) that included 400 to 500 Frenchmen and a large assortment of merchandise.[76]

In 1766 the traffic on the Mississippi was heavy. Despite the difficulty of the upstream trip, large quantities of French merchandise were shipped from New Orleans. In a trip down to New Orleans in the summer, George Morgan passed six French hunting parties in two days and eleven more parties within the next few days. The hunters killed buffalo and bear, which they packed in salt in barrels and sent down to New Orleans. The hunters traveled in large pirogues and boats that carried 3,000 to 5,000 pounds.[77]

In 1767 the convoys were less dependable. Although the French merchants controlled the convoys up the Mississippi, that year they were dependent for merchandise on ships arriving from France. The time of arrival of the ships was crucial. If they did not arrive in time for the French to send a convoy up the Mississippi by spring, the French in Illinois would be forced to buy from Baynton and Wharton.[78] The convoy from New Orleans arrived during that summer with liquor but not enough dry goods because few ships had arrived from France. Less than half the needed Indian goods was taken north as a result. With less competition Baynton and Wharton enjoyed good sales. Most of the trade in fur was transacted in June, and as the French merchandise had not arrived then, Baynton and Wharton received a greater share.[79]

In 1768 no ships with merchandise for trade with the Indians had arrived by February in New Orleans. The only boats to go up the Mississippi were those owned by Monsieur Fagott, who insisted on cash payment to carry any cargo for Baynton and Wharton. As a result, MacNamara, the partner's agent in New Orleans, was unable to send the wine that Morgan had ordered.[80]

The destination of the merchandise from both Fort Pitt and New Orleans were a few settlements clustered in the area where the Missouri and Ohio Rivers joined the Mississippi. There were five groups of consumers in Illinois: the Indians, the French traders who wintered with the Indians, the French farmers in the area, the British army after it occupied the territory, and the British Indian Department, which made large purchases of presents for the Indians to keep them peaceful. The total population of Illinois in 1760 was approximately 2,000, including slaves, compared to 3,000 persons in New Orleans.[81]

The Capitulation of Montreal in 1759 had surrendered the Great Lakes and Vincennes but not Louisiana to the British. Later the Treaty of 1763 ceded to Britain the minor posts considered part of Louisiana. Before 1764, most of the French habitants in Illinois lived in seven villages, Fort Chartres, Prairie du Rocher, Cahokia, Ste. Genevieve, San Filippe, Massiac, and Peoria. Some of the villages were very small. San Filippe had only 20 inhabitants in 1763 and only twelve to fifteen families in 1765.[82] Cahokia had 100 inhabitants in 1763 and 300 French and 80 blacks in 1765.[83] Prairie du Rocher had 100 French inhabitants and 100 slaves in 1765.[84]

Fort Chartres, founded in 1720, was the major military post. This stone fort was built by the French in 1753 and had a garrison of six companies with 300 soldiers and 20 cannon. The fort included two barracks, a guardhouse, two officers' quarters, a powder magazine, a kitchen, and other buildings around a four-acre parade ground. In 1763 there were still nearly 200 French soldiers in the garrison. The French garrison finally transferred the fort to the British in 1765, and it was renamed Fort Cavendish.[85] The village surrounding the fort had 100 inhabitants in 1763 and about 40 families in 1765.[86] Another estimate in 1765 was 1,000 French and 300 slaves.[87] In 1764 Dabbadie estimated the population at 1,400. Pittman in 1766 estimated 2,000. By 1767 the estimate was a little more than 1,000 and the same number was used in 1771.[88]

Kaskaskia was located at the juncture of the Ohio and Mississippi Rivers, the largest town in Illinois in 1765, with 80 houses, 500 white inhabitants and 500 blacks. In 1763 Aubrey estimated the population at 400 persons.[89] From 1744 to 1756, Kaskaskia was the fur depot for the upper Mississippi as well as the lower Missouri, the Illinois, and the Wabash Rivers.[90]

Some colonial traders were working in the Illinois villages. Edward Cole, who had moved to Niagara in 1760 and then to Detroit in 1761, was in Fort Chartres in 1767, trying to restore his finances. He was not doing well, but another Detroit trader, Winston, who had hidden from the Indians at St. Joseph in 1763 and had his goods stolen by Chevalier, had done well in Fort Chartres and planned to pay his debts.[91]

All the estimates indicate that the French farmers did not leave Illinois after the British occupation. Only the merchants and traders crossed the Mississippi to St. Louis. The French trading center was St Louis, established in 1764 west of the Mississippi by Maxent, LeClede, and Company under an exclusive grant from the French government in 1762 for trade with the Indians. The company built a large storehouse and forty homes for families. When the British occupied Illinois, the French garrison from Fort Chartres moved to St. Louis. More than half of the men on the St. Louis militia roster listed their occupation as trader, hunter, or rower.[92] A petition signed by the people of St. Louis and the militia roster showed that most of the population of the town were French from Canada and Illinois; less than 5% were from New Orleans.[93] Within a few months after the city was founded, fifteen bateaux and two pirogues of merchandise left New Orleans for St. Louis.[94] Harry Gordon reported that LaClede at St. Louis had monopolized the trade of the Missouri River, the north Mississippi, and the Illinois, as well as that with the Indians near Green Bay, Lake Michigan, and St. Joseph.[95]

The consumers in Illinois had two options, buy from either the French merchants in New Orleans or the Pennsylvania merchants who sent their merchandise by way of Fort Pitt. One of the largest mercantile firms in Philadelphia, Baynton and Wharton, in 1764 began a major effort to monopolize this business. Baynton and Wharton expected that their lower prices would overcome French resistance to buying British goods. The partners assumed that the Illinois French would be eager to buy after more than five years without supplies from France. Baynton and Wharton presumed that the major market in Illinois would be the Indians. Beginning in 1764 Baynton and Wharton zealously assembled merchandise worth more than £19,000 Pennsylvania ($2,200,00) to do business in Illinois. They planned to provide for 2,500 Indian families at a rate of £38 Pennsylvania (£22 sterling or $4,370) per family based on the 5,000 shirts in the stock. The amount of the shipment was probably based on an estimate of the population provided by George Croghan, who was a partner in the venture. Sir William Johnson had estimated the total market for the Northern Department, the area north of the Ohio River, at 10,000 adult male Indians. Croghan assumed that the French traders would buy goods from Baynton and Wharton to trade up the Missouri River as well as in the older areas, which would have had at least 2,500 families.

In 1764 Sir William Johnson estimated that the 10,000 Northern Department Indian warriors and their families would be a market for merchandise worth £179,594 ($35,918,000) or about £18 sterling ($3,600) per family.[96] Therefore, the Baynton and Wharton estimate of £22 sterling per family in Illinois was only slightly higher than Johnson's estimate.

The Indians had plenty of fur to trade. The Maumee and Wabash Valleys were rich in fur in 1765 because the Seven Years War and Pontiac's Uprising had reduced the level of hunting, allowing the animals to multiply. The Indians were in need, as during the Seven Years War the British navy had prevented French vessels from reaching New Orleans with merchandise and exporting furs to France.

Baynton and Wharton did deliver large amounts of merchandise to Illinois after enormous hardships, but it did not sell quickly as the French refused to buy from the partners. Baynton and Wharton did not have the expertise to deal directly with the Indians in their villages, and any attempt to do so was obstructed by the French. The French purchased some merchandise from Baynton and Wharton, but the sales were on credit, which was difficult to collect, as the French sent their fur and deerskin down the Mississippi River to New Orleans. Morgan complained that he was able to get very little fur from the French.[97]

Renegades from the Great Lakes area who had obtained goods on credit from the British merchants in Canada traded them for furs with the Indians and then absconded to Illinois with the furs. They sold the fur for their own profit rather than returning it to those who had provided the credit. On occasion Frenchmen robbed and murdered their British or colonial employers and took the goods to the ready market in St. Louis. Illinois was a convenient outlet for any outlaw.[98] Later, the Illinois French were prohibited from seeking credit for goods east of the Mississippi River, if they planned to return the fur to St. Louis to repay previous debts.[99]

Therefore, Baynton and Wharton's sales were limited to the few Indians who entered their stores, farmers, and French traders. Consequently, Baynton and Wharton had a huge inventory of goods purchased on credit in Britain for which they were unable to pay. Their best customers were the French farmers.

Colonial merchants purchased provisions from the French farmers with British merchandise and then sold the food to the army. Army provisions had to be purchased locally because during the long trip up from New Orleans provisions were ruined by the heat.[100] The army paid in sterling bills of exchange which Pennsylvania merchants used to pay debts in England. The army bought some provisions directly from the French with bills of exchange, but the farmers were reluctant to accept them because the French merchants in New Orleans accepted British bills of exchange only at steep discounts.[101]

These three markets—the Indians, the French, and the British army combined—were an impressive potential outlet for British goods imported by colonial merchants. On 24 September 1763 news of the Treaty of Paris, signed 4 March 1763, finally reached Fort Chartres in Illinois. The French commander, Villiers, announced to the inhabitants that he was under orders to surrender the colony to the British, but that the people were free to leave and go to new settlements on the west side of the Mississippi that would be under Spanish rule according to the terms of the treaty.[102] By autumn 1763, Florida had been occupied by British troops from Cuba, but no immediate steps had been taken to occupy Illinois.

Theoretically the fur trade passed into the hands of the British in 1763, and only a small amount of trade up the western branches of the Mississippi remained in Spanish hands. However, in practice the French merchants in Illinois retained two-thirds of the fur from throughout the Mississippi Valley. The French strategy was to use the Indians to block the routes along the Wabash, Ohio, and Miami Rivers and to rob or kill any British or colonial traders who ventured south from Detroit or Lake Michigan or west from Fort Pitt. French knowledge of the Indian language and customs and long connections gave the French a distinct advantage over the English.[103] Because of their close ties to the Indians, developed over previous generations of intermarriage and long experience wintering in the villages, the French were able to sell their merchandise to the tribes for as much as ten times its cost.

The British and colonial merchants had to cope with continued French competition. The French were better than the British in dealing with the Indians and constantly used the Indians against the British. The French actually could have driven out the British troops with the help of a few Spanish troops and supplies to fit out the Indians.[104] However, the French had no wish to continue the fighting.

In January 1764 Aubrey reported to Spain that Dabbadie had reconciled the Indians around New Orleans to the treaty between France and England. Aubrey hoped to have the same success with the Indians in the north. As long as the Indians resisted, the British could not reach Illinois via the Ohio River. Therefore, the British were trying to go up the Mississippi, but Aubrey believed that the attempt would fail.[105]

With the end of the Seven Years War in 1763 French ships were free to enter New Orleans with trade goods for the Indians. The timely arrival of ships from France was crucial to dispatch the convoys to Illinois. In 1764 the ships arrived late. The ship *Le Missouri* arrived at Belize in central America on 18

April 1764 with a cargo of merchandise bound for New Orleans from Bordeaux, France, via Santo Domingo. The ship would not reach New Orleans until May, and its cargo was not available for the first convoy. Severe winter weather in the spring of 1764 also delayed the opening of navigation on the Mississippi and trade with Illinois.[106] The first convoy for Illinois with four bateaux and one pirogue, armed and loaded by private merchants, had set off up the Mississippi on 19 April 1764.[107] Not only were the French ships late; they had not taken provisions. On 21 April 1764 Dabbadie was forced to ask the British at Mobile for a loan of flour for New Orleans as the supply was exhausted and the troops were on half rations of rice. The loan was refused, but a British merchant sold a small amount of flour to Dabbadie. On 4 June 1764 Dabbadie purchased flour from Maxent, the St. Louis merchant, who had probably obtained it from Illinois.[108]

The French continued to spread false rumors concerning the intent of the British among the Indians in 1764. General Gage and Colonel Bouquet were convinced in May and June 1764 that the French in Illinois had supplied the ammunition used by the Indians in the uprising in 1763. Gage believed that the French had actually stirred up the trouble in order to keep the fur trade in their own hands. On a positive note for the British, the French merchants in Illinois were short of ammunition and would have had little to give to the Indians.[109] A report from Green Bay relayed information from the Puant, Fox, and Sac tribes that a Frenchman, LeVorn, from Illinois had told them that the English would kill them if they went to Montreal for supplies. Instead of going to Montreal, LeVorn said, he would take goods up to the Wisconsin area from Illinois.[110]

George Croghan suggested to the Board of Trade in June 1764 that a British colony be established on the Mississippi to prevent the Indians from dealing with the French.[111] General Gage had this objective in mind when he ordered the 22nd Regiment to make a second effort to go up the Mississippi. Major Farmer at Mobile was ordered to make treaties with the Indinas allowing the British to pass. Farmer was also ordered to clear the Iberville channel and to establish a post at Natchez. Gage replaced the men who had deserted earlier and provided supplies for the 22nd Regiment, believing the establishment of a post on the upper Mississippi was essential to control French influence in Illinois.[112]

At Oswego, Sir William Johnson received reports as well that the Indians at Detroit had received large amounts of ammunition from the French in Illinois to keep the British away.[113] The governor of New York believed that ammunition for the Indians was being moved up the Ohio River from Fort Chartres. With all communications cut between the rebellious Indians and the British as an aftermath of Pontiac's Uprising, the French in Illinois were reaping the benefits of the fur trade. Colden expected the French to use every excuse to evade or delay the evacuation of their troops from Illinois.[114]

General Gage was concerned about the formation of an alliance between the Indians and the Illinois French who provided supplies. If the tribes on the British frontier withdrew to Illinois and allied themselves to the western Indians, the alliance would be too powerful for the British forces. A campaign in Illinois would cost a great deal, and the colonists would not willingly support a war that far west. On the other hand, Gage did not believe that the French were giving the merchandise to the Indians; rather that the Indians were purchasing the goods with furs.[115]

Contrary to British fears, the French officials and army were actually leaving Illinois. On 2 July 1764 a convoy of 21 bateaux and 7 pirogues arrived in New Orleans from Illinois with 6 French army officers, 63 soldiers, and others.[116] In Illinois on 26 June 1764 St. Ange, a French official, told the Miami, Kickapoo, Mascoutens, Wea, and Piankashaw tribes that they would no longer receive gifts from the French and recommended that the tribes make peace with the British. He indicated that if the tribes surrendered to the British, they would be given as much help as they had received from the French traders. The Indians refused to surrender, but St. Ange gave them some powder anyway. St. Ange learned that the Indians planned to lay siege to Detroit that summer along with the Shawnee, the Mohicans, and the Ottawa.[117]

In August 1764 St. Ange continued his attempts to pacify the Indians. Under pressure from Governor Dabbadie to reduce expenses, St. Ange claimed that some expenditures were unavoidable because the Indians pleaded misery and must be given something.[118] St. Ange told the Indians that they need not continue fighting the English in order to be loyal to the French and that the French wanted peace. The Indians disregarded the French message and refused to stop fighting, saying that they were protecting the French by continuing the war and that they would be mistreated by the English.[119] On 16 August 1764 Dabbadie wrote to Gage expressing his regret regarding the difficulty caused by the Indians. Dabbadie had ordered the post commanders to try to calm the Indians, but they remained bitter. French officials did not oppose British occupation of Illinois because the French would benefit financially by eliminating the cost of maintaining the Illinois forts.[120] On 24 August 1764 Dabbadie sent out a third convoy for Illinois under M. Dernis with seven bateaux and one pirogue and another pirogue for Arkansas with a total of 132 people.[121]

Explaining his policy to the Spanish government, Dabbadie claimed that the Indians must be given a small quantity of powder and bullets because they relied on their guns for hunting, and through hunting they obtained their food and the furs that contributed to the Louisiana trade.[122]

In September 1764 a dispatch arrived informing the French officials that as of 21 April 1764 Louisiana had been ceded to Spain, but no Spanish troops had arrived to occupy New Orleans.[123] In Illinois the Indians attacked a French hunter, so St. Ange prohibited the French traders from going north until relations improved.[124]

Contrary to the official stance of the French officials, Alexander McKee, the British Indian agent at Fort Pitt, reported that the French had sent five large canoes of merchandise to the Shawnee in Ohio. Smallman, another agent, reported that the French had sent supplies to the Shawnee twice during 1764.[125] Bouquet also informed Johnson that Killbuck, the Delaware chief, would tell Johnson privately of intrigue by the French officials who supplied the Indians with powder. Having this information, Johnson was to judge whether the powder was supplied with the connivance of the French commanding officer.[126] Reports that the French sent large quantities of merchandise up the Mississippi were forwarded to Sir William Johnson by the Indians who had traveled to Illinois and had received presents from the French. Johnson proposed that the British increase their level of giving to compete with the French.[127] Captain William Howard at Michilimackinac received a contrary report in November 1764 that the French had sent an officer to St. Joseph to urge the Potawatomi to continue the war.[128]

Yet St. Ange claimed that he had refused to supply the Shawnee because they continued the war with the English. However, St. Ange did give them a little ammunition to prevent antagonism. St. Ange was embarrassed by the Indian demands that created expenses contrary to Dabbadie's orders, but he had to give them something so that the French would not lose their influence. St. Ange claimed that the Indians would not agree to make peace with the English, and if the Indians did not surrender, the British could not take Illinois, leaving St. Ange to deal with the Indians without the means to provide for them.[129] St. Ange belittled the peace made by Colonel Bradstreet in 1764 for he knew that the Indians intended to betray the British when the time was right according to a letter from Pontiac. Pontiac was circulating a belt six feet long and four inches wide to all the nations to request aid in the uprising against the British. The belt was made of beads in a particular pattern that served to remind the carrier of all of the details that he was to convey orally to each group in the same way that beads are used by Catholics in reciting the rosary. Each group of beads represented a part of the message, and a belt six feet long carried a long discourse.[130]

The immediate problem was to pacify the Indians so that British troops could reach Illinois. Neither Gage nor Baynton and Wharton gave up on Illinois. Having failed to occupy Illinois from the south, the British made plans to do so from the north. Bouquet informed Sir William Johnson in late November 1764 that the only way to eliminate French influence was a display of force; therefore, Bouquet proposed a military expedition down the Ohio River to the Mississippi.[131] Colden, the governor of New York, believed that the military expedition to Illinois should go either overland from Philadelphia to Fort Pitt and then down the Ohio, or via Lake Erie, the Miami River, and the Wabash River, rather than attempt to force the Mississippi route.[132]

Early in November 1764 General Gage ordered Colonel Bouquet to send an officer down the Ohio River to Illinois accompanied by Shawnee and Delaware escorts to inform all the tribes that peace had been made with the French.[133] Colonel Bouquet questioned the wisdom of sending a single officer as a messenger down the Ohio River because he would be treated badly by the

Indians aroused by the French. The Indians mistrusted the English officers and felt that the English had no power over the tribes. Bouquet believed that the French must be driven out of Illinois by force. It was impossible to go up the Mississippi because the Indians could fire continually on the boats rowed slowly upstream against the current at only ten miles per day. On the other hand, boats going with the current down the Ohio River moved at fifty miles per day and could outdistance the Indians on land. The plan to send a military expedition down the Ohio had to be kept secret to prevent the French from assembling the Indians to stop the convoy. Once in Illinois, the British could dictate peace terms to the Indians and cut off their supply of ammunition from the French.[134] Among the peace terms that Bouquet recommended to Johnson for the Shawnee and Delaware were free navigation of the Ohio River, prohibition of traders in the Indian villages, and prohibition of French trade with the Indians. The last term could be enforced only after Illinois was occupied.[135]

General Gage in December 1764 ordered Bouquet to proceed with an expedition down the Ohio River as the only way to stop the French in Illinois from assisting the rebellious Indians. He believed that the expedition would convince Pontiac to go over to the British side and that the trouble came from French traders, not the French officials in Illinois.[136] Johnson agreed with Bouquet that the trouble with the Shawnees was caused by French supplies and that the taking of Illinois would end the problem.[137] He wrote to Gage on 18 December 1764 that peace could not be attained as long as the French supplied the Indians, but that the first goal was to obtain the consent of the Indians for the British to occupy Illinois. After the British were in control in Illinois, they could try to win the Indians over from the French.

Johnson proposed in December 1764 to send George Croghan to convene a peace conference at Fort Pitt and then take two or three companies of troops and some intermediary Indians via Sandusky and Lake Erie to the Miami River to meet with Pontiac. After that Croghan would travel overland to Illinois with a large load of gifts on pack horses and promise the troublesome Indians in Illinois that the British would reopen the trade in the spring of 1765.[138]

If no action were taken until the spring of 1765, Johnson argued, the French might stir up the Indians again.[139] Johnson ordered Croghan on 18 December 1764 to travel to Johnson Hall in upper New York to confer with him on the proposed expedition and to meet with the Shawnee and Delaware who were also going to Johnson Hall. At that time, Johnson hoped to obtain the assistance of the friendlier Indians in occupying Illinois. Illinois had to be occupied, and Croghan must enlist Shawnee and Delaware chiefs to accompany him and the troops down the Ohio.[140]

Gage agreed with Johnson that the way to Illinois was blocked by the defiant Indians and the solution lay in either a treaty or force. Forceful passage down the Ohio River was not possible because neither Pennsylvania nor Virginia would provide troops. The French were obstructing a peaceful solution, playing on the fears of the Shawnee and Delaware that the British were insincere. In late

December 1764 the Delaware told Bouquet that the French commandant at Fort Chartres had promised aid to the Indians within a short time, and that meanwhile the French traders would supply ammunition and clothing. The French traders had carried this message to the Delaware and Shawnee at Muskingum.[141]

In a letter to the Board of Trade, Johnson stated that taking Illinois was important for two reasons, first, to prevent the French from stirring up the Indians, and, second, to regain a significant portion of the fur trade then going to the French in New Orleans. Rather than waiting until spring, Johnson hoped that if Croghan obtained the support of the Shawnees and the Twightwees tribes, he could take Illinois by traveling overland during the winter of 1764-65.[142]

Gage finally decided in favor of sending Croghan down the Ohio River with a French-speaking British officer, Lieutenant Alex Frazier of the 78th Regiment, who was ordered to leave Fort Pitt in early January 1765 with letters for the French commander in Illinois.[143] Gage was still waiting for news of the treaty with the Delaware and Shawnee, as Croghan needed their support to persuade some influential Indian chiefs to accompany him down the Ohio. The timing was critical because the 34th Regiment would try to row up the Mississippi from New Orleans in February 1765, and Indian resistance had to be removed if the regiment were to succeed.[144]

In 1765 Louisiana was in an economic depression as an aftermath of the Seven Years War. There was very little commerce, no money was circulating, debts were not paid, and the price of slaves and land was only half that of previous years. Aubrey, the desperate French governor, was anxious for the Spaniards to arrive to take over his duties.[145]

Most of the Illinois French merchants had crossed to the west side of the Mississippi River by 1765. With the reopening of the fur trade in 1765 and the resumption of commerce between France and New Orleans, French business revived. French vagabond traders were scattered throughout the unoccupied area of the west. In 1765 there were between 400 and 500 French traders illegally in British territory.[146] They were working the older territory east of the Mississippi River and the upper Mississippi River.[147] Using St. Louis as their main base, the French traded in great numbers throughout the area of present Illinois, Indiana, Ohio, Michigan, Wisconsin, Minnesota, and west of the Mississippi. The Pennsylvania traders, the Canadians from Montreal, and the French from Illinois competed for the Indian trade south of the Great Lakes and in the Mississippi and Ohio Valleys. The British firmly believed that there would be no peace with the Indians as long as commercial rivalry continued.[148]

Until the Indians were pacified the British army could not occupy Illinois. Croghan had convinced Johnson and Gage that he could pacify the Indians with gifts, and Croghan planned to purchase those gifts from Baynton and Wharton. Croghan informed the partners of the proposed trip and joined in a commercial venture in which he was a partner with a one-quarter share. For the next four years the affairs of Baynton and Wharton, George Croghan, the Indian Department, and the British army in Illinois were intricately connected.

Since 1763 Baynton and Wharton had been making plans to go to Illinois. On 31 May 1763 the partners had sent a huge shipment of goods valued at £13,915 Pennsylvania ($1,600,000) from Philadelphia to Callendar & Spear at Carlisle intended for Illinois. The partners in the venture were Callendar & Spear (45%), Samuel Eldridge (10%), and Baynton and Wharton (45%).[149] When the Ohio River was blocked by Pontiac's Uprising later in 1763, the large stock of merchandise was stranded in Fort Pitt; it was probably sold to the Indian Department in 1764.

In November 1764 George Croghan and Baynton and Wharton planned another trading venture to coincide with the official mission to garrison Illinois under the leadership of Croghan. Baynton and Wharton hastened to form a consortium to gain ascendancy in the Indian trade at Fort Pitt and Illinois. In January 1765 Baynton and Wharton made an illegal arrangement with George Croghan to acquire a large stock of merchandise to be shipped to Fort Pitt for purchase by Croghan with Indian Department funds and used as gifts to the Indians as part of his peace making expedition down the Ohio River. The agreement divided the potential profits, giving Croghan two shares, Robert Field two shares, Baynton and Wharton two shares, Robert Callender one share, and John Baynton one share. The total value of the goods was £19,766 Pennsylvania ($2,273,000), a considerable amount. Each share was valued at £2,470 Pennsylvania ($284,000). Croghan did not advance any cash or merchandise. Although Croghan invested no money, he was to have a share of the profits with the three who had provided the funds. Callender and Field each provided £3,000 Pennsylvania in fur in lieu of cash; Baynton and Wharton provided a large inventory of merchandise. Robert Field, John Jennings, William Long, William Smallman, and Robert Callender were to move the merchandise by wagon to Carlisle and by pack horse from there to Fort Pitt.[150]

Baynton and Wharton put their local political affairs in order. Samuel Wharton wrote to Benjamin Franklin on 19 December 1764 about the proposed trip by Croghan down the Ohio River informing him that Croghan was waiting for orders to negotiate a treaty with the Indians. Wharton emphasized that peace was impossible until the Indians were cut off from contact with their French cohorts in Illinois. Wharton also mentioned that the Pennsylvania Provincial battalions were being disbanded and that the 1st Battalion was paid off in Lancaster on 20 December 1764. Given the unsettled relations with the Indians, the disbandment was a clear indication that the Pennsylvania leadership was transferring frontier defense to the British army.[151]

The financial transactions for the trip began in January 1765.[152] Gage provided Croghan with a credit of £2,000 New York ($252,000) to purchase presents for his mission. Croghan, claiming that the goods available in Fort Pitt were old and damaged, purchased new goods in Philadelphia, including wampum and silver for the conferences.[153] The purchases were made from Thomas Smallman (£2,650 Pennsylvania, $304,750), Robert Field (£1,121 New York, $141,250), and Baynton and Wharton (£1,900 Pennsylvania, $218,500), all of whom were involved in the Baynton and Wharton venture. He also purchased goods worth £2,037 Pennsylvania ($234,300) from Simon Levy and Company with Thomas Smallman as cosigner.[154] In March Johnson sent Croghan's first bill to Gage for £4,043 New York ($509,500). The amount was more than double that allowed by General Gage, who was outraged that Croghan had made such an extravagant purchase without consultation. Croghan's explanation was that silver ornaments were needed to attract and draw in the Wabash Indians.[155]

The plan was to send a first shipment of Indian goods worth £2,190 Pennsylvania ($252,000) for sale to the tribes along with additional merchandise of equal value that Croghan was to purchase to win their favor. Most of the merchandise to be used was already in the hands of Baynton and Wharton, but large amounts were purchased from other merchants and suppliers in Philadelphia. The fact that the partners had to have the shirts made is an example of the complexity of preparing for such a large venture. Each shirt required about 2.5 yards of cloth, probably 90% linen and 10% muslin. First the partners obtained an Indian shirt from Callendar & Spear and had patterns made for the ruffled shirts by Samuel Mason's widow. Nearly 500 thirty-yard pieces of Irish and princess linen, garlix, and muslin were purchased, The materials, including thread, were given to Jane Campbell, Nancy Martin, Hannah Coffin, Margery Fare, Sarah Humphreys, Mrs. Coburne, Dorothy, and Mary Morris, who were engaged to make more than 2,500 Indian shirts from 8 December to 12 December 1764. The finished shirts were delivered by the end of January.[156] The cost of the shirts ranged from 6d to 8¼d. By 8 January 1765 the company's books listed £220 to be paid for shirts at a maximum rate of 26 shirts per £ Pennsylvania, indicating that 5,700 shirts had been made.[157] Considering that there were fewer then 10,000 Indian adult males in the Northern Section of the Indian Department (the territory north of the Ohio River and east of the Mississippi River), the partners expected a major share of the trade.

Wine was purchased from D. & J. Lampiere; Thomas Mayberry provided leather trunks; John and Peter Chevalier were paid £46 for four hogsheads of rum; Wishart & Edward received £291 Pennsylvania ($33,365) for 26 hogsheads of rum; Usher & Malcolm was paid £101 for a ton of sugar; and Samuel Howell and Enoch Hobart also sold rum to the partners. Hannah & Mason and others were paid £305 Pennsylvania for making Indian shirts. A fee of £11 was paid for loading 44 wagons with at least a ton on each wagon.[158]

On 7 December 1764 five wagon loads (each with a load of one to one and a half tons) were sent to Robert Callendar by the three business partners and "etc.," omitting Croghan's name from the transaction. One of the wagons contained five bales of cloth including one bale of blue stroud worth £60 sterling, a bale of twelve scarlet strouds valued at £95 sterling, and a bale of twelve aurora strouds valued at £75 sterling. The value of the five wagon loads was more than £2,000 sterling or £3,400 Pennsylvania ($400,000). On 12 December 1764 five more wagons were sent to Robert Callendar from all four partners (including Croghan's name on this order), and on 14 December 1764 three more wagons were sent. The total amount of goods purchased and shipped to Carlisle for the Illinois venture was £13,914 Pennsylvania ($1,600,000), far more than the original plan to send £2,500 sterling worth.[159] On 24 December 1764 Baynton and Wharton received a shipment on the brigantine *Grace* from their primary supplier in London, Richard Neave, for merchandise valued at £2,809 sterling (at an exchange rate of 175%, £4,916 Pennsylvania, $561,800). The firm was well prepared to enter the western trade.[160] To manage the merchandise when it arrived at Fort Pitt John Jennings was hired for twelve month's service on behalf of the partnership, beginning 3 December 1764.[161]

The value of the goods far exceeded the funds available to Croghan for the purchase of gifts. The remainder was to be sold to the Indians even though in January 1765 trading with the Indians was illegal. The gifts and the merchandise for sale were intermingled in order to disguise which were intended as gifts. Under the pretense that the merchandise was the property of the Indian Department, no license was granted. An indication of the illegal nature was the diversion around Fort Loudon and Lyttleton to avoid detection.[162]

The first convoy of 81 horse loads was dispatched by Robert Callender. As the convoy was bypassing Fort Loudon, a barrel broke and some of the alarmed frontiersmen observed that it was filled with scalping knives. On 6 March 1765 a hundred armed men with blackened faces calling themselves the "Black Boys" followed the convoy to Great Cove on Sidelong hill about five miles from Fort Loudon, whipped the horse drivers, killed three horses, and burned 63 loads of goods valued at £3,000 Pennsylvania ($345,000). The attackers kept the other eighteen loads, mostly liquor. Later some of the attackers were captured and taken to Fort Loudon, but because the local residents favored their action, the prisoners were released.[163] However, the question remained what was to be done with their rifles, an indication that they were Pennsylvania frontiersmen as they were the only ones to have rifles.[164]

When taken before a local grand jury in April 1765, the matter was dropped because of insufficient evidence. The defense claimed that the attack had been committed by men from Virginia. The Black Boys could not be found in May. William Allen, the justice of the peace at Fort Loudon, stated that too many goods were being sent, as five or six horse loads would have supplied the garrison at Fort Pitt.[165] Gage believed that actually many of the members of the grand jury had been involved in the riot. After the attack the people of the area maintained a scout on the road to inspect convoys for any Indian goods.[166]

Johnson believed that the goods destroyed were the property of the British government and wanted to compensate Croghan for the loss with Indian Department funds.[167] Baynton and Wharton also claimed that the contraband dry goods that were burned were the property of the British government but that the liquor that was not destroyed was the property of their partner, Robert Callender.[168] Croghan took the position that he had purchased the dry goods with Indian Department money for Colonel Bouquet, who had promised the Indians that gifts would be available at Fort Pitt.[169] The Indian Department could legally give knives, guns, and dry goods to the Indians even though trading with them was illegal.

Johnson was evidently sympathetic to Croghan. At first he believed incorrectly that Croghan had no interest in the shipment and that Baynton and Wharton were at fault for shipping goods without a pass along with Croghan's presents for the Indians. By April Johnson had learned that Croghan was involved and demanded an explanation.[170] Nevertheless, Johnson asked General Gage for permission to have Baynton and Wharton send to Fort Pitt a second convoy of merchandise because they had prepared a large quantity of merchandise for the Illinois trade. Croghan had reported that his negotiations with the Indians had been successful and that they were ready to do business with the colonists at Fort Chartres. If sent to Fort Pitt, the goods would be held there until trade was opened officially.[171]

Other Pennsylvania merchants raised questions about the Baynton and Wharton shipment. Samuel Wharton instructed John Baynton to say that the goods belonged to Callender, not the Indian Department, and that they were intended to be used for Indian presents. Callender swore that all of the merchandise belonged to the Indian Department. The total value of the goods that were sent in several shipments was in question. Callender indicated that the value of all the shipments was up to £20,000 Pennsylvania ($2,300,000), and those destroyed were worth £6,000 Pennsylvania. Wharton lowered the value of the destroyed goods to £5,000 Pennsylvania and later reduced his estimate again to £3,000. Wharton stated that he did not intend to ship goods illegally. Obviously an illegal activity was taking place when the convoy took a back road to avoid Fort Loudon.[172]

Gage believed neither that Croghan was telling the truth nor that the merchandise was government property. Gage thought Croghan was more interested in trade than in his job as Indian agent and believed that Croghan had conspired with Baynton and Wharton to smuggle Indian goods to Fort Pitt.[173] However, eventually General Gage compensated Croghan £2,000 sterling ($400,000) for the merchandise destroyed at Sidelong, and Samuel Wharton expected Croghan to receive an additional £500 sterling.[174] Added compensation of £1,300 Pennsylvania ($149,500) was made in February 1766.[175] As late as April 1766, Baynton and Wharton corrected an error of £323 Pennsylvania ($37,145) in additional charges for goods destroyed at Sidelong, so in the end the British treasury repaid Baynton and Wharton for all of the goods lost.[176]

Colonel Bouquet at Fort Pitt had provided Croghan with permits to take presents to the Indians because trade with them was still illegal as a result of Pontiac's Uprising.[177] The only goods permitted to pass through Fort Pitt were those intended as gifts of the British government to the Indians. Croghan lied to Colonel Bouquet alleging that the goods were all going to Illinois and the entire stock would be purchased by the Indian Department.[178] In fact, half of the merchandise was the private trading venture of Baynton and Wharton and their partners, including Croghan.

The arrangement was illegal on several counts. The governor of Pennsylvania had not opened the Indian trade, which had been closed during the uprising, and trading with the Indians was still illegal. Croghan, a deputy in the Indian Department, was using his public position for private gain, a practice specifically forbidden by Sir William Johnson. Croghan was already spending anticipated profits; in December 1764 he had drawn large sums of money from Baynton and Wharton to furnish his house and entertain guests in Philadelphia.[179]

Croghan finally started down the Ohio River on 15 May 1765. Lieutenant Alexander Fraser, who had preceded him, had been gathering together Miami Indians since the middle of April. Because of the delay the tribes became restless, especially after receiving messages and gifts from the French encouraging them to continue the war and asserting that the French would supply them.[180] Croghan finally arrived and met with the Shawnee at the Scioto River along with seven French traders who had been at their villages. Another five French traders were with the Delaware. Croghan had asked the Shawnee to include these traders, as they had no licenses from General Gage.[181]

The Indians were hostile. The Miami Indians, with whom Fraser had been dealing on the Wabash, robbed and took him prisoner. Fraser was taken to Illinois, where he was released; he subsequently arrived in New Orleans on 19 June 1765. On 8 June 1765 a party of Kickapoo Indians robbed Croghan of all his goods and took him as a prisoner to Pontiac at Vincennes. However, with the help of the Shawnee, Croghan convinced Pontiac to end the war and permit the British army to take possession of Illinois in July.[182]

Gage was anxious to send troops down the Ohio to Illinois and had ordered Captain Sterling and one hundred men to be ready as soon as Croghan had cleared the way. The troops finally left Fort Pitt on 22 August and arrived in Illinois on 9 October 1765, a long 47-day journey on the low water in the Ohio River during the middle of summer.

Forty miles west of the Wabash River they encountered a French trader with two loaded boats and thirty men.[183] The uncooperative French asked that British and colonial traders be kept out for nine months to allow the French to transfer to the west side of the Mississippi. Captain Sterling had traveled without presents because the Indians had taken those bought by Croghan and there were few goods left at Fort Pitt. As a result, he was forced to buy goods from the French in Illinois at exorbitant prices. The real problem for Sterling in Illinois would occur in the spring, when 3,000 to 4,000 unhappy Indians would arrive expecting presents as they traded their furs.[184]

However, before the colonists could sell large quantities of merchandise to the Indians, the French traders had to be displaced and the Indians convinced to buy from the colonial merchants. The enterprising Illinois French had already effectively monopolized the trade in Ohio, competing with colonial traders to within a few miles of Detroit and Fort Pitt.[185] In 1765 Croghan had forced some French traders out of the Shawnee towns on the Scioto River on the grounds that they had no licenses to trade.[186]

In the summer of 1765 the Indians told Croghan that the French had formed the confederacy of tribes in the Ohio Valley to prevent the British and colonists from reaching Illinois. However, the confederacy was broken after the Delaware, the Shawnee, and the Six Nations from New York made peace at Fort Pitt in 1765. Croghan then had an opportunity to deal with the Ohio Valley Indians and was somewhat successful in settling with them.[187] In June 1765 the Cherokee sent a French trader back to Illinois because the British had urged the tribe to stop trading with the French.[188] Nevertheless, the French continued to lie to the Indians, trying to block the colonists from going down the Ohio River to Illinois.

In November 1765 Johnson informed the Board of Trade in London that the French traders from Illinois were troublesome not only in competing for furs with the British and colonial traders but also, to maintain an edge in the business, in creating bad feelings toward the British. Rather than submit to the British regulations, the French traders were paying higher prices for their goods in St. Louis after the merchandise traveled up the Mississippi from New Orleans.[189] To counter French activity Johnson told the Board of Trade that there must be a strong Indian Department with agents in the Illinois area to gain the friendship of the Indians.[190] Johnson believed that the French actually were making little profit from the trade and that the French government had other motives.

The Spaniards were also suspicious of French involvement with the Indians. They too believed that the French motivation was to bribe the Indians to prevent the British from trading in the Mississippi Valley. Every French trader was considered an agent of the French government to carry out this policy. The French officials remaining in Illinois were sharing in the profits and therefore, encouraged the traders to promote Indian loyalty to the French and hostility to the British. In February 1765 the Shawnee met with British agents, who suspected the French were encouraging the Indians to rob and murder colonial and Canadian traders. Aubrey, the Spanish official at New Orleans, naively reported that he hoped there was no secret understanding between the French and the Indians.[191]

In 1765 Johnson expressed to General Gage his belief that despite the claim of French impartiality, the French governor of Louisiana and other officials were stirring up the Indians and supplying them with arms and provisions. For example, at the same time that a British regiment was unable to ascend the Mississippi because of opposition by the Indians, the French governor of New Orleans sent out in relative safety two convoys of bateaux, one on 19 April 1764 and another on 12 June 1764, with goods destined for Illinois. The second convoy included seventy-seven persons in three boats.[192]

Gage believed that to obtain the trade in Illinois, military occupation was absolutely essential to prevent the illegal export of fur to France and to stop the French from interfering with traders from Detroit, Michilimackinac, and Fort Pitt. He believed that blocking the entrances to the Illinois rivers and the Ohio River with British forts could prevent the French from competing with the traders from Canada and the colonies.[193]

Croghan argued that if the British did not establish posts in Illinois, the French would take the greater share of fur down the Mississippi River. On the other hand, the Detroit merchants believed that the only solution was to remove all restraints on trade and allow the agents of the Detroit merchants to compete with the French traders in the Indian villages rather than being confined to the posts.[194] In 1765 in support of the no-restraint theory the Wabash Indians in Illinois told Croghan that if the British would not send traders to winter with them, they would be forced to go to Illinois to obtain goods.[195]

The Indians were a constant menace to the colonial traders as a result of the ever increasing encouragement by the French to resist the British and colonial traders and keep trading with them. Benefiting the French was the reluctance of the British army to provide gifts to the Indians after Pontiac's Uprising, reinforcing the belief that the British hated the Indians. The Indians expected presents from both the French and the British as part of Indian-white relations. In 1765 the French agent in Illinois reported that the Indians threatened if he did not give them ammunition to attack the British. In quick response Aubrey, the French governor in New Orleans, sent 800 pounds of gunpowder and other presents to Illinois for the Indians.[196]

The French officials did try to maintain peace in 1765. In February some Shawnee chiefs were in New Orleans asking that the French send traders to their towns, who would be repaid well with furs. In return the Shawnee promised the French that the British would never take over the Shawnee territory. The French governor, Dabbadie, promised to send the traders but urged the Indians to make peace with the British and to accept their traders. The Shawnee refused to accept this advice.[197]

The French sent an officer to try to prevent the Indians from harming the English and instructed the voyageurs not to trade ammunition to the Indians. Nevertheless, the French continued to give presents to the Indians to maintain their friendship.[198] There was some effort by the French government to control the incursion of the French into British territory by officially halting communication east across the Mississippi.

The French merchants had moved across the Mississippi to St. Louis but continued to trade. In December 1765 a French merchant, Beaujeu, took an unusually large cargo of merchandise from New Orleans and made numerous gifts to Pontiac, raising the suspicion that the French were working diligently both to convince the inhabitants to move to St. Louis and to encourage them to trade there.[199] Richard Winston and William Long, both agents of Baynton and Wharton at Fort Pitt, received a message from Illinois that British traders were needed there to provide goods for the Indians. However, the Shawnee Indians advised the two agents to wait to go down the Ohio River until spring when the river was deeper.[200]

The colonial merchants hoped that conditions would improve with the transfer of authority to the Spanish. In December 1762 France had ceded Louisiana to Spain to compensate for the loss of Florida in the Treaty of Paris, but the French continued to govern the province until 1766. A Spanish governor, Antonio de Ulloa, was not appointed until 1765 and did not arrive in New Orleans until 1766.[201]

In January 1765 Johnson hoped that the Spanish would take control of Louisiana and remove the French, who continued to arouse the Indians and poison their minds against the British.[202] When Ulloa, the Spanish governor, arrived in 1766, he informed General Gage that Aubrey, his French predecessor, had indeed restrained the Indians to assist the British in occupying the area and that he would continue to create harmony between the Indians and the British.[203] Gage was not convinced and believed otherwise on the basis of reports from his officers. Gage also learned that the Spanish would allow free trade between New Orleans and France while hindering the British.[204] In September 1766 Ulloa required that British and French ships obtain passes from him and have their cargoes approved before unloading. However, he could not enforce the rule, and British ships slipped past New Orleans to dock at places upstream on the Mississippi. According to the terms of the Treaty of Paris, British ships did have the right to use the Mississippi River.[205] In 1767 the Spanish began building forts to control the trade and to bribe the Indians with gifts.

Undaunted the French continued to operate from Illinois, receiving merchandise transported up the Mississippi River and sending furs down to New Orleans for shipment to France. The French were able to trade in the Indian villages while the British army continued to prohibit the unfortunate colonial traders from leaving the posts. This French competition undermined any British attempt to regulate commerce. The profit of the Illinois trade continued to go to the French.

The Pennsylvania merchants tried to compete with the French. Regardless of problems, by 2 August 1765, Baynton and Wharton recorded the net proceeds of the Illinois venture at £10,730 Pennsylvania ($1,233,950).[206] By December 1765 Croghan had paid Baynton and Wharton a total of £3,444 Pennsylvania ($396,000) for his purchases of presents.[207] In 1766 even though the colonials were selling at three times the cost of the merchandise, the colonial traders from Fort Pitt still were charging the Indians less than the French in Illinois.[208] Baynton commented that if he could sell at a profit of 200% he would have an easy time for the rest of his life on the money earned.[209]

The British tried to improve relations with the Indians in 1766. In an attempt to pacify the Indians, Croghan and Johnson constantly pressured Gage to pay for lavish gifts. The conciliation of the Indians with presents was essential because, as were the French inhabitants, the British and colonists were dependent on Indian goodwill for safety. In 1766 Croghan warned that violence would continue if Gage did not order the commandant at Fort Pitt to give presents to the local tribes.[210]

In February 1766 Gage was convinced and urged Croghan to go to Illinois on a pacification mission because of the uncertain situation there with the Indians. Baynton and Wharton, having failed to deliver goods to Illinois in 1765, planned to take advantage of Croghan's mission to capture the Illinois trade from the French and used their connection with Croghan and the Indian Department to make the arrangement. In January 1766 Croghan officially withdrew from the partnership with Baynton and Wharton because of his conflict of interest as a representative of the Indian Department, as well as the inquiry into his role in the shipment of 1765 when merchandise for Indian presents was destroyed, but he remained an ally of the partners.

The Baynton and Wharton agents in Fort Pitt had some disagreement in January 1766, causing the partners some concern about the management as they were sending £8,000 Pennsylvania ($920,000) worth of goods to Fort Pitt to be forwarded to Illinois. One of the agents, Winston, was dealing against the best interests of Baynton and Wharton, so one of the partners considered accompanying the shipment to Illinois. The partners ordered other agents at Fort Pitt, Tull and Vaughn, to prepare boats for the shipment down the Ohio River.[211]

George Morgan, a new partner in the firm of Baynton, Wharton, & Morgan, was to take charge of the shipment of merchandise that would accompany the peace mission under the direction of Croghan. The intent of course was that much of the merchandise would be purchased as presents for the Indians by Croghan in his public capacity. In contrast to the smaller amount, £20,000 Pennsylvania ($2,300,000), sent in 1765, Baynton and Wharton sent an incredible amount of goods, worth £50,000 sterling ($10,000,000), in wagons and on 600 pack horses to Fort Pitt.[212] Morgan established a boat yard at Fort Pitt, where 65 galley bateaux were built to carry the goods.

Croghan immediately began again in 1766 to purchase large amounts of merchandise to be used as presents. Gage authorized the expenditure of £3,445 New York ($434,000), but the exuberant Croghan spent £8,408 New York ($1,060,000), of which £6,480 New York went to Baynton and Wharton for merchandise, including some that was already at Fort Pitt worth £3,445 Pennsylvania.[213] Francis Wade purchased goods worth £1,670 Pennsylvania ($192,000) for Croghan.[214]

In March Gage urged Johnson to get Croghan on the road to Illinois, and although Gage promised to pay for anything necessary to alleviate the situation in Illinois, Gage wanted an exact list of the items.[215] He was very concerned that the colonial merchants succeed in capturing the Illinois market from the French. Currently most of the fur from Illinois was going down the Mississippi and subsequently to France because the French fur traders could sell their beaver at 10d sterling ($8.30) more per pound in New Orleans than was offered in New York City or Philadelphia (probably $51 per pound in New Orleans compared to $43 in New York). Traveling down the Mississippi River was much easier than taking the fur up the Ohio River and then crossing the country from Fort Pitt to Philadelphia.

If the British had merchandise available in Illinois and built forts at the mouth of the Ohio and Illinois Rivers, the French traders could be shut out of British territory and prevented from competing with British and colonial merchants. Keeping the French traders out would alleviate Indian hostility toward the British, which the French encouraged in order to protect their monopoly.[216] If the fur were in British or colonial hands, there was much less chance of its being exported to France even though it went through New Orleans.

The first step was to occupy Illinois and distribute gifts to the Indians. Baynton and Wharton were concerned that the frontiersmen who had destroyed the goods in 1765 would do so again. Robert Callender heard reports that they indeed were planning to intercept the shipment and delayed the cargo at Carlisle. After the partners requested that the governor of Pennsylvania provide protection, the governor wrote to General Gage, asking for British troops. Baynton and Wharton also wrote to Gage, stating that if the frontiersmen destroyed the goods, peace with the Indians, who were expecting presents, would be compromised.[217]

The first step in opening the Illinois market to British goods was taken on 9 March 1766 when John Jennings, William Long, Richard Winston, Thomas Smallman, and others, left Fort Pitt for Illinois with five boats loaded with up to seven tons of merchandise from Baynton and Wharton. Because the cargo was too large to be loaded on the boats, forty bundles of dry goods, kegs of knives, and a bundle of saddles were left behind to be sent later.[218]

General Gage granted permission to the Indian Department to buy large quantities of presents in the expectation that the British at last would be able to control the Illinois territory and fur trade. Croghan was still buying in May and, as Samuel Wharton noted, favored Baynton and Wharton. In June Croghan purchased goods worth £938 Pennsylvania ($108,000) from Baynton and Wharton stocks in Fort Pitt. Croghan planned to equip a group of Indians who would accompany the expedition and to give presents to several chiefs. Croghan also equipped a war party of Iroquois who passed through Fort Pitt on their way to attack tribes in the south.[219]

Perhaps as a consideration for favoring the partners in his purchases, Croghan asked Wharton to pay him £1,300 Pennsylvania ($150,000). Wharton paid Croghan that amount in sterling drafts on Richard Neave, the partner's agent in London, plus £50 Pennsylvania in currency. The purpose of this transfer is not clear.[220]

The second flotilla, which finally set off down the Ohio on 18 June 1766, consisted of thirteen boats, two with Croghan's presents and provisions for Fort Chartres, and the remaining eleven with a cargo that Baynton and Wharton intended to sell on the way down the Ohio and in Illinois.[221] Each boat carried up to seven tons of merchandise, a truly large shipment, and these thirteen were only one group of the 65 boats being built. The charge to the army for the two boat loads of provisions was £1,577 Pennsylvania ($180,000). The value of Baynton and Wharton's cargo was £18,832 Pennsylvania ($2,166,000). Included were guns, brass kettles, matchcoats, strouds, large knives, vermillion, and wampum, on a list that was 26 pages long.[222] Baynton stated that the total venture was the largest shipment ever made down the Ohio and that it would sell at three times its value, still a reasonable price compared to that of French sales.

Baynton expected to do well because French goods from New Orleans were sold at ten times their value. Indicative of the care taken and the excellent political connections, the cargo was insured at a 2% premium negotiated by Benjamin Franklin.[223] The cost of the trip was high. Morgan spent £415 Pennsylvania ($48,000) for wages and other unspecified expenses during the journey.[224]

On the way Croghan distributed presents and Morgan supervised trade with the tribes along the Ohio River. Often the expedition was delayed until trading was completed. The convoy arrived at Fort Chartres on 20 August 1766, and conferences with the Indians began on 25 August with about a thousand Indian men plus women and children. Essential to Croghan's plan was to prove to the tribes that the British could supply them by lavishly distributing presents and provisions, most of which were purchased from Baynton and Wharton. Edward Cole, the commissary charged with distributing the gifts, spent 19,608 livres ($157,000 at $8 per livre) from 1 July to 25 September 1766. He gave Morgan a draft for £1,568 New York ($198,000) in payment for goods given to the Indians. Gage later angrily characterized the amount as unjustified.[225]

The venture did not work out well. Although the conference was very successful in pacifying the Indians, Morgan was disappointed because he had expected to sell far more to Croghan. For example, the partners had sent 5,000 Indian shirts to Illinois, but only about 1,000 warriors attended the conference, leaving 4,000 shirts. Baynton and Wharton had sent merchandise worth £18,832 Pennsylvania ($2,166,000) and had sold £1,722 Pennsylvania ($200,000).[226] The remainder would have to be sold to the hostile French or to the unfriendly Indians who favored the French.

To add to the difficulties the goods had been poorly selected and badly packed. The transportation charges from Philadelphia to Fort Pitt and the cost of building the boats were also a heavy overhead charge on the venture. The venture seemed to end in a complete failure when General Gage refused to honor the bills sent by Croghan for the presents. Though still angry, Gage finally paid Baynton and Wharton with a bill of exchange drawn on the British treasury for £1,290 sterling ($258,000) for the total expenses incurred by Croghan. The bill was promptly sent to Richard Neave, Baynton and Wharton's supplier in London, to pay long delayed obligations.[227] The total amount received for sales in Illinois from May 1766 to 7 January 1767 was only 66,066 livres ($530,000), a small return on an investment that included one cargo that was worth at least £18,832 Pennsylvania ($2,166,000).[228] The remainder of the merchandise would have to be sold to the French in Illinois, who were reluctant buyers. As long as the French had free access to the Indian villages the colonials could not expect to profit without the same privilege.

All of the British efforts to halt the activity of the French traders south of Lake Michigan failed. Johnson proposed to build a fort at the mouth of the Illinois River in 1767 as a last ditch attempt to keep the French traders out of British territory. However, the French continued to court the Indians even after the British army occupied Illinois. Whereas the colonial merchants from New York and Pennsylvania were limited to trading at the posts, the French went directly to the Indian villages.[229] An Albany trader in Detroit in 1767 complained that even after the British occupation, the French traders from Illinois took goods to Vincennes, Vermillion, Ouiatanon, and as far north as Miami.[230]

The British army finally abandoned any pretense of eliminating the French. In 1767 the British commander at Fort Chartres collected fees from French traders and gave them permission to go up the Illinois and Wabash Rivers to trade French merchandise to the Indians. Furs were sent openly from British territory to St. Louis or even directly to New Orleans where they were shipped to France.[231]

The Florida governor, Haldimand, sent an officer to New Orleans in 1767 to check on reports that the French were sending fur there that had been taken from east of the Mississippi. The officer found no evidence of furs being taken from British territory, only farm produce, as was perfectly legal.[232] Even though in 1766 General Gage had abandoned attempts to make the Iberville River navigable to Lakes Pontchartrain and Maurepas after the first attempt had failed in 1764, Haldimand in 1767 hoped to divert the fur trade from New Orleans by deepening the Iberville River and providing a bypass around New Orleans. As they could not be reached from the Florida ports, the British army forts at Natchez and Iberville were dependent on New Orleans for supplies. Opening the Iberville River would alleviate that situation and make access to British ports possible for colonial traders in Illinois.[233] After months of effort in January 1769 Gage and Haldimand finally gave up and abandoned any further attempts to create an alternate route. All of the Illinois trade continued to pass through New Orleans.[234] The competition from New Orleans was continuing in 1768 and seriously reduced the amount of deerskin received at Pensacola, casting doubt in the mind of Haldimand as to whether trade in Florida was worthwhile.[235]

The Illinois trade outlook was dismal. In 1767 Baynton and Wharton were in financial difficulty that eventually led to bankruptcy as a result of the large unsold orders for merchandise sent to Illinois. The purchases of the Indian Department, though substantial, were far less than expected. Before the unsettled accounts caught up with them, Baynton and Wharton hoped that their new partner, George Morgan, could make the Illinois trade profitable. They were the only merchants competing with the Spaniards and French in Illinois in 1767.

With the expectation that Morgan would make a difference, in January Thomas Wharton assured Benjamin Franklin that the firm would make large profits in Illinois.[236]

Instead, a potential source of profit for Baynton and Wharton was the sale of rations to the army in Illinois. Providing a reliable source of rations for the British army at Fort Chartres at the lowest cost had been a major problem for General Gage. In January 1767 Croghan advised Gage that the best way to supply the garrison was to obtain flour, peas, Indian corn, buffalo, and beef at Vincennes. However, the Illinois French farmers would not sell their produce for bills of exchange drawn on the army, the usual way provisions were purchased, because New Orleans merchants would accept British bills of exchange only at a discount of 50% to 60% to discourage the French from selling to the British. The French had no faith in the local paper money left over from the French regime because it fluctuated in value. The farmers would accept only hard cash (Spanish silver dollars and other gold and silver coins) or merchandise.

Therefore, the best way to obtain provisions was either to send specie (usually Spanish silver dollars) to the commanding officer of the garrison (a risky undertaking and hard cash was always in short supply in the colonies) or to have a merchant exchange merchandise for produce, which would then be sold to the army for bills of exchange. Croghan estimated the plan could be accomplished at a cost of 12d Pennsylvania ($5.75) per ration. It was not coincidental that Baynton and Wharton was the only colonial firm in Illinois that had the merchandise to exchange.

The plan would have many benefits: giving the garrison a secure source of provisions, eliminating the burden of transporting the provisions down the Ohio River, giving the French farmers a good market for their grain and beef as an incentive to produce more, breaking the reliance of the French on the French merchants in New Orleans, and encouraging the French who had moved west of the Mississippi to return to Illinois from St. Louis and resume farming.[237] The plan was implemented and Baynton and Wharton began to receive large payments for rations.

In addition to receiving the revenue from providing rations, Baynton and Wharton continued to sell to the Indian Department. Edward Cole, the commissary in Illinois, continued to make large purchases from Baynton and Wharton for gifts to the Indians. In March Baynton and Wharton received bills of exchange from the army in Illinois valued at £1,378 sterling ($275,600). The total from September 1766 to March 1767 was £5,000 New York ($630,000). Gage protested that the Indians went to Cole for presents and then took their fur to trade to the French in St. Louis. The expense for presents in Illinois was vastly more than the amounts for Detroit and Michilimackinac.[238]

The reasons for the heavy expense for presents were that Baynton and Wharton were the only colonial merchants in Illinois, and Croghan had a special relationship with Baynton and Wharton. The main source of revenue for Baynton and Wharton in 1767 was the limited sale of merchandise to the Indian Department, far less than expected earlier, when Gage expected to take complete control of Illinois and the fur trade there. However, the purchases made by Croghan were substantial. For the period 11 September 1766 to 30 April 1767, Croghan purchased 34,155 livres ($273,000).[239] Croghan's transactions in Illinois totaled 121,028 livres ($968,000) by 29 October 1767.[240] Croghan purchased merchandise worth £7,020 New York ($885,000) from Baynton and Wharton from March to October 1767. Cole spent £10,742 New York ($1,353,500) from September 1766 to September 1767, compared to a total from Detroit and Michilimackinac of only £1,100 New York ($138,600).[241] In comparison, the sales of produce to the army for the period 16 October 1766 to August 1768 were only 33,239 livres ($266,000).[242] In December Morgan sent Samuel Young to New Orleans with drafts worth £12,816 New York ($1,615,000) to take to Philadelphia. The two major bills were both drawn on the Indian Department, William Johnson for £3,721 and Edward Cole for £7,020, a total of £10,721 ($1,351,000).[243] In December Morgan informed his partners that the account to be paid by the Indian Department was a handsome one and that he expected the next bill to be even greater.[244]

However, this sum was less than a tenth of the inventory that the partners had sent to Illinois, and they were selling very little to the French and Indians. In May 1767 Baynton and Wharton recorded the proceeds of the sale of fur sent by Morgan to Bartholomew MacNamara, the partner's agent in New Orleans. The total after expenses was only £125 Pennsylvania ($14,375), a paltry sum, considering the scale of the operation.[245] Morgan promised to send a large shipment of fur in the spring of 1768. From December 1766 to May 1767 the partners sent additional merchandise to Illinois worth £3,433 Pennsylvania ($395,000) but had sold very little.[246] In December Morgan placed a large order for merchandise from Baynton and Wharton. His hopes for sales were based on the possibility that ships from France might not arrive at New Orleans in time for the spring convoy up the Mississippi to Illinois in 1768. If such were the case, the French traders would be forced to buy from Baynton and Wharton. Most of the trade with the Indians for pelts was done in June, and if the French merchandise had not arrived, Morgan expected to sell all of his stock at high prices and possibly clear the debts owed for the Illinois venture.[247]

However, most of the French merchants had moved west across the Mississippi and continued to compete not only with Baynton and Wharton but also with the colonial traders on the Wabash, Ohio, and Mississippi Rivers. The French were trading as far north as St. Anthony's Falls (present day Minneapolis). According to Croghan only a huge amount of presents would win the Indians over to the British.[248]

Countering these efforts to win over the Indians were the frontier farmers, who reacted violently to the Indian attacks. Malevolent Indians had ample opportunity to attack the colonial traders, especially on the rivers. In July 1767 the Chippewas attacked two boats on the Ohio River, murdered fourteen men,

and stole £3,000 Pennsylvania ($345,000) worth of merchandise owned by
Baynton and Wharton.[249] In another incident Henry O'Brien, Little, Peter
Brown, and seven others were killed on the Ohio River, and their two boats and
£8,000 Pennsylvania ($920,000) worth of merchandise were stolen. Some of the
merchandise was later recovered and sold by Morgan in Illinois for £353 sterling
($70,000). Thomas Mitchell was killed in a Shawnee village in the fall of 1767,
and John McDonald was killed near Fort Pitt in December 1767.[250]

Fearing the hostile Indians, colonial traders from Illinois could not trade in
Vincennes nor travel up the Illinois or Mississippi Rivers in 1767. The French
had complete control of the area outside the posts. Morgan believed that unless
the British army could control the French and the Indians, it would be better to
abandon Illinois.[251]

In 1768 three colonial traders were killed and their merchandise stolen by
the French. In September a hunting party from Fort Chartres was attacked by
Indians in the Wabash Valley. Nine were killed and eight horse loads of fur
were taken to Vincennes. The Indians considered the hunting ground theirs and
believed that whites had no right to take game without permission. The hunters
had permission from the Indians to hunt buffalo for meat for the garrison but
were killed when they ignored the rule and also hunted deer, bear, and beaver.
Gage noted that the Ohio River was becoming more dangerous in 1768 and told
the commander in Illinois that he should not try to protect any hunters who
broke the rules by hunting furs without permission.[252]

The treacherous activity of the French in 1768 was protested by Gage to
Spanish officials in Illinois, Don Ulloa, the Spanish governor, and Aubrey. They
in turn issued a proclamation forbidding French traders to go east of the
Mississippi and threatening to arrest anyone who incited Indians.[253] In 1768
the Spanish officials in New Orleans began to tighten the trade rules. Only ships
carrying provisions for the city were permitted in the port, and none was
allowed to land woolens or any kind of dry goods except with a permit from
Spain.[254] No traders were permitted to go up the Mississippi without a pass
signed by Ulloa, and the traders were required to report the details of their
business to officials in New Orleans.[255] Ulloa informed Gage that the post
commanders were not to permit Spanish merchants to trade with British or
colonial merchants and that no Spanish traders were to trade with the Indians in
British territory. The only exception was an emergency, with a permit from the
British army commander in the area. No traders from the west side of the
Mississippi were to trade east of the river without a pass from Ulloa.[256] An
attempt was made to enforce this rule. DeLaGauterais was sent to the Choctaw
Indians in the south to drive out the French traders. Any French traders found
east of the Mississippi were to be arrested and taken to Pensacola.[257]

However, the Spanish could not control the situation in 1768. The French
traders from Spanish territory freely crossed the Mississippi and traded with the
Indians in the Ohio, Illinois, and Wabash River valleys. At the same time the
French traders told the Indians to continue to harass the British and said that the

French and Spanish government would assist them if they rose up against the British. General Gage ordered the local British commander at Fort Chartres to change his policy of granting permission to the French to trade with the Indians. He was ordered to arrest any such traders and send them to Fort Pitt for trial and punishment.[258]

Despite the potential riches of the Illinois trade, the Pennsylvanians could not make it pay. The dangers of the trip down the Ohio were ever present. The French refused to buy from them, and the Indians were discontented by the lack of gifts and the misconduct of the traders. Baynton and Wharton lost fourteen men and £3,000 worth of goods in one attack on a convoy.[259]

In February 1768 Morgan was very pessimistic about the possibilities in Illinois. Although he believed that Baynton and Wharton had learned how to profit from Illinois, where immense profits were possible if they could last the course, still they would have to build up the stock of merchandise in Illinois and then wait several years before the trade became profitable. While unpacking a shipment of goods Morgan ordered another long list of merchandise. He hoped that an assortment of the more desirable goods would be sent to prevent the traders from going down river to buy in New Orleans.[260]

Winter was the dead season. Morgan had a party of hunters out to supply meat to the army, but not a single Indian had traveled to Kaskaskia or Fort Chartres to trade since 22 December 1767. However, Morgan had learned that the Indians had a good hunting season and that they would have a large amount of fur to trade in April. Since September 1767 only a few Indians had requested presents from Edward Cole, the Indian Department commissary, who therefore, purchased very little from Morgan. The remittance sent to Baynton and Morgan in February was very small.[261] Sales of merchandise from 12 December 1767 to 16 February 1768, about two months, totaled only 122 livres ($122).[262]

In April business continued to slump. The hunters returned with only ten tons of meat and had to be paid £100 Pennsylvania ($11,500) for wages. Neither the Indians nor any French traders had arrived as expected. Morgan still did not know whether the ships from France had arrived in New Orleans before the spring convoy set off for Illinois. If no goods arrived in the Mississippi convoy, then Morgan expected to do very well.[263]

The major source of revenue continued to be the Indian Department. In April 1768 Morgan sent Baynton and Wharton a draft from Cole for presents for £1,969 New York ($248,000), but Morgan was aware that a move to reduce such expenditures was under way and he could not anticipate how much would be spent in the future.[264] True enough, General Gage was enraged at the amount being spent in Illinois, which exceeded the total of all other posts north of the Ohio River. In March he had responded to Shelburne concerning the high cost of the Illinois garrison, whose cost was greater than the entire volume of trade. Furthermore, the French traders incited the Indians against the British and took the furs from up the Ohio and Wabash Rivers. Gage promised that he would reduce expenses and had already refused to pay some bills.[265] Colonel

Reed, the commanding officer, was ordered to return to Fort Pitt, and the commissary of provisions was removed. Gage suggested to Johnson that he remove Edward Cole, the Indian Department commissary, as well and threatened to approve no more expenditures for Illinois.[266]

While Gage was fuming over the lavish expenditures in Illinois, Baynton and Wharton were desperately in need of cash. They pleaded for immediate payment of the large bills from Illinois, but Johnson informed them that clearing the bills through General Gage took time. Gage finally released £6,266 New York ($790,000) to Johnson on 30 May.[267] On the same day Wharton went to New York with additional bills drawn on Croghan for £1,197 Pennsylvania ($138,000) but was refused immediate payment.[268]

From 26 March to September 1768 Indian gifts, including guns and rum, worth only £1,601 New York ($202,000) were purchased from Baynton and Wharton in Illinois. The British army commander, Colonel Wilkins, estimated that Morgan was getting only 5% of the furs, and the remainder were going down to New Orleans to French merchants.[269] Business in Illinois was very poor. When the Indians and traders went to St. Louis and Fort Chartres, Morgan offered merchandise at half price payable the following year in fur. He was refused on the grounds that all of the traders had debts in New Orleans, where they had to send their fur. Business was so bad in New Orleans that its merchants sent agents to St. Louis to collect debts immediately when the traders traveled in from the Indian villages. The traders also feared to deal with Morgan because of Spanish rules prohibiting such deals.[270] In July some of the French traders went to Morgan and asked for goods on credit but could give no security, so Morgan refused. The result was that Morgan was able to send bills for only £702 New York ($88,500), most of which were for provisions sold to the army.[271]

The crushing blow that would finally destroy Baynton and Wharton was the award of the army ration contract to David Franks. William Murray was on his way in July with a cargo of merchandise including silver ornaments, linen, twenty rifles, rum, sugar, and other Indian goods worth £1,200 Pennsylvania ($138,000), a comparatively small amount. As a private venture Murray was taking shoes and stockings worth £400 Pennsylvania to sell to the soldiers. Morgan did not believe Murray would do well unless he spoke French fluently. Morgan intended to try to buy the entire cargo from Murray when he arrived. Because of the award of the ration contract, Morgan had given up hunting parties, but he wanted to subcontract the meat ration from Murray and send out hunters again.[272]

In August 1768 John Campbell, an agent of Baynton and Wharton, set off from Fort Pitt with merchandise for Illinois, including French Indian guns. The Illinois store was out of rum, so Campbell put a double crew on his boat to paddle day and night to make the trip quickly. Because the water was high and the boat loaded only at two-thirds capacity, Campbell hoped to get over the falls without making a portage.[273]

By the end of October 1768 Morgan was very pessimistic about the prospects of Baynton and Wharton. The local French traders were heavily in debt to the New Orleans merchants, who sent agents to Illinois to collect furs to pay those debts. Therefore, Morgan had little opportunity to obtain pelts in trade. In addition, Cole was being removed, thereby ending his large purchases for presents to the Indians even though Colonel Wilkins, who had assumed Cole's duties, was favorable to Morgan. The competition for the sale of rations was not serious. William Murray, the local agent of the ration contractor David Franks, had sold his cargo of shoes and stockings during the trip down the Ohio River, and his remaining merchandise was unsalable, except silver ornaments and rum. Despite the poor business, Morgan was able to send a remittance of £2,156 New York ($272,000), which was Cole's last sale to Baynton and Wharton.[274]

The affairs of Baynton and Wharton were in complete disarray. They paid out about £2,300 Pennsylvania ($265,000) for miscellaneous items in September, and the single sale of peltry was only £131 Pennsylvania ($15,000).[275] Even the final large draft from Edward Cole would cover only a single month's expenses. The French and their influence on the Indians had led to the downfall of Baynton and Wharton.

However, the competition from Illinois continued to challenge the merchants of Montreal, Fort Pitt, and Albany and was a significant factor in the abandonment of restriction of trade only from the posts. Furs taken from Illinois could be exported legally only to England or to the American colonies under the British navigation Laws. Nevertheless, once in New Orleans, furs from Illinois often were sent either to France or to some other European country under the guise that they were from west of the Mississippi. Various plans were devised to stop the illegal trade in furs. The most extensive was building a post at Point Iberville and deepening the river to provide access to the sea from the Mississippi on British soil. Construction of a canal had been attempted twice and had failed. Forts were considered too expensive and not effective, and even bribes in the form of presents to the Indians were tried, but no attempted solution could halt the illegal export of pelts down the Mississippi.[276]

The British rules restricting trade with the Indians to the confines of designated posts handicapped the British and colonial traders. The French working for British merchants in Canada violated the rules with ease, but the Pennsylvania, New York, and Virginia traders were hamstrung. The occupation of Illinois in 1765 gave the colonial merchants an opportunity to supply both the army and Indians, but again the French traders frustrated the Pennsylvania merchants. Much of the fur continued to go down river to New Orleans despite fear of the furs rotting in the warm climate and the greater prevalence of vermin. Down river transport was easier, and the price of furs in New Orleans was greater than in the colonies. Even the colonial merchants who established themselves in Illinois were forced to ship their fur south rather than use the more difficult route via the Ohio River and overland to Philadelphia.[277]

Table 4.1 Balance Sheet for Illinois
(£ sterling in thousands)

Assets in

| | |
|---|---|
| Merchandise from New Orleans | £30 |
| Merchandise from Pennsylvania | £20 |
| Colonial produce (rum, flour, meat) | £25 |
| (Merchandise from Pennsylvania sold to French farmers for provisions) (£14) | |
| Provisions from French farmers | £24 |
| Total | £99 |

Assets out

| | |
|---|---|
| Fur to New Orleans and France | £95 |
| Fur to Philadelphia | £5 |
| Bills of exchange from army | £50 |
| Total | £150 |

The merchandise used in Illinois was from New Orleans, Pennsylvania, and Michilimackinac. Some of the goods from Pennsylvania were bartered to the French farmers to obtain provisions for sale to the army, and others were traded to French merchants. Very little was bartered directly with the Indians.

The French who traded with the Indians in the area south and west of the Great Lakes took the greatest share of the furs produced in that area even though the Indians received less for their furs than they could have obtained from the British or colonial merchants.[278] The French traders obtained most of their goods from New Orleans throughout 1765 to 1768, paying for it with fur. Goods were purchased from colonial merchants only when the supply from the south was late.

The net result was a loss of a large share of the fur trade, as most of the fur went down the Mississippi to New Orleans and then to France. The major profit for the colonial merchants was the sale of rations to the army and presents to the Indian Department. Therefore, when the army left after 1768, the value of the area dropped significantly. With New Orleans in Spanish hands, the Mississippi fur trade was of little value. The only economic benefit was the sale of British goods by way of West Florida or Fort Pitt.

## NOTES

1. Morgan to Clarkson and Jennings, 24 June 1768, Baynton, Wharton & Morgan Papers, Microfilm, 10 Rolls, Original in Pennsylvania Historical Commission [BWM], Roll 5; Baynton and Wharton Journal B, 19 February 1767, BWM, Roll 8.

2. Captain Harry Gordon's Journal 13 October 1766 quoted in Charles A. Hanna, *The Wilderness Trail*, 14 vols. (New York: G. P. Putnam's, 1911), vol. 2, p. 55.

3. J. Marsh to Haldimand, 20 November 1767, *Illinois State Historical Collections* (Springfield: Trustees of the Illinois State Historical Library, 1903–) [IHC], vol. 16, p. 116.

4. Bartholomew MacNamara to Morgan, 24 January 1767, BWM, Roll 5.

5. Francois X. Martin, *History of Louisiana, from the Earliest Period* (New Orleans: Lyman and Beardslee, 1827–29), vol. 1, p. 179.

6. Croghan to Gage, 16 January 1767, Shelburne Manuscripts, p. 153, quoted in Douglas Dunham, "The French Element in the American Fur Trade," Ph.D. Dis., University of Michigan, 1950, Microfilm in State Historical Society of Wisconsin, p. 91.

7. J. Marsh to Haldimand, 20 November 1767, IHC, vol 16, p. 116.

8. J. Marsh to Haldimand, 20 November 1767, IHC, vol. 16, p. 114.

9. Morgan to Baynton and Wharton, 20 June 1768, IHC, vol. 16, pp. 326–31; Morgan to Baynton and Wharton, IHC, vol. 16, pp. 360–62.

10. Bartholomew MacNamara to Morgan, 24 January 1767, BWM, Roll 5.

11. Morgan to Bartholomew MacNamara, 20 June 1768, BWM, Roll 5.

12. Shelburne Opposition to Townsend, 30 March 1767, IHC, vol. 11, p. 539.

13. George Johnstone to John Pownall, 19 February 1765, IHC, vol. 10, p. 439.

14. Aubrey to the Minister, 27 January 1766, IHC, vol. 11, pp. 144–46.

15. Croghan to Gage, 16 January 1767, Shelburne Manuscripts, p. 153, quoted in Dunham, p. 91.

16. Gage to Shelburne, 17 January 1767, IHC, vol. 11, p. 497.

17. Croghan to Gage, 16 January 1767, quoted in Dunham, p. 91.

18. Wilkins to Barrington, 5 December 1769, IHC, vol. 16, p. 834.

19. Aubrey to the Minister, 27 January 1766, IHC, vol. 11, pp. 144–46.

20. Dunham, p. 72.

21. Fraser to Haldimand, 4 May 1766, IHC, vol. 11, p. 229.

22. J. Marsh to Haldimand, 20 November 1767, IHC, vol 16, p. 116

23. Gage to Hillsborough, 16 June 1768, IHC, vol. 16, p. 318.

24. Remarks of Gage on the Barrington Plan of 1766, 10 May 1766, IHC, vol. 11, pp. 243–44.

25. Baynton and Wharton to William Franklin, 10 December 1766, IHC, vol. 11, pp. 447–49.

26. Baynton and Wharton to Clarkson, Jennings and Long, 19 March 1767, BWM, Roll 3.

27. Baynton and Wharton, Journal C, 19 September 1767, BWM, Roll 9.

28. Baynton and Wharton, Journal C, 8 September 1767, BWM, Roll 9.

29. Baynton and Wharton to William Franklin, 10 December 1766, IHC, vol. 11, pp. 447–49.

30. Morgan to Baynton, 30 October 1768, IHC, vol 16, p. 436.

31. BWM, Roll 6, Frames 821–28.

32. Morgan to Baynton and Wharton, 11 December 1767, IHC, vol. 16, p. 133.

33. Morgan to Baynton and Wharton, 5 April 1768, IHC, vol. 16, pp. 227–28.

34. Baynton, Wharton, & Morgan to Lauchlin Macleane, 9 October 1767 in Clarence W. Alvord and Clarence Carter, eds., *Trade and Politics, 1767–1769, Illinois State Historical Collections* (Springfield: Trustees of the Illinois State Historical Library, 1921), vol. 16, [Alvord], p. 84; Virginia D. Harrington, *The New York Merchant on the Eve of the Revolution* (New York: Columbia University Press, 1935), p. 240.

35. Gage to Johnson, 19 January 1767, Edmund B. O'Callaghan, ed., *Documentary History of the State of New York*, 4 vols. (Albany: Weed, Parsons, 1849–1851), [DHNY], vol. 2, p. 485; Gage to Johnson, 25 January 1767, DHNY, vol. 2, p. 486.

36. Forbes to Gage, 15 April 1768, IHC, vol. 16, p. 241.

37. Gage to Shelburne, 23 December 1766, IHC, vol. 11, p. 462.

38. Samuel Young to Morgan, 18 February 1768, BWM, Roll 5.

39. Paul C. Phillips, *The Fur Trade*, 2 vols. (Norman: University of Oklahoma Press, 1961), vol. 1, p. 596.

40. Haldimand to Gage, 17 June 1767, IHC, vol. 11, p. 579.

41. Gage to Hillsborough, 17 August 1768, IHC, vol. 16, p. 377; Haldimand to Gage, 25 February 1768, IHC, vol. 16, pp. 176-77.

42. Croghan to Gage, 16 January 1767, IHC, vol. 11, pp. 492-93; Gage to Shelburne, 17 January 1767, IHC, vol. 11, p. 497.

43. Clinton N. Howard, *The British Development of West Florida, 1763-1769* (Berkeley and Los Angeles: University of California Press, 1947), pp. 27-28.

44. Howard, pp. 17, 39; Linda Sellers, *Charleston Business on the Eve of the Revolution* (Chapel Hill: University of North Carolina Press, 1934), pp. 169-70.

45. Farmer to Gage, 11 March 1765, IHC, vol. 10, p. 465.

46. Daniel Clark to Baynton and Wharton, 28 April 1764, BWM Microfilm, Roll 3.

47. Cornelius Tucker to Bernard Gratz, 31 July 1766, Etting Collection, Historical Society of Pennsylvania.

48. Baynton and Wharton, Journal C, 4 June 1767, BWM, Roll 9; Virginia D. Harrington, *The New York Merchant on the Eve of the Revolution* (New York: Columbia University Press, 1935), p. 240.

49. Samuel Young to Morgan, 18 February 1768, BWM, Roll 5.

50. Theodore C. and Marguerite J. Pease, *George Rogers Clark and the Revolution in Illinois, 1763-1787* (Springfield: Illinois State Historical Society, 1929), pp. 8-9.

51. Theodore C. and Marguerite J. Pease, *George Rogers Clark and the Revolution in Illinois, 1763-1787* (Springfield: Illinois State Historical Society, 1929), p. 20; Wayne E. Stevens, *The Northwest Fur Trade, 1763-1800* (Urbana: University of Illinois, 1928), p. 26.

52. Gage to Halifax, 10 August 1765, IHC, vol 11, p. 68.

53. John Baynton to Captain Harris, 17 May 1769, BWM, Roll 5.

54. Morgan to Rumsey, 19 September 1769, IHC, vol. 16, p. 601.

55. Charles H. Ambler, *A History of Transportation in the Ohio Valley* (Glendale, CA: Arthur H. Clark, 1932), p. 25.

56. Hamilton, p. 6.

57. Jack M. Sosin, *The Revolutionary Frontier, 1763-1783* (New York: Holt Rinehart & Winston, 1967), p. 31.

58. Charles H. Ambler, *West Virginia, the Mountain State* (Englewood Cliffs, NJ: Prentice-Hall, 1958), p. 53.

59. Morgan to his wife, 28 June 1766, IHC, vol. 11, p. 314; Bouquet to Gage, 27 May 1764, IHC, vol. 11, p. 252.

60. Clarence W. Alvord, *The Illinois Country 1673-1818* (Springfield: Illinois Centennial Commission), 1920, p. 275.

61. Gage to Reed, 15 July 1767, IHC, vol. 11, pp. 583-84.

62. Gage to Reed, 15 July 1767, IHC, vol. 11, p. 584.

63. John Campbell to Baynton and Wharton, 28 October 1767, BWM, Roll 3; Bernard and Michael Gratz to William Murray, 7 July 1768, Gratz Letter Book, Etting Collection, Historical Society of Pennsylvania; Phyn to Johnson, 15 April 1768, IHC, vol. 16, pp. 242-44.

64. Phyn to Johnson, 15 April 1768, IHC, vol. 16, pp. 242–44.

65. M. devilliers to Dabbadie, 13 March 1764, *IHC*, vol. 10, p. 225; Stevens, p. 155.

66. John Lees, *Journal of [John Lees] a Quebec Merchant* (Detroit: Society of the Colonial Wars of the State of Michigan, 1911), p. 43.

67. Instructions to Gauterais, 1 January 1765, IHC, vol. 10, p. 407; *IHC*, vol. 16, p. 336; Dunham, p. 81; Alvord, *Illinois Country*, p. 213.

68. Shelburne Opposition to Townsend, 30 March 1767, IHC, vol. 11, p. 540.

69. Jenning's Journal, 24 June 1768, IHC, vol. 16, p. 336.

70. Morgan's Journal, 24 November to 18 December 1766, IHC, vol. 11, pp. 440–47.

71. Martin, p. 201; M. Clarkson Diary, 20 February 1767, IHC, vol. 11, p. 363.

72. Samuel Young to Morgan, 18 February 1768, BWM, Roll 5.

73. Alvord, *Illinois Country*, p. 213; Phyn to Johnson, 15 April 1768, IHC, vol. 16, pp. 242–44.

74. Fraser to Lt. Col. Campbell, 20 May 1765, IHC, vol. 10, pp. 495–96; Gage to Governor Penn, 16 June 1765, *Pennsylvania Colonial Records*, vol. 9, p. 268.

75. Capucin to Baptiste Campeau, 7 June 1765, JMss, vol. 4, p. 764.

76. Harry Gordon to Johnson, 10 August 1765, IHC, vol. 11, pp. 67–68.

77. Morgan's Journal, 24 November 1766, IHC, vol. 11, p. 440.

78. Morgan to Baynton and Wharton, 24 December 1767, BWM, Roll 5.

79. Morgan to Baynton and Wharton, 11 December 1767, IHC, vol. 16, p. 134; Morgan to Baynton and Wharton, 5 April 1768, IHC, vol. 16, pp. 226–27.

80. Samuel Young to Morgan, 18 February 1768, BWM, Roll 5.

81. Dabbadie to the Minister, 10 January 1764, IHC, vol. 10, p. 209; Franklin B. Hough, *Diary of the Siege of Detroit...* (Albany, NY: J. Munsell, 1860), pp. 155-56; Dunham, pp. 97–98.

82. IHC, vol. 10, p. xxxi.

83. IHC, vol. 10, p. xxxi.

84. Sterling to Gage, 15 December 1765, IHC, vol. 11, p. 125; IHC, vol. 10, p. xxvi.

85. Robert G. Ferris, *Explorers and Settlers* (Washington, DC: US Department of the Interior, 1968), p. 212.

86. Alvord, *Illinois Country,* (Springfield: Illinois Centennial Commission, 1920), p. 192; IHC, vol. 10, p. xxxi, Phillips, p. 596.

87. Theodore C. Pease and Marguerite J. Pease, *George Rogers Clark and the Revolution in Illinois, 1763–1787* (Springfield: Illinois State Historical Society, 1929), p. 3.

88. Alvord, *Illinois Country*, p. 202; Dabbadie to the Minister, 10 January 1764, IHC, vol. 10, p. 209.

89. IHC, vol. 10, p. xxv.

90. Phillips, p. 501.

91. Cole to Edgar, 3 August 1767, Edgar Papers, XV.

92. Hough, pp. 155–56; Pease, *Clark and the Revolution in Illinois*, p. 3; Dunham, pp. 97–98.

93. Dunham, pp. 97–98.

94. Dunham, p. 70.

95. Dunham, p. 71.

96. IHC, vol. 10, pp. 338–39.

97. Morgan to McNamara, 20 June 1768, BWM, Roll 5.

98. *Wisconsin Historical Collections*, vol. 18, pp. 263–68.

99. Phillips, p. 598.

100. Dabbadie to Minister, 10 January 1764, IHC, vol. 10, p. 209.

101. CO 5 86, p. 301 and CO 5 87, p. 67, quoted in Phillips, p. 598.

102. Villiers to Inhabitants of Fort Chartres, 27 September 1763, JMss, vol. 10, p. 821.

103. Gage to Shelburne, 11 November 1766, Reid, p. 26.

104. Dabbadie to Minister, 10 January 1764, IHC, vol.10, p. 209.

105. Aubrey to Minister, 15 January 1764, IHC, vol. 10, pp. 214–15.

106. Journal of Dabbadie, 21 May 1764, IHC, vol. 10, pp. 186–87.

107. Journal of M. Dabbadie, 19 April 1764, IHC, vol. 10, pp. 182–83.

108. Journal of Dabbadie, 21 May 1764, IHC, vol. 10, pp. 186–87.

109. Bouquet to Gage, 27 May 1764, *Canadian Archives*, 1889, p. 66; Gage to Bouquet, June 5, 1764, *Canadian Archives*, 1889, p. 67; Gage to Johnson, April 30, 1764, JMss, vol 11., pp. 167–68.

110. Trader's Reports, Gladwin MSS, 1764, Reuben G. Thwaites, *The British Regime in Wisconsin, Collections of the State Historical Society of Wisconsin*, vol. 18 (1908), p. 268.

111. Croghan to the Board of Trade, 8 June 1764, Canadian Archives Microfilm II, State Historical Society of Wisconsin.

112. Gage to Halifax, 21 May 1764, IHC, vol. 10, pp. 248–49.

113. Johnson to Gage, 29 June 1764, JMss, vol. 11, p. 245.

114. Johnson to Gage, 29 June 1764, JMss, vol. 11, p. 245.

115. Colden to Halifax, 9 July 1764, *Colden Papers, New York Historical Society Collections*, 1876, p. 335; Gage to Halifax, 13 July 1764, IHC, vol. 10, pp. 283–84.

116. Journal of Dabbadie, 2 July 1764, IHC, vol. 10, pp. 189–90.

117. St. Ange to Dabbadie, 15 July 1764, IHC, vol. 10, pp. 289–91.

118. St. Ange to Dabbadie, 12 August 1764, IHC, vol. 10, pp. 292–93.

119. St. Ange to Dabbadie, 12 August 1764, IHC, vol. 10, p. 294.

120. Dabbadie to Gage, 16 August 1764, IHC, vol. 10, pp. 300–1.

121. Journal of Dabbadie, 20 August 1764, IHC, vol. 10, p. 196.

122. Dabbadie to the Minister, 10 September 1764, IHC, vol. 10, p. 312.

123. Dabbadie to the Minister, 30 September 1764, IHC, vol. 10, pp. 314–15.

124. St. Ange to Dabbadie, 30 September 1764, IHC, vol. 10, p. 296.

125. Alex McKee to Johnson, 17 November 1764, JMss, vol. 11, p. 475.

126. Bouquet to Johnson, 30 November 1764, JMss, vol. 4, p. 607.

127. Johnson to Gage, 30 September 1764, JMss, vol. 11, pp. 364–65.

128. Journal of William Howard, 3 November 1764, JMss, vol. 11, p. 696.

129. St. Ange to Dabbadie, 9 November 1764, IHC, vol. 10, pp. 356–57.

130. St. Ange to Dabbadie, 9 November 1764, IHC, vol. 10, pp. 355–56.

131. Bouquet to Johnson, 30 November 1764, *Canadian Archives*, 1889, p. 34.

132. Colden to Lords of Trade, 12 October 1764, NYCD, vol. 7, p. 668.

133. Gage to Bouquet, 9 November 1764, IHC, vol. 10, pp. 353–54.

134. Bouquet to Gage, 30 November 1764, IHC, vol. 10, pp. 366–67.

135. Gage to Johnson, 6 December 1764, IHC, vol. 10, p. 369.

136. Gage to Bouquet, 7 December 1764, IHC, vol. 10, p. 371.

137. Johnson to Bouquet, 17 December 1764, JMss, vol. 4, p. 620.

138. Johnson to Gage, 18 December 1764, JMss, vol. 4, p. 625.

139. Johnson to Gage, 18 December 1764, JMss, vol. 4, p. 625.

140. Johnson to Croghan, 18 December 1764, JMss, vol. 11, pp. 509–10.

141. Gage to Bouquet, 20 December 1764, Canadian Archives, 1889, p. 74; Indian Intelligence, 22 December 1764, JMss, vol. 4, pp. 627–28.

142. Johnson to the Lords of Trade, 26 December 1764, IHC, vol. 10, p. 394.

143. Gage to Bouquet, 24 December 1764, Canadian Archives, 1889, p. 74.

144. Gage to Johnson, 31 December 1764, JMss, vol. 11, pp. 515–17.

145. Aubrey to the Minister, 12 February 1765, IHC, vol. 10, p. 436.

146. Pease, p. 8.

147. Wilkins to Barrington, 5 December 1769, IHC, vol. 16, p. 633.

148. Johnson to Lords of Trade, 16 November 1765, NYCD, vol. 7, pp. 776–77.

149. Journal A, 28 February 1764, BWM Microfilm, Roll 7.

150. Wainwright, p. 212.

151. Samuel Wharton to Benjamin Franklin, 19 December 1764, IHC, vol. 10, pp. 376–77.

152. Baynton and Wharton, Journal A, 29 January 1765, BWM, Roll 8.

153. Croghan to Johnson, 18 February 1765, JMss, vol. 11, p. 576.

154. Croghan to Simon Levy and Company, 23 March 1765 in Byars, pp. 69–71; Gage to Governor Penn, 30 March 1765, PA, 1st Series, vol. 4, p. 215; Johnson to Gage, 13 July 1765, JMss, vol. 11, p. 843.

155. Johnson to Gage, 9 March 1765, IHC, vol. 10, pp. 463–64; Gage to Johnson, 31 March 1765, JMss, vol. 4, p. 703.

156. Baynton and Wharton Memo Book, 8, 11, 12, and 27 December 1764, BWM, Roll 10.

157. Baynton and Wharton Memo Book, 22 December 1764, BWM, Roll 10.

158. Baynton and Wharton Journal A, 28 January 1765, BWM, Roll 8; Baynton and Wharton Journal A, June 1765, BWM, Roll 8; Baynton and Wharton Journal A, 4 January 1765, BWM, Roll 8.

159. Baynton and Wharton, Memo Book, 7–14 December 1764, BWM, Roll 10; Baynton and Wharton, Journal A, 2 August 1765, BWM, Roll 7.

160. Baynton and Wharton, Journal A, 24 December 1764, BWM, Roll 8.

161. Baynton and Wharton, Memo Book, 3 December 1764, BWM, Roll 10.

162. Governor John Penn to Johnson, 21 March 1765, JMss, vol. 11, pp. 343–45; Gage to Governor John Penn, 30 March 1765; PA, 1st Series, vol. 4, p. 215.

163. Lieutenant Charles Grant to Bouquet, 9 March 1765, Canadian Archives, 1889, p. 279; Lt. Colonel Reid to Gage, 4 June 1765, Pennsylvania Colonial Records, vol. 9, p. 269; Lieutenant McCullough to Bouquet, 7 March 1765, Canadian Archives, 1889, p. 278.

164. Callender to Bouquet, 11 March 1765, Canadian Archives, 1889, p. 279.

165. Statement of Ralph Nailer, 2 June 1765, PA, 1st Series, vol. 4, p. 225; Governor John Penn to Johnson, 23 May 1765, JMss, vol. 11, p. 746; Governor John Penn to Gage, 28 June 1765, Pennsylvania Colonial Records, vol. 9, p. 275.

166. Gage to Governor John Penn, 5 July 1765, Pennsylvania Colonial Records, vol. 9, p. 281.

167. Johnson to Gage, 3 April 1764, JMss, vol. 11, pp. 664–45; Johnson to Gage, 4 May 1765, JMss, vol. 4, p. 735.

168. Gage to Johnson, 8 May 1765, JMss, vol. 4, pp. 737–38.

169. Croghan to Benjamin Franklin, 12 December 1765, IHC, vol. 11, p. 61.

170. Johnson to Croghan, 4 April 1765, JMss, vol. 4, p. 706; Johnson to Croghan, 8 April 1765, JMss, vol. 11, p. 680.

171. Johnson to Gage, 3 April 1765, JMss, vol. 4, p. 705; Samuel Wharton to Johnson, 14 April 1765, JMss, vol. 4, pp. 712–16.

172. Francis Wade to Johnson, 26 April 1765, JMss, vol 4, p. 729; Samuel Wharton to John Baynton, 15 March 1765, BWM, Roll 5.

173. Gage to Johnson, 15 April 1765, JMss, vol. 4, p. 717.

174. Samuel Wharton to Baynton and Wharton, 28 November 1765, BWM, Roll 5; Gage to Johnson, 21 April 1765, JMss, vol. 4, p. 721.

175. Baynton and Wharton Journal B, 28 February 1766, BWM, Roll 8.

176. Baynton and Wharton Journal B, 17 April 1766, BWM, Roll 8.

177. Bouquet to Johnson, 25 January 1765, JMss, vol. 4, p. 640.

178. Wainwright, p. 214.

179. Baynton and Wharton, Journal A, December 1764, BWM, Roll 8.

180. Alexander Fraser to Campbell, 17 May 1765, IHC, vol. 10, pp. 493–94; Fraser to Johnson, 18 May 1765, JMss, vol. 11, p. 743; Fraser to Campbell, 20 May 1765, IHC, vol. 10, p. 497.

181. Croghan's Journal, 20 and 26 May 1765 in Thwaites, *Western Travels*, vol. 1, pp. 131–34; Croghan to Gage, 26 May 1765, IHC, vol. 11, p. 22.

182. Campbell to Johnson, 15 July 1768, JMss, vol. 11, pp. 854–55; Wainwright, pp. 219–21; Johnson to Colden, 15 August 1765, JMss, vol. 4, p. 823.

183. Gage to Johnson, 30 June 1765 JMss, vol. 4, p. 779; Johnson to Gage, 13 July 1765, JMss, vol. 11, p. 843; MacDonald to Johnson, 24 July 1765, JMss, vol. 11, p. 850; Hutchins to Johnson, 31 August 1765, IHC, vol. 11, pp. 79–80; Sterling to Gage, 18 October 1765, IHC, vol. 11, p. 107.

184. Memorial of French Merchants to Gage, 17 October 1765, IHC, vol. 11, pp. 111–14; Sterling to Gage, 18 October 1765, IHC, vol. 11, p. 107; Eddington to ____, 17 October 1765, IHC, vol. 11, p. 105.

185. Hough, p. 143; Stevens, pp. 25–26.

186. Croghan Journal, 20 May 1765, Thwaites, *Western Travels*, vol. 1, pp. 131, 134.

187. Croghan to Murray, 12 July 1765, IHC, vol. 11, pp. 58–59.

188. Capucin to Baptiste Campeau, 7 June 1765, JMss, vol. 4, p. 766.

189. Carleton to Shelburne, 2 March 1768, *Canadian Archives Report*, 1886, p. clxxi.

190. Johnson to the Lords of Trade, 16 November 1765, NYCD, vol. 7, pp. 776–77.

191. Fraser to Haldimand, 4 May 1766, IHC, vol. 11, pp. 228–29.

192. IHC, Vol. 10, pp. 183–88.

193. Gage to Johnson, 25 January 1767, DHNY, vol. 2, p. 486.

194. Croghan's Journal, November, 1765, Thwaites, vol. 1, p. 172; Dunham, p. 93.

195. Croghan's Journal, 30 August 1765, Thwaites, vol. 1, p. 159.

196. Aubrey to the Minister, 12 February 1765, IHC, vol. 10, pp. 433–35.

197. Speech by Shawnee Chief Charlot Kaske, 24 February 1765, IHC, vol. 10, pp. 445–47.

198. Aubrey to the Minister, 25 February 1765, IHC, vol. 10, pp. 455–57.

199. Lt. Fraser to Gage, 16 December 1765, IHC, vol. 11, pp. 130–31.

200. Winston to Baynton and Wharton, 16 December 1765, BWM, Roll 5.

201. Dunham, p. 73.

202. Johnson to Colden, 22 January 1765, IHC, vol. 10, p. 417.

203. Ulloa to Gage, 1 April 1766, IHC, vol. 11, p. 208.

204. Gage to Conway, 24 June 1766, IHC, vol. 11, p. 322.

205. Phillips, p. 596.

206. Baynton and Wharton, Journal A, 2 August 1765, BWM, Roll 7.

207. Baynton and Wharton, Journal A, December 1765, BWM, Roll 8.

208. Fraser to Haldimand, 4 May 1766, IHC, vol. 11, p. 229.

209. Baynton to Mary Morgan, 11 July 1766, IHC, vol. 11, p. 337.

210. Croghan to Johnson, 18 April 1766, JMss, vol. 6, pp. 181–82.

211. Baynton and Wharton to Tull and Vaughn, 6 February 1766, BWM, Roll 1; Baynton and Wharton to Smallman, 6 February 1766, BWM, Roll 5.

212. Remarks of Gage on Barrington Plan, 10 May 1766, IHC, vol. 11, p. 244.

213. Baynton and Wharton, Journal A, January 1766, BWM, Roll 8; Gage to Johnson, 7 April 1766, IHC, vol. 11, pp. 212-13.

214. Baynton and Wharton, Journal A, January 1766, BWM, Roll 8.

215. Gage to Johnson, 3 March 1766, IHC, vol. 11, pp. 158–59; Gage to Croghan, 16 April 1766, IHC, vol. 11, pp. 216–17.

216. Gage to Conway, 15 July 1766, IHC, vol. 11, p. 340.

217. Council Minutes, 6 March 1766, Pennsylvania Colonial Records, vol. 9, p. 303; Robert Callender to Baynton and Wharton, 2 March 1766, Pennsylvania Colonial Records, vol. 9, p. 302; Baynton and Wharton to Gage, 7 March 1766, IHC, vol. 11, pp. 165–66.

218. Dobson to Baynton and Wharton, 9 March 1766, IHC, vol. 11, pp. 166–67.

219. Baynton and Wharton, 12 June 1766, JMss, vol. 5, pp. 260–61; Bill of Goods, 10 June 1766, IHC, vol. 11, p. 233.

220. Samuel Wharton to John Baynton, 30 May 1766, BWM, Roll 2; Baynton and Wharton, Journal B, 3 May 1766, BWM, Roll 8.

221. Morgan to his wife, 20 June 1766, IHC, vol. 11, p. 311.

222. Baynton and Wharton Journal, 5 June 1766 to 12 November 1766, BWM, Roll 7; Baynton and Wharton, Journal B, 4 December 1766, BWM, Roll 8.

223. Baynton to Mary Morgan, 11 July 1766, IHC, vol. 11, p. 337; Baynton and Wharton, Journal B, 11 August 1766, BWM, Roll 8.

224. Baynton and Wharton, Journal B, 25 March 1767, BWM, Roll 8.

225. Edward Cole Account, 25 September 1766, JMss, vol. 5, p. 382; Croghan to Johnson, 10 September 1766, IHC, vol. 11, p. 373; Cole to Johnson, 12 November 1766, BWM, Roll 7.

226. Baynton and Wharton, Journal B, 4 December 1766, BWM, Roll 8.

227. Baynton and Wharton, Journal B, 13 October 1766, BWM, Roll 8.

228. Baynton and Wharton, Ledger A, Fort Chartres, BWM, Roll 9.

229. Gage to Johnson, 1 September 1765, JMss, vol. 5, p. 368.

230. Van Schaack to Hay, 4 September 1767, IHC, vol. 16, pp. 3-4.

231. Morgan to Baynton and Wharton, 10 December 1767, IHC, vol. 16, p. 130.

232. Dunham, p. 89; Clarence W. Alvord, The Mississippi Valley in British Politics, 2 vols. (Cleveland: Arthur H. Clark, 1917), vol. 1, p. 304; Pease, p. 11.

233. Gage to Shelburne, 23 December 1766, IHC, vol. 11, p. 459; Haldimand to Gage, 17 June 1767, IHC, vol. 11, pp. 575–56; Gage to Hillsborough, 17 August 1768, IHC, vol. 16, p. 378.

234. Gage to Hillsborough, 6 January 1769, IHC, vol. 16, p. 486.

235. Haldimand to Thomas Willing, 20 April 1768, *Canadian Archives*, 1886, p. 465.

236. Thomas Wharton to B. Franklin, 14 January 1767, IHC, vol. 11, p. 481.

237. Croghan to Gage, 12 January 1767, IHC, vol. 11, pp. 479–81.

238. Baynton and Wharton, Journal B, 24 March 1767, BWM, Roll 8; Gage to Johnson, 20 July 1767, JMss, vol. 5, p. 601.

239. Baynton and Wharton, Ledger A, Fort Chartres, BWM, Roll 9.

240. Baynton and Wharton, Ledger A, Fort Chartres, BWM, Roll 9.

241. Gage to Johnson, 4 April 1768, IHC, vol. 16, p. 221.

242. Baynton and Wharton, Ledger A, Fort Chartres, BWM, Roll 9.

243. Morgan to MacNamara, 20 December 1767, IHC, vol. 16, p. 135; Morgan to Baynton and Wharton, 11 December 1767, IHC, vol. 16, p. 137.

244. Cole to Croghan, 25 October 1767, IHC, vol. 16, p. 98; Morgan to Baynton and Wharton, 2 December 1767, IHC, vol. 16, p. 127.

245. Baynton and Wharton, Journal B, 7 May 1767, BWM, Roll 8.

246. Baynton and Wharton, Journal B, 27 May 1768, BWM, Roll 8.

247. Morgan to Baynton and Wharton, 11 December 1767, IHC, vol. 16, p. 134.

248. Croghan to Gage, 16 January 1767, IHC, vol. 11, pp. 491–92.

249. Wharton to B. Franklin, 4 October 1767, IHC, vol. 16, pp. 66–67.

250. Morgan to Baynton and Wharton, 6 December 1767, IHC, vol. 16, p. 128; Morgan to Baynton and Wharton, February 1768, IHC, vol. 16, p. 164; *Pennsylvania Colonial Records*, vol. 9, pp. 469–70.

251. Morgan to Baynton and Wharton, 10 December 1767, IHC, vol. 16, p. 130.

252. Gage to Hillsborough, 20 June 1768, NYCD, vol. 8, pp. 76–77; Gage to Wilkins, 11 October 1768, IHC, vol. 16, pp 418–19; Gage to Johnson, 10 October 1768, JMss, vol. 6, p. 433; Gage to Hillsborough, 9 October 1768, IHC, vol. 16, p. 414.

253. Phillips, p. 597.

254. Samuel Young to Morgan, 18 February 1768, BWM, Roll 5.

255. Gage to Hillsborough, 9 October 1768, IHC, vol. 16, p. 414.

256. Ulloa to Gage, 29 August 1768, IHC, vol. 16, p. 386.

257. Gage to Shelburne, 24 April 1768, IHC, vol 16, p. 269.

258. Gage to Haldimand, 26 April 1768, IHC, vol. 16, p. 273; Gage to Shelburne, 24 April 1768, IHC, vol. 16, pp. 267–68.

259. Dunham, p. 79; W. N. Franklin, "Pennsylvania-Virginia Rivalry," *Mississippi Valley Historical Review*, vol. 20, p. 477; Thomas P. Abernathy, *Western Lands and the American Revolution* (New York: D. Appleton-Century, 1937), p. 28.

260. Morgan to Baynton and Wharton, February 1768, IHC, vol. 16, pp. 163–64.

261. Morgan to Baynton and Wharton, February 1768, IHC, vol. 16, pp. 161–62.

262. Baynton and Wharton, Ledger A, Fort Chartres, BWM, Roll 9.

263. Morgan to Baynton and Wharton, 5 April 1768, IHC, vol. 16, pp. 226–27; Morgan to Baynton and Wharton, 18 April 1768, IHC, vol. 16, p. 257; Morgan to Baynton and Wharton, 23 April 1768, IHC, vol. 16, pp. 260–61.

264. Morgan to Baynton and Wharton, 5 April 1768, IHC, vol. 16, p. 229.

265. Gage to Shelburne, 12 March 1768, IHC, vol. 16, p. 211.

266. Gage to Johnson, 18 April 1768, JMss, vol. 6, p. 199; Morgan to Baynton and Wharton, 5 April 1768, IHC, vol. 16, p. 229; Gage to Johnson, 7 August 1768, JMss, vol. 6, p. 312; Johnson to Gage, 24 August 1768, IHC, vol. 16, p. 384.

267. Maturin to Baynton and Wharton, 7 May 1768, IHC, vol. 16, p. 278; Baynton and Wharton to Johnson, 8 May 1768, IHC, vol. 16, p. 279; Johnson to Baynton and Wharton, IHC, vol. 16, pp. 290-91.

268. Wetherhead to Johnson, 30 May 1768, JMss, vol. 6, p. 234.

269. Account of Baynton and Wharton, 13 September 1768, Jmss, vol. 6, pp. 389-90; Wilkins to Gage, 13 September 1768, IHC, vol. 16, p. 390.

270. Morgan to Baynton and Wharton, 20 June 1768, IHC, vol. 16, p. 324.

271. Morgan to Baynton and Wharton, 11 July 1768, IHC, vol. 16, p. 349; Morgan to Baynton and Wharton, 20 July 1768, IHC, vol. 16, p. 359.

272. Morgan to Baynton and Wharton, 20 July 1768, IHC, vol. 16, pp. 358-62.

273. Campbell to Baynton and Wharton, 20 August 1768, BWM, Roll 3.

274. Morgan to Baynton and Wharton, 30 October 1768, IHC, vol. 16, pp. 442-447; Croghan to Johnson, 25 December 1768, JMss, vol. 6, pp. 552-53.

275. Baynton and Wharton, Journal C, 1 October 1768, BWM, Roll 9.

276. Pease, pp. 8-9.

277. Dunham, pp. 100-1.

278. Johnson to Lords of Trade, 16 November 1765, NYCD, vol. 7, p. 776.

# 5

## THE ARMY

The British army mission in North America in 1765 was to occupy the new territory acquired in 1763 by the Treaty of Paris ending the Seven Years War. From 1765 to 1768 a minimum of fifteen regiments were stationed in various colonies. The regiments stationed in the west supported the Indian Department in its efforts to maintain peace with the tribes and enforced trade regulations. In performing its supportive role, the army became a heavy consumer as well; it was the largest source of money on the frontier in the form of bills of exchange for the colonial merchants. Total army annual expenditures in America were approximately £400,000 sterling including £5,000 to £33,000 sterling in presents for the Indians. A large percentage of the army's purchases were made from colonial merchants in Canada, the Great Lakes, Pennsylvania, and Illinois. These expenditures absorbed nearly half the deficit of the balance of trade between the thirteen colonies and Great Britain.

Contemporary documents referred to the cost of the army as £400,000 sterling. Table 5.1 indicates a lower figure for the years 1764 to 1769, but I may have missed some expenses in creating the table. The pay and rations were established amounts for each regiment. Also included in this figure were uniforms, bedding, candles, and other routine expenses. Ordnance included replacement weapons, ammunition, and cannon. Other expense was a miscellaneous category, as was extraordinaries, which included the cost of repairing barracks and forts, transportation of troops and supplies, gifts to the Indians, and the overhead expense of the Indian Department. The army payments reduced the deficit in the balance of trade with Britain substantially.

The bills of exchange from the army expenditures helped considerably in balancing the huge deficit in the colonial trade with Britain. The £300,000 sterling surplus in the trade with southern Europe paid for most of the remaining deficit. The overall result was a manageable deficit until Parliament attempted to pass on much of the cost of the army in America to the colonists.

The concept of a large army in America was new in 1754. Before then, there were fewer than 4,000 British soldiers in the thirteen colonies and in the West Indies, costing about £195,000 sterling annually. Of these troops, only 790 were stationed in the thirteen colonies at a small cost of about £13,500 annually.[1] During the Seven Years War with France and later Spain, military policy had changed drastically, and in 1754 the decision was made to commit several regular army regiments to America. In 1755 General Edward Braddock was sent to America as commander-in-chief and with him two understrength regiments of regulars to be fleshed out with American recruits after arrival in the colonies.

Table 5.1 Military Expense and the Balance of Trade[2]
(£ sterling in thousands)

| Year | 1765 | 1766 | 1767 | 1768 |
|---|---|---|---|---|
| Regiments | 20 | 15 | 19 | 16 |
| Pay and rations | £266 | £200 | £248 | £211 |
| Ordnance | 40 | 40 | 40 | 40 |
| Other | 38 | 29 | 21 | 19 |
| Extraordinaries | 87 | 66 | 20 | 61 |
| Total army cost | 431 | 351 | 329 | 332 |
| Army costs plus exports | 1,583 | 1,379 | 1,425 | 1,583 |
| Imports | 1,944 | 1,804 | 1,900 | 2,157 |
| Balance | (361) | (425) | (475) | (574) |

The British army in the 1760s was organized in regiments, which usually had one battalion. However, some regiments, for example, the 60th Royal Americans and the 42nd Black Watch, had two or more battalions. In 1766 the authorized strength of a peacetime British battalion was a colonel, a lieutenant colonel, a major, seven captains, nine lieutenants, eight ensigns, a chaplain, an adjutant, a quartermaster, a surgeon, a surgeon's mate, eighteen sergeants, nine drummers, and 441 men, for a total of 500.[3]

The British organization was designed for warfare in Europe and ill suited to America. The weight of the equipment each soldier was supposed to carry on the march was 64 pounds, too much on rough forest trails. The British troops were not trained to fight in the forest. At the battle of Bushy Run in Ohio, 95 Indians attacked 600 British troops, killing 60 of them and forcing the others to retreat. Later the British formed ranger companies and light infantry to be trained to fight the Indians, but the bulk of the regiments were still cumbersome and unsuited for Indian warfare.[4]

In October 1761 over 20% of the entire British army was in North America, 23,000 men of a total of 108,000.[5] After the defeat of the French in Canada in 1760, the focus of the fighting turned from the frontier to the West Indies. In 1761 most of the regiments left Canada, depriving the colonial merchants of a good market. In 1762 after capturing Cuba many regiments returned to Canada and the thirteen colonies. However, they were badly depleted by sickness.

Sickness was a major problem of the British army in America. The regiments in the West Indies in 1762 suffered from an epidemic of yellow fever. In August 1762 four battalions were returned from Cuba, including two battalions of the 42nd Royal Highlanders, Montgomery's Highlanders, and the 17th Regiment, all of which had many men so seriously ill that they were not fit for duty. When troops were needed to reinforce Detroit in 1763, only small detachments could be sent from these regiments. Scurvy was also a problem; in 1759 more than half the troops at Quebec were ill with scurvy caused by the lack of vitamin C in the ration.[6]

Sickness continued to be a problem in the south. In November 1765 the 21st and 31st Regiments in Mobile and Pensacola were suffering and the commander, Colonel Bouquet, died of illness.[7] In 1767 reinforcements for the 21st and 31st Regiments in Florida were held in New York City until the sickly season had passed to save them from the fate of the men in Florida.[8]

Discipline and drinking were major problems. A trader, Colbeck, was drunk at Fort Niagara with the sergeants of the garrison for fourteen days while his men stayed in the storehouse, drunk as well, with a "seraglio" of Indian women.[9] The formal relations between officer and men and the rigid patterns of barracks life, which were necessary to sustain order in the army, were almost impossible to maintain in the one-or-two company garrisons. The splitting of the regiments into small garrisons destroyed the discipline of the troops.[10]

One obvious indication of the problems of the army was the high rate of desertion. Gage sent returning deserters to Grenada rather than back to their old regiments for fear that they would desert again. Men were needed constantly to fill the ranks of the regiments reduced by sickness and desertion. In October 1762 the First and Second Battalions of the 42nd Royal Highlanders were combined, and a cadre was sent back to Scotland to recruit new men.[11] In January 1767 Lt. Col. Prevost took 188 recruits from Hamburg, Germany to New York City to fill the 60th Regiment, which originally had consisted mainly of Germans. Despite official policy to the contrary, many regiments recruited Americans to replace their losses.

Duty in America apparently was not considered a hardship by the British troops. In 1767 the 14th, 46th, 28th, and two battalions of the 42nd Regiment were rotated back to Britain. From these five battalions 450 men volunteered to remain in America and were transferred to the 21st and 31st Regiments in Florida. In 1769 about half, 266 men, of the 9th and 34th Regiments volunteered to remain in America when their regiments were sent back to Great Britain.[12] This apparent contradiction between desertion and wishing to remain in America can be explained by family ties and the slack discipline in the American garrisons. Back in England the returning soldiers would face the rigid discipline of the army barracks.

The peacetime existence of the regiments in America that created the unique environment began in 1762. The regiments in America were scattered in small garrisons in Canada, on the frontier, in South Carolina, and in Georgia. In December 1762 the army of 8,000 men was distributed as follows:

| | |
|---|---|
| Canada | 3,650 |
| Nova Scotia, Cape Breton Island, Newfoundland | 1,700 |
| Upper New York Posts | 1,250 |
| Western Pennsylvania | 400 |
| Michigan | 350 |
| South Carolina and Georgia | 450 |
| New York City area | 200 |

In February 1763 the army in America was authorized to include fourteen battalions plus the 55th Regiment, which was to be sent to Ireland in 1765. The total strength, including ten companies of artillery, was 8,050 officers and men.

Parliament questioned the need for the army in America. In 1763 political pressure was exerted in London to reduce its high cost. There were varying viewpoints in London on the size and use of the army. Because Britain had defeated France and Spain in 1763, it was obliged to make territorial demands. With a view to future wars rather than economic gains, Canada and Florida were taken as strategic bases. The decision was made to garrison the American colonies with fifteen battalions with an additional five battalions in the British West Indies to guard against slave revolts. The obvious need was to defend the new possessions, but was such a large force required, and was occupation in mind when the troops were stationed there?

The peace was signed in Paris on 10 February 1763, but even before, on 1 February the king and Lord Ligonier, the British commander-in-chief, had agreed to ask Parliament for an overall peacetime army of eighty-five regiments. However, because of parliamentary objections, this number was reduced to seventy-five. Initial discussion took place in February and the intent of Parliament was that the colonies should assist in financing the army in America. On 24 February 1763, a meeting of the king's ministers called for an army in Britain of about the same size as that before the war, but an increase of the North American army to 7,500 men.[13] On 25 February Parliament authorized seventy-five regiments and stipulated that England would support the battalions in America for the first year, but after that the cost would be borne by the colonists.[14] The plan called for twenty regiments consisting of 7,500 men to be maintained in North America, including the continental colonies and the West Indies.[15] In March 1763 the House of Commons approved the measure for the maintenance of the twenty regiments in America with the understanding that American taxation would supply £50,000 sterling of the estimated cost of £250,000.[16] The colonists welcomed the profits from supplying the army but did not wish to be taxed to pay for it.

On 8 June 1763 the Board of Trade reported to Secretary Egremont that part of the overall plan for North America should be a sizable military force to defend against possible French or Indian uprisings and also to provide military government for the Indian territory and to protect the Indians from abuse. On 14 July 1763 Egremont informed the Board of the king's approval.[17]

A probable unstated reason for having these troops in America was the practical matter of maintaining a reserve of regiments for the general defense of the empire. By stationing the units in America, the traditional aversion of the British people to a standing army could be prevented. Furthermore, the American deployment promised American revenue to support fifteen of the regiments.[18] To reduce the army in America to fifteen regiments, some were disbanded in 1763 including the Third and Fourth Battalions of the 60th Royal American Regiment and the 77th, 78th, and 80th Scottish Regiments.[19]

On 12 February 1763 the secretary at war ordered General Amherst to submit a plan for the distribution of the troops that would be cost effective and at the same time accomplish their mission. Not until April did Amherst reply that the Mississippi River and Canada would require the most troops to guard against a Spanish invasion and to control the Indians. Other soldiers would be needed in Florida, but none was to be assigned to the seaboard communities.[20]

Of the fifteen battalions (350 to 500 men each) in North America, seven were along the St. Lawrence Valley and four were in Florida. Four regiments were assigned to the frontier in 1763, two were in northern and western New York, one was scattered along the Great Lakes, and one was in Fort Pitt. By August 1763 no battalions were stationed in the densely settled parts of the original thirteen colonies.[21]

The official explanation for the large peacetime army in America was to manage the Indians and to control the newly acquired territory. The British government expected that the troops in strategically located posts could protect the traders from robbery and murder by the Indians. At first the colonial merchants did not see the frontier posts as symbols of oppression but rather as a means to aid them in their economic struggle to wrest the trade from the French as well as potential customers for colonial products. Although the army could protect the traders and prevent unscrupulous traders from using excessive amounts of rum in the posts, it could not safeguard colonial traders in the Indian villages. In 1764 after Pontiac's Uprising, traders were required to remain in the posts. This rule benefited the French, who ignored it and were therefore able to acquire most of the fur in the villages, as the Indians preferred to have the traders go to them rather than go the posts.

There was little that the troops could do to control the French. Most of the 70,000 French people in Canada were farmers who had practically no concern for life outside their village and were not a threat to English rule. Local leadership in Canada was weak as the so-called seigneurs were, in effect, only landowners with titles dating back no more than one or two generations. Civil servants who had ruled Canada before 1760 returned to France under the provisions of the Capitulation of Montreal.[22] However, the French merchants in Montreal and Quebec stayed and competed with the colonial traders. The army was ineffective in managing either the Indians or the French.

Disaffection of the Indians was always a threat. The French encouraged the Indians to oppose the British and supplied them with weapons. French intrigue inspired Pontiac's Uprising, which initially was successful. Many smaller posts were taken by the Indians and numerous colonial traders were killed in the wilderness. The British were slow to react. Many of the regiments were still in the Caribbean after the conquest of Cuba. The regiments that had returned were reduced by sickness from their wartime strength of 1,000 men to a few hundred. Of the eleven regiments in Canada, New York, and Pennsylvania, the 47th, 17th, First Battalion of the 42nd, and the 77th were sickly from service in the West Indies, and the remainder on occupation duty had been scattered in small units, which seriously reduced their effectiveness. Nevertheless, these weak forces, after suffering numerous defeats in 1763, were able to hold Detroit, Niagara, and Fort Pitt and in the following year regain control.

Only a minimal number of troops were needed to garrison the few forts that were reestablished in 1764. An army of fewer than 1,000 under Colonel Bouquet was adequate to create order in the Ohio Valley, and a similar force under Colonel Bradstreet returned peace to the Great Lakes in 1764. An occupation force of perhaps four battalions distributed on the Great Lakes, the Ohio River, and the Mississippi would have been sufficient, plus at least two additional regiments in reserve, the number normally assigned until 1768. The other nine regiments assigned occupation duties in Canada and Florida were excessive and not related to the fur trade.

The matter of raising the money to support the army in America remained a thorny issue. In September 1763 the Treasury Board in London ordered the draft of a bill for colonial stamp duties to raise revenue to defray military expenses. On 9 March 1764 Lord Grenville presented a resolution to the House of Commons for duties on colonial imports and exports, which was subsequently enacted as the Sugar Act of 1764. This act specifically stated that the revenue was to be used to defray the expense of defending the American colonies.[23] Further strengthening the English position, in March 1764 a resolution was adopted in Parliament to the effect that the expense of defending the British colonies in America should be met by stamp duties.[24] The Stamp Act of 1765 required the use of receipts for "defraying the expenses of defending, protecting, and securing" the colonies.[25]

In the fall of 1765 the British government was concerned about reducing the cost of the army in America, which was £430,000 sterling that year, a sizable portion of a total expense for running the British government of £10 million. The normal expense for maintaining fifteen battalions was about £190,000 sterling plus an additional £200,000 for other charges. The extraordinary expenses added even more to move troops, transport rations, and build and repair the forts. One warrant to cover part of the cost of moving Bouquet's force to subdue the Indians in 1764 was £24,675 New York ($3,110,000). The charges included hiring wagons, pack horses, bullock and sheep drivers, and providing pasture and forage for the animals.[26]

In March 1765 General Gage had suggested that the army be reduced on the frontier. In October Viscount Barrington in London went further to save money by recommending that the troops be withdrawn completely from the frontier posts and transferred to the east coast, where they would be cheaper to feed and available if needed.[27] Gage responded in December, agreeing that maintaining the army on the frontier was too expensive. However, he questioned the possible negative effect on the fur trade if the forts were abandoned. The forts had been of little value during the uprising and the Rule of 1764 confining trade to the post had not protected the Indians from fraud. However, the lack of rules before 1763 actually had led to the uprising and the garrisons could help control and limit the French influence on the Indians. The garrisons would also prevent white settlers from crossing the mountains, and thereby further antagonizing the Indians. For those reasons Gage favored retaining the posts, at least those in Illinois. Barrington's reaction was to defer any decision on the matter.[28]

The colonial merchants' strong opposition to the Stamp Act in 1765 caused political problems in London. The Rockingham Whigs, who assumed power in July 1765 with weak support from George III, were more conciliatory to the colonists than the previous Grenville ministry. Faced by an alliance of members of Parliament favorable to the West Indies planters and the colonists, Rockingham proposed to repeal the Stamp Act.[29] The Stamp Act was creating problems for the army as well. Gage had difficulty selling sterling bills of exchange for New York currency, which was used to meet the expenses of the army and the Indian Department as late as June 1766. The merchants had no need for the bills because they were still unwilling to pay their debts in England as part of the protest against the Stamp Act.[30] The Stamp Act was repealed in March 1766, depriving the treasury of a third of the funds earmarked to pay for the army in America.[31]

Attempts to reduce the cost of the army were initiated in 1765. A system of rotation of regiments was instituted to ease the burden of serving in unhealthy areas. Five regiments were to be rotated in 1765, five in 1766, and three in 1768. By 1769 the plan had been completed though behind schedule. Future rotation was abandoned because of the high cost of moving the troops.[32]

The initial rotation was under way by September 1765. The 34th Regiment was on its way to relieve the 100 men from the 42nd Regiment in Illinois; the bulk of the 42nd Regiment was in Fort Pitt; the 59th and 29th Regiments from Ireland relieved the 45th and 40th Regiments in Newfoundland and Nova Scotia; the 52nd Regiment arrived in Quebec in August to replace the 44th Regiment; and the 21st and 31st Regiments were sent to Florida to relieve the 22nd and 35th Regiments which had suffered from tropical diseases in the West Indies and later in Florida.[33]

In 1765 the British had garrisons at Detroit, Michilimackinac, Green Bay, Sault Ste. Marie (between Lake Superior and Lake Huron), and Kaministiqua on Lake Superior.[34] In 1764 Johnson had recommended that additional posts be established to accommodate the colonial traders who were restricted to trading at posts. This action was not carried out because of the disasters that had overtaken the weakly defended small posts during Pontiac's Uprising.[35]

Pressure to cut costs by abandoning posts and reassembling the scattered regiments continued in 1766. In May 1766 Secretary at War Barrington again proposed to withdraw the soldiers from the western posts because of the difficulty and expense of supplying them in the west at the end of long trade routes. Furthermore, discipline deteriorated when the regiments were split into small detachments, and they could not be quickly assembled for police duty, as was discovered during the Stamp Act riots. Barrington was not convinced that troops could even control the natives at the small posts, and besides, experience had shown that the they were willing to trade at the larger posts. The only function of the smaller posts was to provide a protected place for the colonial merchants to trade and that was no longer necessary because the Indians travel to the major posts at Detroit, Michilimackinac, and Fort Pitt.[36] Therefore, the reason for maintaining the army scattered throughout the west was no longer valid.[37]

Barrington's plan recommended that the troops be concentrated in Florida, Canada, and Nova Scotia, where they would be cheaper to maintain and more readily available for riot duty.[38] Barrington specifically ordered that no regiments be sent to New England as the colonists would be provoked needlessly.[39]

Gage's reaction was favorable because the Indians were more peaceful, and he specifically mentioned the opposition to the Stamp Act as a reason for moving the regiments to the east.[40] In March 1766 of the fifteen battalions in North America the 29th was in Newfoundland, the 59th was in Nova Scotia, the 52nd and 28th were in Quebec, and the 15th and four companies of the 14th were in Montreal, the First Battalion of the 60th was in Ticonderoga and other New York posts, seven companies of the 17th were in Detroit, two companies of the 17th were in Michilimackinac, the 46th was at Niagara, the 34th was in Illinois, the 42nd was at Fort Pitt with a few companies near Philadelphia, the Second Battalion of the 60th Regiment had a few companies in New York City and the remainder of the regiment was en route to stations in upper New York, and the 9th, 21st, and 31st were in Florida. The 28th Regiment was on its way to the British Isles after more than eight years of service in Canada, and the 46th Regiment was also bound for Britain after a long assignment at Fort Niagara.[41] The many old and infirm men of the 46th Regiment would be discharged and replaced with recruits from Britain. By July the 28th and 46th Regiments were in New York City, while the Second Battalion of the 60th Regiment was on its way to relieve the 17th Regiment at Detroit and Michilimackinac.[42]

Sir William Johnson objected to abandoning the small posts because he believed that without them the French would be free to hatch plots with the Indians against the British.[43] Johnson also objected to closing the posts becasue doing so would reduce the means to control either the colonial or the French traders. The colonial traders had abused the Indians in the past and used too much rum in the trade, a practice that had led to Pontiac's Uprising in 1763. If the abuse were rekindled, then war could be expected and the profits of the fur trade lost. Johnson believed that within a few years the profits from trade with the Indians would more than pay for the cost of the garrisons.[44]

There was also objection in England to abandoning the forts, which would reduce the colonists' efforts to trade with the Indians. Richard Jackson, a close associate of Shelburne in London, presented a report condemning the proposal to abandon the frontier as the Indians would not travel 500 to 1,000 miles to trade with the colonists at the large posts. Jackson suggested that even though the number of regiments was reduced, a strong garrison should be maintained in Illinois to supervise the colonial merchants.[45] Gage agreed that even though many posts would be closed, some would remain, Oswego, Niagara, Fort Erie, Detroit, Michilimackinac, Fort Stanwix, and Fort Pitt.[46] The British government agreed with Gage that posts should be sustained in the newly acquired territory to hold the lines of communication open as well as to control the Canadians and to protect the Indians from abuse by the traders.[47]

Of all the posts, the most expensive to maintain was Fort Chartres in Illinois. Far from any other post with no competition except from New Orleans, rations and merchandise could be sold to the army at great profit by colonial merchants. The price of merchandise in Illinois was astronomical. In 1765 the profit hungry French merchants were selling a gallon of French brandy for a pound sterling ($200) compared to only 3/- New York ($18.90) for a gallon of rum in New York and 8/- Pennsylvania ($46) in Fort Pitt.[48] The colonial merchants could sell at half the price of the French merchants and still make a huge profit even with the cost of transportation from Philadelphia.

The first task was for the army to reach Illinois, not a simple matter. In 1764 the British selected the 22nd Regiment to make the expedition up the Mississippi from Florida. The 22nd Regiment had 351 men, having been reinforced by drafting all the men from the Third Battalion of the 60th Royal American Regiment not entitled to discharge when the battalion was disbanded at Pensacola. In addition, many of the men who were discharged from the Royal American regiment were persuaded to reenlist in the 22nd Regiment.

The expedition began with an attempt to find a passage at Iberville, but the waterway was clogged with trees. The regiment then went to New Orleans on 12 February 1764 to prepare for the trip up the Mississippi; there, 30 of the troops deserted. Finally on 27 February 1764 the regiment set out with 320 soldiers, 30 women, and 17 children in ten bateaux and two pirogues. By 15 March 1764, 50 more men had deserted and 7 had died. On 19 and 20 March Indians attacked the expedition 200 miles north of New Orleans, forcing the regiment to retreat to New Orleans on 26 March 1764.[49]

Whereas the British were unable to move troops up the Mississippi, the French had no difficulty. Even though the British regiment could not ascend the Mississippi because of Indian opposition, the French governor safely sent two convoys of bateaux, one on 19 April 1764 and another 11 May 1764. The convoys carried goods for both the Illinois and the Arkansas trade. The second convoy included 77 persons in three bateaux under the command of Berard with supplies for the French garrison in Illinois.[50]

In February 1765 Lieutenant Ross of the 34th Regiment traveled from Fort Pitt to Illinois and found that the Indians there were still not ready for peace. Pontiac had from 1,500 to 3,000 warriors ready to block any attempt of the British to travel up the Mississippi.[51] Regardless of this threat the British planned to send the 34th Regiment on its way north from New Orleans. The British asked the French governor, Aubrey, for permission to encamp 160 men at New Orleans in preparation for the trip north. Aubrey refused on the ground that the soldiers would desert. On the other hand, Aubrey successfully prevented the Indians from attacking the British convoy in the summer of 1765.[52]

Meanwhile, the British were able to send Captain Sterling, three officers, and one hundred men of the 42nd Black Watch Regiment in eight boats down the Ohio in September 1765.[53] In October Captain Sterling with the Black Watch took command of Fort Chartres and the French troops went to St. Louis. St. Ange, the French commander, assisted Captain Sterling in dealing with the Indians rather than urging them to cause trouble.[54] The 34th Regiment from Florida arrived later on 2 December 1765 with 140 men, meeting no opposition from the Indians. Because the soldiers were not skilled boatmen, the trip lasted five months and five days!

Provisions at Fort Chartres were short in 1766 for several reasons: the length of the trip up the Mississippi, the lack of supplies from Fort Pitt, and the refusal of the French to sell food to the army. The expected recruits, rations, clothing, barracks utensils, bedding, and ammunition had not arrived by the fall of 1766. Because of the shortage of food and with winter approaching, the men of the 42nd Regiment were sent down the Mississippi rather than up the Ohio to their regiment in Fort Pitt. The boats would then be available to carry up the one hundred new recruits for the 34th Regiment in the spring of 1767.[55]

The expense of maintaining a garrison in Illinois was enormous. In 1765 the 34th Regiment cost the British treasury in "extraordinaries" (expenses over and above pay and rations) £13,883 sterling ($2,776,600) for preparations to go to Illinois and £4,683 sterling ($936,600) in 1766 in addition to the normal charge for pay and rations of about £12,000 sterling a year.[56]

Because of the length of the trip from New Orleans in 1766, many of the presents for the Indians were damaged and replacements were required. The commander, Colonel Robert Farmar, insisted that new presents be delivered by spring, a sentiment that was supported by Croghan, who feared the Indians would cause trouble otherwise.[57] The commissary in Illinois, Edward Cole, spent £1,568 New York ($200,000) from 1 July to 25 September 1766 at a rate of £10,000 New York ($1,260,000) per year, which Gage thought excessive in comparison to Detroit and to Michilimackinac.[58] A third of the purchases were from Baynton and Wharton.

In July 1767 Baynton and Wharton were pressing Johnson for payment of two bills from the Indian Department in Illinois, one from Croghan for £1,744 New York and another from Edward Cole, the commissary, for £3,721 New York, a total of £5,465 New York ($690,000), which Johnson considered far too high.[59] This total compares to the £4,852 New York ($611,000) in Indian Department expense that led to the removal of Major Rogers from Michilimackinac in 1768. Croghan promised to be more frugal in the future and Cole was instructed to spend less. Illinois provides an example of the high cost of maintaining a western outpost. The army spent British sterling for pay, rations, repairs and maintenance of facilities, and various services, most of which were provided by local merchants and artisans.

In 1764 a new more tightly controlled method to pay military expenses in America was introduced. In the future the treasury would present an estimate of expenses to Parliament for approval. All additional expenditures made by the commander-in-chief in America or the governor of a colony would have to be approved by the treasury before being paid.[60]

Most of the money was used for pay and rations. The British treasury engaged money contractors who provided cash in America for army pay through agents at a commission of 2% of the total. The Spanish dollars or colonial currency was purchased in New York City from bankers and merchants with sterling bills of exchange. The contract to deliver rations included a fixed cost per ration, which was paid to the contractor in sterling bills of exchange. Currency to pay the troops and rations were both purchased with sterling bills of exchange used by colonial merchants to pay for imports from Britain.

The British contractors engaged colonial merchants to transact the business in America. In 1755 Gerard Beekman was engaged to provide pay, rations, and clothing for the army in America, receiving a 5% commission for purchases of food and merchandise and 2.5% for providing cash. Beekman was paid in sterling bills, Spanish dollars, or Jamaican rum.[61] Sir Samuel Fluyder and John Drummond (both members of Parliament) and Moses Franks (the patriarch of the family, which had many relatives in business in America) replaced Colebrooke, Nesbitt, and John Thomlinson as money contractors in 1766.[62]

The money contractors also appointed agents in America. In 1761 Ward Apthorpe, a New York merchant, purchased 2,000 Spanish dollars ($86,000) from John Collins, an agent of Baynton and Wharton in Quebec, with a sterling bill of exchange. The dollars were used to pay the soldiers then in Quebec. Collins also sold dollars worth £400 sterling ($80,000) to Alexander Campbell, the paymaster of the 74th Regiment, for a bill drawn on George Ross of London, presumably an agent for the money contractor in London.[63]

An appropriation of £20,175 sterling ($4,035,000) was made annually to pay a British regiment of 1,145 men, but only £10,585 sterling ($2,117,000) was paid to the troops; the remainder was held back for various expenses including clothing.[64] The regiments in Quebec in 1761 were probably at half strength of around 500 men and would have received less than £5,000 sterling per year or £417 sterling ($83,335) per month. The two sales of cash by Collins probably represented a month's pay to two regiments.

The major source of profit was in selling rations to the British army. Before 1760 the ration contract had been held by Sir William Baker, a member of Parliament, and Christopher Kilby, a Connecticut merchant. The next contractors were Sir Samuel Fludyer and Adam Drummond. In 1762 a new contract was let to Sir James Colebrooke, his brother George Colebrooke, Arnold Nesbitt, and Moses Franks at 4¾d sterling ($3.94) per ration with transportation charges in America to be paid for by the government. Oliver DeLancey and John Watts continued as agents in New York while David Franks and his associates became the agents in Philadelphia.[65] In 1764 the contractors appointed David Franks, John Inglis, and David Barclay of Philadelphia as agents to provide rations at a rate of 4¾d per day per man.[66]

The agents for the contractors also made money selling luxury items to the army: tea, coffee, chocolate, wine, rum, sugar, molasses, tobacco, cloth, and other dry goods.[67] The army officers were free to purchase these items from other merchants. Collins sold miscellaneous products, including rum, to the army.[68] Colonel Prevost purchased clothing for his regiment, the 60th Royal Americans, from Duncan Phyn in 1764.[69]

The major task was providing food for the troops. In 1766 the contracted cost was 6d sterling per ration, food for one soldier for one day. In 1766 a deduction of 2½d per day was made from the pay of the soldier for his rations, which were supposed to cost £22,242 sterling ($4,448,000) for fifteen battalions then in America. The cost for rations in 1766 was £72,729 ($14,546,000).[70] Estimating each battalion at a peacetime strength of 500 men, there were 7,500 soldiers in America. The daily amount of the estimated £22,242 sterling would have been £61 sterling or 2½d ($2.08) per man per day. Instead the actual daily amount in 1766 was £199 sterling or 7½d ($6.24) per man per day, three times the estimated amount and more than the 4¾d ($3.94) provided by the contract. Much of the difference resulted from transportation costs not included in the contract price. Because of the cost of transportation, feeding the regiments on the frontier was much more expensive than feeding those on the coast. The cost of the rations alone in 1766 demonstrated clearly the value of the military market to the colonial economy.

Feeding a regiment of 300 men could be a profitable enterprise. The standard ration was a pound of flour and a pound of beef per day, 9,000 pounds of each per month for a regiment. In 1762 flour sold at Fort Pitt for £2 Pennsylvania ($230) per hundredweight ($2.30 per pound) and beef at 7d Pennsylvania ($3.36) per pound. Venison sold for only 2d Pennsylvania per pound.[71] The cost of a ration at Fort Pitt therefore was approximately 7d sterling ($5.66).

The cost of a similar ration in New York City was less than 6d sterling. In New York City in 1762 beef sold at £4 New York ($504) per barrel (220 pounds) and wheat at £1 New York ($126) per bushel. The 60 pounds of wheat in a bushel could be ground into 60 pounds of flour at approximately 3d sterling ($2.10) per pound plus an allowance for grinding the wheat. The cost of beef was less that 3d sterling ($2.29) per pound for a total of a little more that 5d sterling ($4.39) for a ration. The price of a ration at New York City was significantly lower than the 7d at Fort Pitt and only slightly higher than the contract price of 4¾d sterling. The New York prices quoted were considered high because of poor crops for the past two years caused by drought.[72]

The cost of feeding a regiment of 300 men for a month at Fort Pitt prices was £103.10 sterling ($20,700) for the flour and £150 ($30,240) for the beef for a total of £253.10 ($50,940). Rations in Illinois were higher as transportation from Fort Pitt to Illinois added more to the cost. The London contractors had bid the ration at 4¾d sterling a day ($3.94) and were obviously looking for a better price that the 7d sterling ($5.66) possible with Fort Pitt prices even though the army paid more than the contract price to cover transportation.

Providing rations to the 34th Regiment in Illinois was a major part of the ration contract because of the difficulty of either transporting food there or purchasing it locally. By 1766 the 34th Regiment was established in Illinois, and its enormous cost was reflected in the bills of exchange and accounts sent to Gage. The rations alone cost as much as £15,000 sterling ($3,000,000) per year. The average cost of rations for a regiment elsewhere in America was only £4,849 ($970,000). The transportation to Illinois further increased the burden. To supply the regiment required that 45 boats be sent annually down the Ohio River at a cost of about £5,200 sterling ($1,000,000).[73]

The magnitude of the ration problem in Illinois can be better understood from the details. In 1765 the 34th Regiment was issued 6,178 rations, enough for 44 days for 140 men, for its trip up from Mobile to New Orleans. However, given the consumption of 48,121 rations during the 155 days to reach Illinois, the ration strength including women and other attached personnel was probably about 300 persons.

The rations issued in Mobile included 4,014 pounds of flour, 3,260 pounds of bread, 420 pounds of beef, 4,558 pounds of pork, 63 pounds of butter, 180 gallons of peas, and 304 gallons of rum (9,728 gills).[74]

The ration for a day was a pound of bread, a pound of meat and a gill of rum. The expedition therefore had rations for about 25 days to reach New

Orleans. The regiment was resupplied at New Orleans with 24,484 rations (82 days for 300 persons). The regiment probably stopped for some days at the Yassov River to wait for supply boats from New Orleans. A supply convoy evidently did catch up with the regiment at the Yassov River and issued the regiment 17,459 rations (58 days for 300 persons).

The 34th Regiment consumed a total of 48,121 rations on its journey from Mobile to Illinois: 6,178 from Mobile to New Orleans, 24,484 from New Orleans to the Yassov River, and 17,459 from the Yassov to Illinois. The customary charge to the regiment of the rations was £501 sterling ($100,200) or 2½d sterling per ration.[75] The actual cost was probably four times that amount. Flour sold at 10/- New York per hundredweight ($0.63, a little less than 1d sterling per pound) and beef at 10d New York ($5.23 a little more than 6d sterling) per pound in New York in 1768.[76] The cost of the pound of beef and the pound of flour in New York would have been 7d sterling ($5.86). Rum sold at about 4/- New York ($25.20) per quart or less than 4d sterling ($3.15) per gill, increasing the cost of the ration to about 11d sterling, more than four times the allotted price. A total purchase of colonial food and rum of £2,000 sterling ($400,000) was a considerable amount and did nothing more than feed a regiment on its way to Illinois.

When the regiment arrived in Illinois it was very short of provisions. The commander, Colonel Robert Farmar, was able to purchase 50,000 pounds of flour in Illinois, which was sufficient for 221 days, so he was feeding about 226 persons including the women who normally accompanied a regiment in the eighteenth century. The flour would last until July 1766 and meat could be obtained from hunting buffalo. However, many Indians were expected in the spring and the French custom was to feed them a double ration (two pounds of bread and two pounds of meat). More flour was needed, and Farmar pressed Gage to ensure that a supply would arrive from Fort Pitt early in the spring of 1766.[77]

A major task confronted General Gage—how was he to continue to feed the 34th Regiment at any cost? The long route from Philadelphia was 1,400 miles and lasted many weeks. Gage's plan to buy food locally faced difficulty because many of the French farmers were reluctant to sell to the British. The substitution of corn meal for flour and buffalo for beef was a temporary solution. There were large herds of buffalo along the Ohio River only a hundred miles from Fort Pitt in 1766.[78] In March 1766 the 34th Regiment was very short of food and had lived on bread and Indian corn for four days. They hoped that hunters would supply three boat loads of buffalo meat within a few days.[79]

The commandant at Fort Pitt was ordered to use Indians in canoes to supply the provisions, while waiting for boats to be built at Fort Pitt to transport provisions and the new men who had been recruited in Pennsylvania to fill the depleted ranks of the 34th Regiment. The regiment was still short of food in July 1766. Even though Indian corn meal was substituted for wheat flour, there was not enough to provide the full daily ration. Gage suggested that a military colony be created in Illinois to raise the food needed by the garrison.[80]

The commanding officer in Illinois was free to purchase his supplies from whomever he wished until the contractor was able to provide the ration. Most of the ration business was enjoyed by Baynton and Wharton, who maintained good relations with the commander. When Morgan established a store at Vincennes under the management of Alexander Williamson, he described the manner in which rations were gathered for the army. Williamson had past experience as a guide, which was of great benefit in dealing with the Indians. Williamson was warned to tell his friends in Detroit that business was very bad; otherwise they might go to Vincennes and compete with him. The local French farmers paid for merchandise with flour, tobacco, Indian corn, and hogs. Flour was accepted only at a price approved by Morgan and in quantities that could be sold to the army. All tobacco of good quality was to be taken at 20 sols ($4.20) per pound, made into "carrots" and sent to Kaskaskia. Indian corn was to be taken only in quantities that could be fed to hogs and cattle that had been purchased. Hogs were to be purchased at 18 sols ($3.78) per pound. When a hundred pigs had been purchased, Williamson was to hire two people to drive them to Kaskaskia, preferably in October or November. Cattle were purchased at 10 sols ($2.10) per pound or 200 livres ($1,600) for a three-year-old ox and delivered to Kaskaskia. Cows were sold at 150 livres ($1,200) in Kaskaskia so they were purchased for less.[81]

Baynton and Wharton attempted to obtain the ration contract in 1767 on a permanent basis. In January they sent proposals to General Gage and to Lauchlin MacCleane in London with the offer of a bribe to MacCleane to use his personal influence in presenting their proposal to the British treasury. Baynton and Wharton proposed to feed a regiment of 500 men in Illinois for a period of five, six, or seven years using buffalo meat, flour, corn meal, and peas at a cost of 1/- sterling ($10) delivered to Fort Chartres. Given the price of beef and flour at Fort Pitt and the cost of transportation, this offer was reasonable. With the substitutions of buffalo and corn meal available in Illinois, Baynton and Wharton expected to make a substantial profit, about £3,000 sterling ($600,000) on a gross of £10,000 sterling ($2,000,000).[82] The partners asked for an advance of £3,000 sterling ($600,000) to deposit a stock of provisions for 500 men. They also asked that no stills be set up in Illinois to compete with their sale of rum to the troops.

The advantage of the Baynton and Wharton offer was that it would be a more reliable source of food for the army in Illinois. The Ohio River was navigable only two months in the spring and two months in the fall when the water level was higher. During the summer and winter the troops were often short of food. In September 1766 the 34th Regiment had rations for only two months on hand, a slim margin. Adding danger to the complexity of finding food, the Indians could block movement on the Ohio River at any time.

In 1767 the ration contract for the American seaboard colonies was held by Sir Samuel Fluyder, a member of Parliament; Adam Drummond, also a member of Parliament; and Moses Franks, a Jewish merchant in London. The latter's brother, David Franks, was their Philadelphia agent and also the competitor of Baynton and Wharton in frontier trade.[83] David Franks offered to provide rations to Illinois for 9½ pence sterling ($7.90) per ration deposited at Fort Pitt which required the army to build boats and transport the food down the Ohio River. Baynton and Wharton estimated that transportation down the Ohio River cost the army over £5,000 sterling per year. The proposal of Baynton and Wharton would have reduced the cost of feeding the troops in Illinois by about £5,000 sterling by providing a daily ration at 12d sterling delivered to Fort Chartres, rather than Franks's offer of 9½p delivered to Fort Pitt with the government's paying the cost of transporting the food down the Ohio.[84]

Baynton and Wharton estimated their offer would save the army 50% and guarantee that the food would be available, whereas currently the troops were not being fed. In addition, buying grain from the French farmers would make them more friendly to the British. The French farmers would not accept army bills of exchange or paper money in payment for their produce whereas Baynton and Wharton would barter merchandise that the farmers needed. The partners claimed to have £30,000 sterling ($6,000,000) in merchandise in Illinois that could be used for this purpose.[85]

The partners' proposal was forwarded to Shelburne with the comment that Baynton and Wharton were the most extensive traders in North America and that the proposal proved that the Illinois garrison could be supplied at a reasonable cost.[86] Morgan very much wanted the contract, believing that if it were awarded to his firm, they would get the entire trade in Illinois. If not, he felt they should withdraw from Illinois, as it would be better to lose £10,000 than to send more goods and lose £20,000.[87] His hopes grew dim as Robert Leake, the commissary-general in New York City, advised Gage to reject Morgan's proposal on the grounds that buffalo meat would not remain edible for six months and could not be stored for emergencies. Leake warned that a more permanent supply was necessary in the event of an Indian siege.[88] Because of the danger of an Indian uprising in Illinois, the garrison must have a one-year supply on hand and the buffalo would spoil. Leake suggested that each spring the rations contractor be required to send salt pork, which would not spoil, in barrels sufficient to feel 300 men for nine months.[89]

In April 1767 the 34th Regiment had enough provisions but no reserve stocks. Gage expected Colonel Reed, commander of the 34th Regiment, to have a year's supply of rations in Fort Chartres at all times in the event of an Indian attack. The Indians could take the fort only by making a surprise attack or by starving the garrison out. In July 1767 Gage sent Reed £1,000 sterling ($200,000) in Spanish dollars to buy food locally.[90]

In July 1767 Baynton and Wharton hoped to supply the 34th Regiment with provisions until the contract was settled in England. Colonel Reed refused to deal with Baynton and Wharton, preferring instead a French merchant, Daniel Blouin. Baynton and Wharton asked Gage to order Reed to buy from them but had not succeeded by August.

In 1767 Franks found that delivering provisions to Illinois was no simple matter and asked that the price be raised to 15d sterling ($12.50). By August 1767 Gage was convinced that Baynton and Wharton were the better source in view of David Franks's offer which was 3d higher than Baynton and Wharton's offer.[91] Gage was outraged by Franks's proposal and wished that he could deal with Baynton and Wharton.[92] Despite Gage's preference of dealing with Baynton and Wharton, the contract remained in the hands of David Franks.[93] Because Franks had powerful connections in Parliament, he retained the contract to supply the garrison in Illinois at 9½p sterling delivered at Fort Pitt and the army had to move the rations to Fort Chartres. Franks and Company had no experience in shipping on the Ohio River, had no boats, and had no stock ready to move. Baynton and Wharton believed that Franks and Company would need eighteen months to begin delivery.

Baynton and Wharton took advantage of the situation and continued to supply the garrison both fresh and salted meat, flour, and corn.[94] The returns were sizable, as indicated by the payment of £6,035 sterling to them for military expenses.[95] They intended to send four boats to Fort Chartres and supplies for hunters to Fort Pitt.[96] Wharton calculated that 52 hunters and boatmen from Fort Pitt could obtain 80 tons of buffalo meat at a cost of £2,061 Pennsylvania ($237,000) or 3d per pound.[97] Providing the buffalo meat to the Illinois garrison was very profitable. Morgan had been selling meat to the army and to the agent of David Franks in early 1768 because the contractor was not able to provide meat from Fort Pitt. The hunting parties were successful, and the net profit from the sale of meat was £3,000 Pennsylvania ($345,000).[98] Morgan hoped to supply the meat to the contractor and even the complete ration at 13½p Pennsylvania ($6.48 compared to the $11.20 the contractors received from the British government).[99]

Other sales were made to the 34th Regiment. In September 1767 rum worth £621 Pennsylvania ($71,415) was sold to the regiment and in October Colonel Reed paid £521 Pennsylvania for provisions.[100] At the end of 1767 Reed continued to prefer to buy rations from Blouin even though he failed to deliver sufficient quantities. Morgan, the partners' agent in Illinois, complained that unless they received the full ration contract they would not do well. The only time Morgan could sell Indian goods was in the spring, and without revenue from sale of food to the army, the firm might as well abandon the Illinois business and take a loss of £10,000 to £20,000 Pennsylvania ($2,300,000).[101]

In March 1768 Morgan tried to overcome the resistance of the army to Baynton and Wharton by offering fresh beef at 8d New York ($4.24) per pound and flour at 10/- New York per hundredweight ($0.63 per pound). As an additional proposal to meet the army's concern for reserve stock, Morgan offered salted beef guaranteed not to spoil for a year at 10d New York per pound.[102] Even though the local French merchants offered provisions at a lower cost, Forbes, the post commander, ordered that the supplies be purchased from Morgan for reasons that he would not state.[103] Hunters Morgan had sent out early in the spring returned in April with nine tons of meat that could be sold to the army, sixty venison hams, and fifty-five buffalo tongues that could be sold to the French inhabitants and to the Spanish army in St. Louis. Morgan was so successful that he planned to send more hunters out the following spring with the goal of shipping buffalo meat to New Orleans for sale or even to New York and Philadelphia.[104]

In the summer of 1768 the 18th Regiment arrived from Fort Pitt with large quantities of rations and other supplies, reducing the market for Baynton and Wharton. Colonel Wilkins, the commander, gave preference to Morgan, who had 7.5 tons of beef on hand, which the army promised to buy at 8d Pennsylvania ($4) per pound. Morgan also sent out French hunters to supply ten tons of buffalo meat for sale to William Murray, the agent for David Franks and Company who held the ration contract. Murray had ordered 17.5 tons of meat from Morgan for the army.[105]

Baynton and Wharton's offer in 1768 to supply the contractor with ten tons of flour at a low price was rejected. The French in Illinois would not sell flour to the army for less than 37/6 Pennsylvania ($215) per hundredweight plus a 3/- delivery charge to Fort Chartres if it were paid for with British treasury bills of exchange. This was an exorbitant premium. Earlier in March Morgan had offered to supply the army with flour at 10/- New York ($60.30) per hundred- weight. He was able to buy from the French at much lower prices because he offered in exchange slaves, Spanish dollars, or private bills of exchange, which were acceptable to the farmers. Morgan had slaves for sale as his fellow agent in Illinois, Matthew Clarkson, had imported a shipment from New Orleans to trade to French farmers for produce that Clarkson intended to sell to the British army for treasury bills of exchange.[106] The farmers were willing to take private bills because they could collect immediately, rather than waiting a time for the government bills to be paid.

David Franks planned to ship a year's supply of flour from Fort Pitt to reduce the demand by the army and force the French farmers to lower their price. At the same time, Morgan would no longer be able to buy flour from the farmers and sell to the army at a high price because of the lack of an alterna- tive.[107] To address the meat problem, in June 1768 Franks shipped 400 bushels of salt to Illinois, evidence that he intended to send out his own hunters to obtain buffalo meat and eliminate the middle man, Morgan.

Franks's difficulty stemmed in part from the lack of experience of his agents (George Gibson and Henry Prather) in Illinois. Prior to working for Franks, they had traveled from Philadelphia to purchase fur from Baynton and Wharton agents on behalf of Joseph Simon and Bernard and Michael Gratz, all of whom had ties with David Franks.[108]

To provide more experienced representation, in July 1768 Bernard and Michael Gratz sent William Murray and Ephraim(?) Douglas to Illinois to represent David Franks. Murray left Fort Pitt on a large boat loaded with his merchandise and military stores and joined another boat loaded with military supplies.[109] Murray's merchandise included his personal goods worth £350; merchandise from Franks and Levy; supplies from the ration contractor, Moses Franks, Arnold Drummond & Company, worth £600; and £100 in silver work purchased from Henry Simons by Drummond & Company "at a high price." The merchants represented in this list indicate the powerful group working with David Franks.

Morgan intended to purchase the entire cargo from Murray if possible, but Murray sold the shoes and rum in his cargo on the trip down the Ohio River. However, he was willing to sell the remainder to Morgan. Morgan did not want the rum and the silver but was willing to deal on the other goods.[110]

By July 1766 Murray was in business and sending additional orders for merchandise to Bernard and Michael Gratz, who shipped two wagon loads of rum to Fort Pitt and later sent two wagon loads of merchandise plus two "Dutch" (Conestoga) wagon loads to Aenas MacKay, their agent at Fort Pitt, for shipment to Illinois in the fall.[111]

By the summer of 1768, David Franks was awarded the contract to supply the Illinois troops at 13½d per ration because the Baynton and Wharton bid was based on unacceptable buffalo meat. Morgan still hoped that his partners could sub-contract to supply the food to David Franks at a lower rate.[112] The loss of this contract was a major blow to Baynton and Wharton and the prime cause of their failure.

Adding to Morgan's woes, Gage dismissed the commissary, Edward Cole, and ended the exorbitant expenditures for presents that had greatly benefited the partnership. As a result, they were fortunate to sell their stock to David Franks and his associates at reduced prices.[113]

However, it was a hollow victory for Franks and his colleagues because the Illinois garrison was soon reduced along with Fort Pitt. The reduction of the garrison in Illinois and the abandonment of Fort Pitt were part of the overall withdrawal of garrisons from the frontier prompted by economic and political considerations. The boom of selling to the army in Illinois was over.

The cost of occupying Illinois could not be contained, nor could the colonial merchants wrest the fur trade from the French, who continued to ship merchandise from New Orleans to St. Louis and sell it to the farmers and to the French traders, who paid higher prices for the merchandise than offered by Baynton and Wharton. The French passed on the higher cost to the Indians, who refused to deal with colonial traders.[114] The French farmers were reluctant to accept British bills of exchange for provisions and demanded payment in specie, usually Spanish dollars.[115]

The French merchants in Illinois continued to control trade with the Indians in 1768. A possible solution was the construction of forts to prevent the French traders from reaching the Indian villages. Baynton and Wharton wanted the British government to intervene by increasing the Illinois garrison to 500 men and building forts to block the movement of the French traders at Massaic at the mouth of the Ohio River as well as Cahokia at the mouth of the Illinois River on the Mississippi, and at Green Bay.[116] Colonel Wilkins, the Illinois garrison commander, suggested that forts be established at Cahokia to block access to rivers leading to the Chicago area, as well as at Massaic to block access to the Ohio Valley and the rivers leading north to the Detroit area and at Vincennes on the Wabash River. Wilkins believed that these forts would stop the illegal trade of the French and provide a market for British merchandise.[117] However, Gage did not believe that the forts would control the situation. He thought that the small Indian villages would have to be consolidated and the cost would not justify the end. The Indian trade was not great, and Baynton and Wharton was about to go bankrupt.[118]

The die was cast in 1766 when the British army began cutting expenses and moving to the coast, reducing its value to the colonial economy while increasing the potential threat of the use of the troops against the colonists. Despite objections, on 11 December 1766 instructions were sent to Gage from London to cut military spending, and though he replied that all efforts were being made to do so, political pressure continued from London.[119]

General Gage was already considering using the army to control the colonists on the seaboard. In May 1766 Gage informed Conway in London that there were three regiments available for duty on the east coast. In August 1766 Gage planned to send a regiment to Philadelphia and ordered Governor Penn to make provisions for quartering and feeding the troops.[120]

One of the objections to the budget presented to the House of Commons in January 1767 was the £400,000 sterling for the army in America. Because the need for the army increased with the growing American defiance of British sovereignty, many in Parliament believed that the colonists should pay a share of the cost.[121] Ironically, the Americans were being asked to support an army that would be used to force them to pay more taxes.

Shelburne tried to find some way of collecting taxes in America without opposition. In December 1766 he suggested a quit rent of 2/- sterling ($100) for each one hundred acres of land owned privately in America.[122] The Chancellor of the Exchequer, Charles Townshend, proposed a series of measures to raise money to support the army in America. In January 1767 his budget included taxes in America estimated to yield £110,000 sterling ($2,200,000).[123]

In early 1767 the parliamentary demand for cutting the cost of the army in America could not be ignored. George Grenville in London proposed that the cost of the army be reduced and that Townshend find methods to raise money in America to pay the entire expense. The opposition party in Parliament on 25 February 1767 reduced the British land tax from 4/- in the pound sterling (a 20% tax on the assessed valuation of the land owned) to 3/- in the pound (15%), reducing the total revenue by £500,000 sterling, which was greater than the estimated cost of the army in America of £400,000 sterling.[124]

Shelburne was still considering what to do with the army. Even though the role of the Indian Department was a factor, the British objective was to reduce expenses by withdrawing the army from the frontier. Three facts dictated the withdrawal: the army was not able to control the fur trade; nor could it prevent settlers from moving into Indian land; and the Americans refused to pay taxes to maintain the army.[125]

In addition to moving the troops to the coast, Lord William Barrington, the secretary of war in London, planned to eliminate the Indian Department and cut the extraordinary expenses, saving a total of £300,000 sterling.[126] In December 1766 Gage had been given full control of the extraordinary expenses in America with instructions to economize. The chief items were fuel, bedding, and utensils for the troops; provisions and other supplies for the frontier posts; feeding of the troops; repairs to the forts and barracks; and Indian Department costs.[127]

By April 1767 Gage showed his cooperation when he reported on his actions to achieve the savings. Fuel, bedding, and other such items had been reduced to the bare minimum mandated in regulations, and everything was obtained at the lowest price possible. The transportation costs had been reduced by obtaining provisions from local farms at Detroit, Michilimackinac, and Illinois. In the future the contractor for rations would be required to include transportation as part of the ration fee. Repairs to forts were limited to those needed for defense. Barracks were to be repaired only if necessary to protect the troops from the weather. However, Gage had little hope of reducing the Indian Department. He suggested that perhaps New York and South Carolina might assume part of the burden, as they had before 1755.[128]

General Gage was critical of the Indian Department commissaries appointed by Johnson, especially in Illinois. Gage thought that the commissaries, despite orders to the contrary, seemed to be spending more rather than less.[129] The Indian Department cost of only £11,884 sterling in 1766 increased to about £16,000 sterling in 1767.

The major reduction was in the extraordinaries. The 1766 extraordinaries of about £66,000 were cut to £20,415 in 1767. The "other" expenses, a wide range of miscellaneous charges, were cut from £29,195 in 1766 to £20,695 sterling in 1767. The reduction from the 1766 figures in these two lines was from £95,195 to £41,110, a saving of £54,085 ($10,817,000). The basic cost of fifteen battalions and ordnance remained the same.[130]

Despite the thrifty rhetoric, the army continued to spend money lavishly at the posts. In November 1767 Phyn and Ellice sent Hayman Levy, one of their agents in New York City, bills of exchange totaling £937 New York ($118,000) drawn by Captain Patrick Sinclair, James Sterling, Captain (John?) Brown, Fras. Hereford, Captain G. Sowers, and Lieutenant Gordon. All of these individuals were probably at Detroit, and most were army officers or merchants dealing with the army. The proceeds of these bills were used to buy a bill for £600 sterling ($120,000) to pay debts owed by Phyn and Ellice in Britain.

Given the continued spending by the army, the Americans objected not to its presence but to taxes to maintain it thus cutting off a rich source of sterling bills to pay for colonial imports. Gage made the point to Shelburne that the colonists did not see the army as a burden but rather as a market for the farmers and the merchants.[131]

However, the colonists did resist any move to make them pay army expenses. In August 1767 Gage was having trouble finding quarters for the regiments moving through New York City as part of the rotation program. He complained that he had received little help from the city.[132] Finally in September the New York Assembly voted £3,000 New York ($378,000) to pay for the cost of billeting troops in the city.[133]

In 1767 most of the troops were still in Canada, in Florida, and on the frontier rather than in the heavily populated areas. In February 1767 the 14th, 29th, and 15th Regiments were in Quebec, Montreal, and nearby posts; the Second Battalion of the 60th and half of the 17th were in the Great Lakes and upper New York area; the 9th and 31st were in Florida; and part of the 42nd was at Fort Pitt. The First Battalion of the 60th was divided between Quebec and the frontier posts in Georgia. In the settled areas were five companies of the 17th in New York City and six companies of the 42nd in Philadelphia preparing to leave for Ireland and England. The 28th was in New Jersey and the 46th in New York awaiting transportation to Ireland.

Five battalions were rotated out of America in 1767 including four that went to Ireland (46th, 28th, 42nd, and 27th). The 17th Regiment returned to England. Efforts were made to convince the men in the departing regiments to volunteer to serve in the remaining regiments and many did so. A factor in the success of the voluntary transfers was that many of the soldiers were Americans who had been recruited in the colonies to provide replacements for losses. The Americans presumably would prefer to remain rather than leave their families behind in the colonies. Only a remnant of about 100 men in each regiment returned to England. Of the four battalions sent to Ireland a total of 500 men departed and 450 chose to remain in America.[134]

The 27th Regiment was scheduled to leave Quebec when it was relieved by the 10th Regiment. General Gage hoped that the volunteers from the 27th would fill the regiments in Canada and Nova Scotia. The two battalions of the 60th Royal Americans had been filled with recruits from Germany.[135] The men from the 42nd Regiment at Fort Pitt who volunteered to serve with the 21st Regiment in Florida were sent with a provisions convoy to Illinois and went down the Mississippi to Mobile. Those who volunteered to serve with the 34th Regiment remained at Fort Pitt under officers of the 18th Regiment. The plan was to have four companies of the 34th in Illinois and the remainder of the regiment at Fort Pitt, as opposed to the previous assignment of a regiment at Illinois and another at Fort Pitt.[136]

To replace the departing regiments the 16th and 26th Regiments arrived in New York from Ireland in July and the 18th Regiment went to Philadelphia. The 17th, 46th, and 28th Regiments, and part of the 42nd, left in late July. Because of the lack of troops to replace the three companies of the 42nd at Fort Pitt, they had to remain until relieved by companies from the 18th and 34th.[137] The disposition of the troops was governed by instructions from Lord Shelburne to leave as few troops as possible in the small posts on the frontier and concentrate the regiments at the major posts.[138]

Townshend objected to the withdrawal from the frontier and proposed instead to tax the colonists to pay for the army. The Townshend taxes failed to raise a significant amount of money for the army and had the bitter effect of creating another round of opposition in America.[139] Townshend died in September 1767 and Shelburne regained control of American policy. Shelburne, who opposed taxing the Americans, informed the cabinet that the management of the Indians and the fur trade were of great importance, but reducing their cost was necessary. The Stamp Act had failed to provide money to support the army, which could not control the fur trade anyway. The Plan of 1764, which called for restricting the colonial traders to the garrisoned posts, also had failed. Therefore, Shelburne's solution to reduce the cost of the army was to abandon the frontier altogether.[140]

On 5 October 1767 Lord Shelburne forwarded to the Board of Trade a plan for the future of the west that had a significant bearing on the role of the army. The plan included the previous Barrington proposal to decrease military expenditures by withdrawing the garrisons from the west but also proposed replacing them with new settlements of colonists to create a barrier against the Spaniards and manage the Indians.[141] The presentation of the Board of Trade to the king on 7 March 1768 included only moderate features of the Shelburne plan, withdrawing the troops in the Indian territory not directly involved with the tribes and favoring additional colonies. This proposal became the blueprint for withdrawal and subsequent reduction in costs.[142] The Indian Department was to be reduced as Detroit, Michilimackinac, and Niagara would be sufficient for trading purposes.[143]

In general, the proposals of the Board of Trade found favor with Hillsborough, Shelburne's successor as head of the Board of Trade, who believed that most of the troops should be in Canada and Florida with three battalions in New York, New Jersey, and Pennsylvania, reducing the number of smaller western posts.[144] General Gage also agreed that most of the western posts should be abandoned, but believed that some should remain to protect the frontier and the fur trade. Gage had little to say for the need of Fort Chartres because its only purpose was to prevent the French and Spanish from moving up the Mississippi and did not achieve even this goal. There was little trade at Fort Chartres, which served only as a link in the route to Illinois and was one of the most costly to maintain and difficult to supply in the event of trouble. Other than the three main posts, Gage recommended that a few men remain to hold supply lines open at Crown Point, Ticonderoga, Oswagatchie, and Fort Erie.[145]

The economy move was under way in 1768. In July Baynton and Wharton received only £310 Pennsylvania ($35,650) in bills from the army in Illinois. In the summer the firm sent only two boat loads of goods to Illinois and had trouble finding ten boatmen.[146] Gage was still trying to reduce expenses, especially for the transport of provisions and other supplies from Fort Pitt. The army built its own boats at Fort Pitt and used recruits for the 34th Regiment as boatmen. Expenses could have been reduced if the army had been able to purchase food in Illinois, but that source was dependent on a good harvest and a surplus of produce. Despite all efforts, the cost of maintaining the regiment in Illinois was too high.[147]

The cost of the army in America continued to cause conflict in England. London demanded that the cost be even further reduced. In 1768 Gage made strenuous efforts to do so by restricting expenditures for extraordinaries, those expenses in excess of the regular appropriation for food, clothing, and pay. The extraordinaries included Indian Department expenditures, transportation charges, and other variable charges. Gage also made a major saving by refusing to authorize repairs on the various posts, particularly on the frontier.[148] However, savings on these minor expenditures had little impact on the overall cost of the army.

Although the "other" expense remained constant in 1768, a total of £19,067 sterling compared to £20,695 in 1767, the extraordinaries leapt from £20,415 in 1767 to £61,805 in 1768. In October 1768 Benjamin Franklin wrote that Shelburne was astonished at the growing charges in America. Major Farmar in Illinois had drawn £30,000 sterling ($6 million) for extraordinary charges to move the 34th Regiment to Illinois and maintain it there.[149] Baynton and Wharton continued to receive large sums from the army. In June 1768 the firm received bills of exchange drawn on the army for £6,035 sterling ($1,200,000), a substantial sum that could be used to pay Baynton and Wharton's accounts in London.[150]

Hillsborough continued to press Gage to concentrate the troops in four large groups in the middle colonies, Quebec, Halifax, and St. Augustine. Detachments were to be used to occupy the small posts in the Great Lakes, Newfoundland, and West Florida.[151] However, Gage continued to disperse the troops. In 1768 the 8th, 52nd, and 15th Regiments and the First Battalion of the 60th Regiment were in Canada; the 10th, 29th, 14th, and 59th Regiments were in Newfoundland and Nova Scotia; the Second Battalion of the 60th Regiment was in Detroit and Michilimackinac; the 26th Regiment was in New York; the 18th and part of the 34th Regiments were in Pennsylvania; the other half of the 34th was in Illinois; and the 9th, 21st, 16th, and 31st were in Florida.[152]

Gage continued to rotate regiments from the frontier. In March a detachment of the 21st Regiment was sent from Fort Pitt by way of Illinois to rejoin its regiment in Florida. In September 1768 seven companies of the 18th Regiment replaced the companies of the 34th Regiment in Illinois and Fort Pitt, returning the 34th to Philadelphia.[153]

Gage's rotation of regiments upset the colonial merchants. In February 1768 Lieutenant Williams of the 17th Regiment left an outstanding bill of £72 New York ($9,000) owed to Phyn and Ellice, which they tried to collect; then they threatened to send the account to England to force the lieutenant to pay.[154] In June John Campbell expressed sorrow that the 34th Regiment was leaving Fort Pitt because, although they needed linen and other items, they had canceled their orders.[155] In December Campbell wrote that he was glad to be rid of the 34th Regiment.[156]

The major differences in army expenditures resulted from the concentration of the troops on the seaboard, where rations, barracks, and other needs were paid for locally. For example, payments to the Quartermaster General at Albany totaled £6,000 sterling in 1764 and £19,110 in 1765 for supplying the troops in upper New York and on the Great Lakes. By 1770 only £1,724 was paid for this service. Payments for similar services to the Deputy Quartermaster General in New York City were £13,197 in 1764 and £30,613 in 1765 but dropped to £10,997 in 1770. In contrast, charges to the Barrack Master General were non-existent in 1764 but were £18,976 in 1770 and £19,169 in 1772.[157] In the early 1760s most of the extraordinaries went to western merchants who provided boats and food for the troops. After 1768, the money was used for rent.

Sir William Johnson was also under pressure to cut the expenses of the Indian Department. In April 1768 Hillsborough, determined to cut the costs of the department in America, set an absolute limit of £1,000 for Johnson and £3,000 for presents and contingent expenses.[158] Johnson complained continually about the lack of funds to buy gifts for the Indians. In July he told Gage that returning the management of the Indians to the colonies would cost more in the long run and blamed the merchants for the problems. The current allocation of funds did not provide for the salaries of deputies, gunsmiths, or interpreters for the Indian Department, all very necessary to maintain good relations. Only £3,000 sterling ($600,000) had been allowed for presents, an amount far too small.[159] In August Johnson also complained to London of the lack of money to pay deputies and interpreters and suggested an allocation of £1,000 sterling for salaries and £4,000 for presents which he hoped could be stretched to meet the demand.[160]

In late 1768 Johnson planned to hold a conference at Fort Stanwix to reach an agreement with the Indians to purchase some of their land for settlement. Johnson anticipated the cost including the expenses of the conference at £10,000 sterling ($2 million). Hillsborough considered the amount unreasonable and believed that the Indians would take less for their land.[161]

Johnson and his commissaries in the posts continued to spend large sums. In May 1768 in New York four merchants presented bills each in excess of £100 New York ($12,600) to pay Indian Department expenses. The British treasury sent a warrant to Johnson for £1,397 sterling ($280,000).[162] In December Gage sent two warrants to Johnson, one for £7,200 sterling ($1,440,000) and another for £905 sterling ($181,000).[163] These two warrants alone exceeded the £4,000 sterling limit imposed by Hillsborough.

Hillsborough did not obtain immediate results in relations to the posts either.

In April 1768 he had ordered that the small posts be abandoned to reduce cost and concentrate the army in large bodies. He recommended retaining Fort Chartres, Crown Point, Fort Pitt, Detroit, Niagara, and Michilimackinac. Gage promised to carry out the plan as soon as possible but suggested that Fort Erie on the Niagara River and Oswego on Lake Ontario also be retained.[164]

After lengthy debates, in June 1768 Gage was ordered to withdraw from all minor posts in the interior. The order was carried out, and the troops were sent to the major cities on the seacoast to quell anticipated difficulties. From 1769 to 1773, an average of four regiments were in Boston and three in Pennsylvania and New York. The Montreal and Quebec garrisons were reduced from four or more to two regiments.

Before 1769 there was little concern in America that the army would be used to control the colonists. The shift in British policy toward America in 1754 was caused by the threat of the French and their Indian allies. Nearly a third of the entire British army had been employed in handling this threat. The need for an army of occupation in 1760 could not be ignored. Britain had pushed the French and Spanish menace further from the colonies, but the French and Indian population remained in the newly acquired areas, and some form of control was needed.[165] For Britain to have no control over new territory acquired by a war was illogical.

The dispositions of troops from 1760 to 1767 clearly indicate the role of the army. Those in Canada were scattered in the populated area as evidence of English rule. About two regiments were generally assigned to the posts in upper New York and the Great Lakes. The line of communication from Philadelphia and Fort Pitt usually required a regiment. Several companies were used in the frontier posts in Georgia, and a regiment was posted in Illinois after 1765, and two or more in Florida. Other than troops awaiting transportation or traveling to new locations, those stationed in the urban centers were limited to a few companies in New York and Philadelphia. New York was the headquarters of the commander-in-chief, where a few troops were required for ceremonial purposes, general housekeeping duties, and maintenance of the supply service for garrisons up state. Philadelphia was the supply depot for the troops in the west.

In 1760 the British intended the army to control the newly acquired territory. Had the regiments been placed in America simply for convenience, as has been suggested, they would not have been scattered in the small posts, an assignment detrimental to discipline.

The presence of the army on the frontier was necessary. Parliament had been convinced that control of the wilderness was essential for the security of the colonies and for the preservation of the fur trade. Stability in the wilderness would preclude revolts by tribes which were likely if they did not have access to the European traders. Control of the trade through imperial regulation of the western territories was possible only with the presence of the army. The regiments would have been concentrated on the seaboard if they had been intended for police work before 1769.

British military expenditures somewhat relieved the postwar economic depression in the colonies and lessened the bitter feelings against Britain. British budgetary problems led to an attempt to obtain some of the needed funds from the colonists who were supposedly benefiting from this added security and commerce. The Stamp Act was written specifically for the support of the regular army and British-paid officials in America.[166] The colonies in turn refused to accept financial responsibility for the west and argued that the Indian trade was a matter of imperial responsibility. This divisive attitude created serious political difficulties in the relations between the colonists and the mother country. To counteract opposition and to reduce costs, the army was removed from the Indian territory, ending its usefulness to the Americans and creating further difficulties.[167] The savings were trivial compared to the political effects of surrendering western trade to the French.

The colonial resentment of the presence of the army before 1768 was due not to its function as defender of the frontier but to the British government's expectation that the colonies pay for part of the expense. The colonial merchants had no wish to provide the revenue to maintain the army themselves. The taxation issue was not opposition to sending gold to Britain but rather meeting imperial expenses with American tax money instead of British tax money.

The objections of the colonists centered on the taxation issue rather than on the presence of troops. The merchants, in particular, were aware of the mechanics of the situation. Even though they welcomed the flow of British money to support the army and the Indian Department, if the source of this money was a tax such as the Stamp Tax, it would be paid out of their pockets rather than the English taxpayer's, and the net results would be a loss to the colonial economy and a more adverse balance of trade.

This change in pattern of expenditures meant a substantial loss in income to the colonial merchants on the frontier. Before 1768, the army was considered a profitable market, as well as a shield against the Indians and a controlling factor in the west. During the Seven Years War the colonists had agreed to tax themselves to support the war, but only after the promise of reimbursement from England.[168] From 1759 to 1761, over a million pounds sterling of English money was spent annually, providing a tremendous stimulus to the colonial economy. In 1762 this figure dropped sharply to little over a half million, as the army was sent to the West Indies, but it jumped to £750,000 in 1763 as a result of Pontiac's Uprising and the return of the troops. From 1764 on, when the troop strength was reduced to the peacetime level, the figures dropped to less than £400,000 except in one year. Comparing these figures to the export and import figures indicates clearly that military expenditures, in the form of purchases of American goods and services, were an important factor in balancing the payments between America and the mother country.

In 1760 the total of exports and military expenditures was £1,943,000, compared to imports of £2,612,000. In 1764 exports and military expenditures dropped to £1,487,000 and imports decreased to £2,249,000. In both years the adverse balance was about £600,000, but the percentage of military expenses decreased. Americans replaced military spending with exports. The critical deficit in the balance of trade occurred in 1772, when military expenditures made up only 20% of the combined export–military expenditure figure. In that year the deficit expanded to over £1,400,000 ($28,000,000), clearly indicating the significance of military expenditures to the balance of trade.

The distribution of the army was not favorable to the colonial merchants. Although the colonials did ship provisions to the regiments on the Atlantic coast, the French farmers benefited most in Canada and Illinois.

Table 5.2 Expenditures of the British Army by Area
(£ sterling in thousands)

| Canada and Upper Lakes | £40 |
| Nova Scotia and Newfoundland | £120 |
| New York and Lower Lakes | £70 |
| Pennsylvania and Ohio Valley | £30 |
| Illinois | £50 |
| Florida | £90 |
| Total | £400 |

Of the £400,000 sterling expended by the army, the French farmers received as much as £200,000 sterling, much of it in the form of British manufactured goods rather than products of the thirteen colonies (see Table 5.2). Although some of the British goods were purchased originally by colonial merchants and the bills of exchange from the army were used to pay for the merchandise in Britian, still the business was of less value to the colonial economy than the sale of farm produce from the thirteen colonies. Before 1769 the attempt to deprive the colonial merchants of much of the sterling produced by military expenditures aroused the colonial merchants, not the threat imposed by the army. American merchants did build favorable balances by trade with the West Indies, southern Europe, and Africa, but the army was probably the major source of sterling bills. The economic return derived from the presence of the forces made the army one of the major "industries" in the colonies. The pay of the enlisted men was spent for their needs, including rum, not provided by the service. The money for rations was taken by the colonial suppliers who provided the barrels of beef, pork, and flour. The cost of repairs to the forts was paid to local artisans. A relatively small amount of the money was spent in Britain.[169] Merchants supplying the army were acutely aware of the value of bills of exchange drawn by the regiments to pay for provisions and supplies.

The British government was well aware of the economic benefit that the army provided to the Americans. Gage stated very clearly that the merchants of New York had made fortunes doing business with the army and that the farmers had done well selling their produce. The army was definitely not a burden on America.[170] The mission of the army had been to control the new territory and facilitate trade with the Indians. Had the army been successful in facilitating trade between the colonial merchants and the Indians, the merchants would have benefited substantially. Because the army failed to deliver the Indian market to the colonial merchants and ceased to be a market itself when it was withdrawn from the western posts, what had been anticipated as a great stimulus to the frontier economy was lost.

## NOTES

1. Shy, p. 34; Bernhard Knollenberg, *Origin of the American Revolution: 1759-1766* (New York: Free Press, 1965), p. 87.

2. Amounts rounded off to nearest thousand. The exact numbers are in Chart H, in Walter S. Dunn, Jr., "Western Commerce, 1760-1774," Ph.D. Dis., University of Wisconsin, 1971.

Row 3 (Cost) was derived by multiplying the number of regiments by £12,210, the peace cost of a regiment. The cost of the headquarters was estimated at £16,000 per year. Shelburne Papers, vol. 57, p. 231, Clements Library, University of Michigan.

Row 4 (Ordnance) was the average cost of the ordnance. John Shy, *Toward Lexington: The Role of the British Army in the Coming American Revolution* (Princeton, NJ: Princeton University Press, 1965) pp. 336-40.

Row 5 (Other) are actual "other" expenses for a wide variety of activities including reimbursing the colonies for military expenses. Shelburne Papers, vol. 154D.

Row 6 (Extraordinaries) was based partially on actual in the Gage Account Books and estimates based on average amounts per regiment for the missing years.

Row 7 (Total) The actual total for 1766 was £319,606. Shelburne Papers, vol. 57, p. 231.

3. Knollenberg, pp. 87-88; English Establishment 15 August 1766, *Pennsylvania Colonial Records*, 10 vols. (Philadelphia: J. Severns, 1851-52), vol. 9, p. 320.

4. Review of Trade, 22 September 1767, Edmund B. O'Callaghan and Fernold Berthold, eds., *Documents Relating to the Colonial History of the State of New York*, 15 vols. (Albany: Weed, Parsons, 1853-1887) [NYCD], vol. 7, p. 962; Knollenberg, pp. 88-89.

5. Shelburne Papers, vol. 137, p. 59.

6. Shy, pp. 106-7; Calvin Goodrich, *The First Michigan Frontier* (Ann Arbor: University of Michigan Press, 1940), pp. 87-88; Lawrence H. Gipson, *The Coming of the Revolution, 1759-1766* (New York: Harper & Rowe, 1962), p. 267.

7. Gage to Conway, 9 November 1765, *Illinois State Historical Collections* (Springfield: Trustees of the Illinois State Historical Library, 1903-) [IHC], vol. 9, p. 115.

8. Gage to Shelburne, 24 August 1767, IHC, vol. 11, p. 592.

9. Sterling to John Duncan, January 10, 1762, Sterling Letter Book, Clements Library.

10. Hillsborough to Gage, 15 April 1768, IHC, vol. 16, pp. 247-50.

11. William Corry to Johnson, 18 October 1762, Sir William Johnson, *The Papers of Sir William Johnson*, 14 vols. (Albany: The State University of New York Press, 1921–1965) [JMss], vol. 3, p. 908.

12. Gage to Shelburne, 17 January 1767, IHC, vol. 11, p. 497; Gage to Shelburne, 24 August 1767, IHC, vol. 11, p. 592; Hillsborough to Gage, 11 June 1768, IHC, vol. 16, pp. 297–99; Shy, p. 278.

13. Knollenberg, p. 34.

14. Knollenberg, p. 35; Jack M. Sosin, *Whitehall and the Wilderness: The Middle West in British Colonial Policy, 1760–1775* (Lincoln: University of Nebraska Press, 1961), pp. 25–26.

15. Shy, pp. 79–80.

16. Merrill Jensen, *The Founding of a Nation* (New York: Oxford University Press, 1968), p. 60.

17. Ibid., pp. 98–99.

18. Ibid., p. 94.

19. Shy, pp. 115–16.

20. Sosin, p. 37.

21. Amherst Papers, Clements Library, vol. 3, p. 81.

22. Gustave Lanctot, *Les Canadians Francais et Leurs Voisins du Sud* (Montreal: Bernard Valiquettes, 1941), p. 94.

23. Knollenberg, pp. 142–43.

24. Ibid., p. 47.

25. Ibid., p. 207.

26. Account Book, vol. 2, 2 May 1765, Gage Papers, Clements Library.

27. Barrington to Gage, 10 October 1765 in Sosin, p. 115.

28. Gage Report, 18 December 1765 in Sosin, p. 116.

29. Vincent T. Harlow, *The Founding of the Second British Empire, 1763–1793*, 2 vols. (London: Longmans, Green, 1952), pp. 151, 181; Keith Feiling, *A History of England* (New York: McGraw-Hill, 1951), p. 704; Erick Eyck, *Pitt versus Fox, Father and Son* (London, G. Bell and Sons, 1950), pp. 144–45.

30. Gage to Johnson, 2 June 1766, IHC, vol. 11, pp. 246–47.

31. Jensen, p. 174; Sosin, p. 95.

32. Shy, pp. 274–75, 282.

33. Gage to Conway, 23 September 1765, IHC, vol. 11, pp. 86–87.

34. Franklin B. Hough, *Diary of the Siege of Detroit...* (Albany, NY: J. Munsell, 1860), p. 450; Sosin, pp. 36–37.

35. NYCD, vol. 7, p. 973.

36. Barrington to Gage, 8 May 1766, Gage Manuscripts in Shy, p. 237.

37. Shy, p. 237.

38. Jensen, p. 230.

39. Barrington Plan, 10 May 1766, IHC, vol. 11, pp. 239–43.

40. Harry Gordon to Johnson, 4 March 1766, IHC, vol. 11, p. 161; Gage to Conway, 28 March 1766, IHC, vol. 11, p. 200.

41. Shelburne Papers, Clements Library, vol. 57, pp. 208–9; Shy, p. 238; Army Dispositions, 1766, IHC, vol. 11, p. 200.

42. Gage to Conway, 24 June 1766, IHC, vol. 11, p. 324; Gage to Conway, 15 July 1766, IHC, vol. 11, p. 339.

43. Johnson to Gage, 20 May 1767, NYCD, vol. 2, p. 496.

44. Johnson to Gage, 7 January 1766, JMss, vol. 5, pp. 3–4.

45. Richard Jackson's Opinion, November 1766, IHC, vol. 11, pp. 422–30.

46. Gage to Johnson, 3 February 1766, JMss, vol. 5, p. 30.

47. Amherst to Johnson, 9 August 1761, JMss, vol. 3, p. 516; Hillsborough to Gage, 15 April 1768, IHC, vol. 16, pp. 247–50.

48. Eddington to—, 17 October 1765, IHC, vol. 11, p. 106.

49. Shy, pp. 152–53; Report of Robertson, 8 March 1764, IHC, vol. 10, pp. 216–17, 220; IHC, vol. 10, pp. xli–xlii; Gage to Halifax, April 14, 1764, IHC, vol. 10, p. 225; Loftus Attempt Up the Mississippi, March 1764, IHC, vol. 10, p. 227.

50. Journal of Dabbadie, June 12, 1764, IHC, vol. 10, p. 188; Dabbadie to Minister, June 29, 1764, IHC, vol. 10, pp. 270–77.

51. Aubrey to the Minister, 4 February 1765, IHC, vol. 10, p. 428; Lt. Ross to Major Farmer, 21 February 1765, IHC, vol. 10, pp. 442–43.

52. Aubrey to the Minister, 27 January 1766, IHC, vol. 11, pp. 143–44; Aubrey to the Minister, 12 March ibid, IHC, vol. 11, pp. 181–87.

53. Gage to Conway, 23 September 1765, IHC, vol. 11, pp. 86–87; Aubrey to the Minister, 27 January 1766, IHC, vol. 11, p. 139; Gage to Governor Penn, 15 June 1766, IHC, vol. 11, p. 259.

54. Cession of Fort de Chartres, 10 October 1765, IHC, vol. 11, p. 91; Sterling to Gage, 18 October 1765, IHC, vol. 11, p. 110.

55. Farmar to Gage, 16 to 19 December 1765, IHC, vol. 11, pp. 131–33; Gage to Farmar, 7 July 1766, IHC, vol. 11, pp. 332–33; Croghan to Johnson, 26 March 1766, JMss, vol. 5, p. 109.

56. Shy, p. 154.

57. Robert farmer to Stuart, 16 December 1765, IHC, vol. 11, pp. 131–33; Croghan to Johnson, 27 December 1765, JMss, vol. 4, p. 886.

58. Clarence W. Alvord, *The Illinois Country 1673-1818* (Springfield: Illinois Centennial Commission, 1920), p. 278.

59. Johnson to Gage, 11 July 1767, Edmund B. O'Callaghan, ed., *Documentary History of the State of New York*, 4 vols. (Albany: Weed, Parsons, 1849-1851), vol. 2, p. 499.

60. Shy, p. 241.

61. Virginia D. Harrington, *The New York Merchant on the Eve of the Revolution* (New York: Columbia University Press, 1935), p. 296.

62. Shy, pp. 332–37.

63. John Collins to Baynton and Wharton, 30 January 1761, Baynton, Wharton, and Morgan Papers, Microfilm, 10 Rolls, Original in Pennsylvania Historical Commission [BWM], Roll 2.

64. Stanley M. Pargellis, *Lord Loudoun in North America* (New Haven: Oxford University Press, 1933), p. 122.

65. Shy, p. 333.

66. 7 June 1764, *Michigan Pioneer and Historical Collections*, 40 vols. (Lansing: Wynkoop, Hallenbeck, Crawford, 1874-1929), vol. 19, pp. 261–62.

67. Harrington, pp. 300–301.

68. John Collins to Baynton and Wharton, 30 January 1761, BWM, Roll 2.

69. Phyn and Ellice to Colonel Prevost, 12 February 1768, Phyn & Ellis Papers, Microfilm in the Buffalo and Erie County Historical Society [PEBF].

70. Shy, pp. 336–40.

71. James Kenny, "Journal of James Kenny, 1761-1763." *The Pennsylvania Magazine of History and Biography*, vol. 37 (1913), 4 February 1762, pp. 37-40.

72. Harrington, pp. 314-15.

73. Alvord, *Illinois Country*, p. 275.

74. Receipt by Farmar, 24 May 1765, IHC, vol. 10, p. 499.

75. Receipt of Farmar, 4 March 1766, IHC, vol. 11, p. 160.

76. Morgan(?) to Captain Gordon Forbes, 17 March 1768, BWM, Roll 6.

77. Farmar to Gage, 16-19 December 1765, IHC, vol. 11, pp. 131-33.

78. Richard E. Banta, *The Ohio* (New York: Rinehart, 1949), p. 111.

79. Farmar to Gage, 19 March 1766, IHC, vol. 11, p. 191.

80. Gage to Conway, 28 March 1766, IHC, vol. 11, pp. 197-99; Gage to Farmar, 7 July 1766, IHC, vol. 11, pp. 331-32.

81. Morgan to Williamson, 8 July 1768, IHC, vol. 16, pp. 344-45.

82. MacCleane to Shelburne, January 1767, IHC, vol. 11, pp. 478-79.

83. Gage to Read, 15 July, 1767, IHC, vol. 11, pp. 584-85; Baynton, Wharton, and Morgan Proposals, 9 January 1767, IHC, vol. 11, pp. 471-76.

84. Baynton, Wharton, and Morgan to Lauchlin MacCleane, 9 January 1767, IHC, vol. 11, pp. 473-75.

85. Baynton and Wharton to Lauchlin MacCleane, 9 January 1767, IHC, vol. 11, pp. 473-76; Baynton and Wharton to Gage, 5 January 1767, IHC, vol. 11, p. 471; Baynton and Wharton to the Lords of the Treasury, 9 January 1767, IHC, vol. 11, p. 477.

86. MacCleane to Shelburne, January 1767, IHC, vol. 11, pp. 478-79.

87. Morgan to Baynton, 10 December 1767, IHC, vol. 16, p. 131.

88. Leake to Gage, 24 February 1768, BWM Film, Roll 6.

89. Leake to Gage, 24 February 1768, BWM, Roll 6.

90. Gage to Reed, 15 July 1767, IHC, vol. 11, pp. 584-85.

91. Wharton to Baynton, 21 August 1767, BWM Film, Roll 5.

92. Samuel Wharton to Baynton, 21 August 1767, BWM, Roll 5.

93. Morgan to Baynton and Wharton, 11 July 1768, IHC, vol. 16, pp. 347-48.

94. Morgan to Captain Gordon Forbes, 17 March 1768, BWM Film, Roll 6.

95. Baynton, Wharton, and Morgan Memo Book, 2 June 1768, BWM Film, Roll 10.

96. Baynton to Wharton, 17 August 1767, BWM, Roll 2.

97. Ibid.

98. Morgan to Baynton and Wharton, 20 June 1768, IHC, vol. 16, pp. 326-31.

99. Morgan to Baynton and Wharton, 11 July 1768, IHC, vol. 16, pp. 347-48; Morgan to Baynton and Wharton, 20 July 1768, IHC, vol. 16, pp. 360-62.

100. Baynton and Wharton, Journal C, 19 September 1767, BWM, Roll 9; Baynton and Wharton, Journal C, 12 October 1767, BWM, Roll 9.

101. Morgan to Baynton and Wharton, 10 December 1767, IHC, vol. 16, pp. 128-131.

102. Morgan to Captain Gordon Forbes, 17 March 1768, BWM, Roll 6.

103. Morgan to Baynton and Wharton, 5 April 1768, IHC, vol. 16, p. 229.

104. Morgan to Baynton and Wharton, 5 April 1768, IHC, vol. 16, pp. 222-24.

105. Morgan to Baynton and Wharton, 30 October 1768, IHC, vol. 16, p. 443.

106. John Baynton to Samuel Wharton, 17 August 1767, BWM, Roll 2.

107. Morgan to Baynton and Wharton, 11 July 1768, IHC, vol. 16, p. 348; Morgan to Baynton and Wharton, 20 July 1768, IHC, vol. 16, p. 360.

108. Whiteman, p. 69; John Campbell to Baynton and Wharton, 24 June 1768, BWM, Roll 3.

109. Murray to B. and M. Gratz, July 1768, IHC, vol. 16, p. 343.

110. Morgan to Baynton and Wharton, 20 July 1768, IHC, vol. 16, p. 358; M. Gratz to William Murray, 8 July 1768, IHC, vol. 16, pp. 342–43; Morgan to Baynton and Wharton, 30 October 1768, IHC, vol. 16, pp. 442–43.

111. M. Gratz to William Murray, 7 July 1768, IHC, vol 16., p. 341; B. & M. Gratz to Aenas MacKay, 15 August 1768, IHC, vol. 16, pp. 375–76.

112. Morgan to Baynton, Wharton, and Morgan, 11 July 1768, IHC, vol. 16, pp. 347–48.

113. Charles A. Thomas, "Successful Merchants in the Illinois Country," *Journal of the Illinois State Historical Society*, vol. 30 (1938), pp. 439–40.

114. Carleton to Shelburne, 2 March 1768, *Canadian Archives Report,* 1886 (Ottawa: Canadian Archives, 1887), p. clxxi.

115. Wilkins to Gage, 13 September 1768, IHC, vol. 16, pp. 388–90.

116. Baynton and Wharton to Lauchlin Macleane, 9 October 1767, IHC, vol. 16, p. 85.

117. Wilkins to Gage, 13 September 1778, IHC, vol. 16, pp. 388–90.

118. Gage to Hillsborough, 16 june 1768, IHC, vol. 16, pp. 317–18.

119. Gage to Shelburne, 4 April 1767, IHC, vol. 11, pp. 552–54.

120. Gage to Conway, 6 May 1766, Gage Correspondence, vol. 1, p. 90 in Shy, pp. 110–11; Gage to Governor Penn, 15 August 1766, *Pennsylvania Colonial Records*, vol. 11, p. 318.

121. Sosin, p. 130.

122. Shelburne to the Governors in America, 11 December 1766, NYCD, vol. 7, p. 880.

123. Harlow, pp. 185–88; Feiling, p. 706.

124. Sosin, p. 130; Jensen, pp. 223–24; Harlow, p. 186.

125. Shy, pp. 260–63.

126. Sosin, p. 132.

127. Gage to Shelburne, 4 April 1767, IHC, vol. 11, pp. 552–53; Shy, pp. 243–44.

128. Gage to Shelburne, 4 April 1767, IHC, vol. 11, p. 553.

129. Gage to Johnson, 13 April 1767, JMss, vol. 5, pp. 534–36; Gage to Johnson, 11 May 1767, JMss, vol. 5, p. 547.

130. Charts H and I in Dunn, *Western Commerce*; Sosin, p. 132.

131. Gage to Shelburne, 17 January 1767, IHC, vol. 11, pp. 495–96.

132. Gage to Shelburne, 24 August 1767, IHC, vol. 11, p. 593.

133. Peter Hasenclever to Johnson, 28 September 1767, JMss, vol. 5, p. 704.

134. Shy, p. 278.

135. Gage to Shelburne, 24 August 1767, IHC, vol. 11, p. 592.

136. Gage to Shelburne, 24 August 1767, IHC, vol. 11, p. 592.

137. Gage to Shelburne, 24 August 1767, IHC, vol. 11, pp. 591–92.

138. Gage to Shelburne, 3 April 1767, IHC, vol. 11, pp. 544–50.

139. Harlow, pp. 186–90; Eyck, pp. 164–65.

140. Shelburne's Minutes of the Cabinet, 11 September 1767, IHC, vol 16, pp. 12–13.

141. Shelburne's Minutes of the Cabinet, 11 September 1767, IHC, vol. 16, pp. 79–80.

142. R. A. Humphreys, "Shelburne and British Colonial Policy, 1766–1768," *English Historical Review*, vol. 50 (1935), p. 265.

143. NYCD, vol. 8, pp. 19–34.

144. Benjamin Franklin to William Franklin, 13 March 1768, IHC, vol. 16, p. 215.

145. Gage to Hillsborough, 16 June 1768, IHC, vol. 16, pp. 315–20.

146. John Campbell to Baynton and Wharton, 24 July 1768, BWM, Roll 3.

147. Gage to Barrington, 11 October 1768, IHC, vol. 11, p. 399.

148. Shy, pp. 327–30.

149. B. Franklin to W. Franklin, 11 October 1768, IHC, vol. 11, p. 400.

150. Baynton and Wharton Memo Book, 2 June 1768, BWM, Roll 10.

151. Hillsborough to Gage, 15 April 1768, IHC, vol. 16, p. 252.

152. Gage to Hillsborough, 18 June 1768, IHC, vol. 16, pp. 321–24; Shy, pp. 269–73.

153. Gage to Hillsborough, 12 March 1768, IHC, vol. 16, p. 211; Gage to Hillsborough, 17 August 1768, IHC, vol. 16, p. 378.

154. Phyn and Ellice to Captain Alexander Grant, 27 February 1768, PEBF.

155. John Campbell to Baynton and Wharton, 24 June 1768, BWM, Roll 3.

156. John Campbell to Baynton and Wharton, 2 December 1768, BWM, Roll 3.

157. Account Books, vols. 1 and 9, Gage Papers, Clements Library.

158. Hillsborough to Gage, 15 April 1768, IHC, vol. 16, pp. 247–50.

159. Johnson to Gage, 20 July 1768, JMss, vol. 6, p. 279.

160. Johnson to Hillsborough, 17 August 1768, NYCD, vol. 8, pp. 95–96.

161. Hillsborough to Johnson, 12 October 1768, NYCD, vol. 8, p. 102.

162. William Newton to Johnson, 9 May 1768, JMss, vol. 6, p. 216.

163. Gage to Johnson, 5 December 1768, JMss, vol. 6, pp. 511–12.

164. Hillsborough to Gage, 15 April 1768, IHC, vol. 16, pp. 247–50; Gage to Hillsborough, 16 June 1768, IHC, vol. 16, pp. 315–16, 320.

165. Sosin, pp. 3–4.

166. Sosin, p. 4.

167. Shy, pp. 402–3.

168. Shy, p. 45.

169. Shy, p. 265.

170. Gage to Shelburne, 17 January 1767, IHC, vol. 11, pp. 495–96.

# CONCLUSION

The period from 1765 to 1768 was marked by conflict and competition as many newcomers tried to take advantage of the opportunities offered by the colonial frontier. The problems began with the capitulation of Montreal in 1759, which ended the Seven Years War in America and opened the area north of the Ohio River and east of the Mississippi to British and colonial merchants.

Prior to 1760 the colonists had few difficulties with the British government and exploited the frontier as far as they could in the face of French resistance. With the French army removed, the frontier became a vast new market, made up of Indians who traded their fur; the British army which occupied the area; the Indian Department which was charged with the management of the tribes; and an increasing number of white settlers.

Even though the French had lost Canada to England at the end of the Seven Years War and the Canadians were forced to ship their furs to Britain rather than France, still the French retained control of the Indian trade at the retail level. Despite the advantage of low-cost merchandise offered by the colonial traders from New York and Pennsylvania, the French continued to hold the trade because of a century of experience with the Indians and a close affiliation with the tribes. Many of the French voyageurs and winterers were part Indian and had wives and children in the villages they served. The fur trade was their way of life, just as farming was a way of life in midwestern America in the early twentieth century. Despite any obstacle, the French fought to maintain their position in the Indian trade. The colonial traders, with the possible exception of the Oswego traders, had no such commitment.

The French merchants encouraged the Indians to dispose of the colonial traders during Pontiac's Uprising, and the threat to their lives discouraged the colonists from resuming their competition after peace was made with the Indians. The French rid themselves of the colonial merchants in Montreal by simply refusing to pay them for goods taken on credit and buying instead from the English and Scottish merchants. The colonists in Quebec and Montreal had to charge higher prices for dry goods than the British because of the additional cost of shipping the merchandise to Quebec from Philadelphia or New York. The exception was rum distilled in the colonies, which could be sold at lower prices than British or West Indian imports. The only competition to colonial rum was cheap British brandy, which was so bad that it had to be mixed with strong Jamaican rum to make it palatable.

The French in Canada bought merchandise from the new British merchants who entered the fur trade in 1765 and also began ordering directly from England. The new British merchants replaced the colonials as wholesalers and assisted the French in regaining their monopoly of the Indian trade in 1765. The French voyageurs not only held their grasp on their sphere as they has before 1760, but as new subjects of King George III enjoyed the added advantage of being able to compete in areas previously dominated by colonial traders from New York and Pennsylvania.

Unlike in Canada, where the French had no option other than to buy from the British or the colonists, in Illinois the French had access to New Orleans, which offered the opportunity both to import goods from France and to export furs from that port. The French hat industry was cut off from its previous supply of fur from Canada in 1760 and sought a new supply from New Orleans to satisfy the rage for beaver hats in Europe. Even after control was transferred to Spain, the port remained open to French ships, which carried merchandise for the Indian trade and took away £100,000 sterling in fur. The French traders in Illinois were encouraged by high beaver prices in New Orleans to compete vigorously for the furs south of the Great Lakes and to expand their market up the Mississippi and Missouri Rivers. To maintain their monopoly in Illinois, the French refused to buy goods from Philadelphia, even though they were cheaper than the French goods taken up the Mississippi River from New Orleans.

The colonial traders did retain a small portion of the frontier commerce despite the competition of the Canadians from the north and the Illinois French from the west. In New York and the lower lakes, the Albany Dutch were forced to settle for trading with the Indians who traveled to the posts at Oswego, Niagara, and Detroit. The Albany traders were supplied by New York City and Schenectady merchants such as Phyn and Ellice, who managed to make a reasonable profit through careful management.

In Pennsylvania the merchants were handicapped by the restriction to trading with Indians who traveled to Fort Pitt and Fort Augusta. Later the traders ventured forth into the wilderness and dealt with the Shawnee in the Ohio River valley. In Illinois, Baynton and Wharton, a Quaker firm, tried through illegal means to monopolize the trade as soon as that area was occupied by the British army. Their all-out venture in Illinois, blocked by the French, bankrupted the firm as the French refused to buy from them and prevented the Indians from doing so. Because of the political connections of David Franks,

Baynton and Wharton received another setback when they were later deprived of the lucrative army rations contract.

The targets of all of these ventures were the furs and deerskin the Indians were eager to trade for European goods as well as the bills of exchange from the lavish expenditures of the British army stationed in America.

The frontier was not only a source of fur, but a lucrative market for British manufactured goods and colonial produce. The market included the Indians, the white settlers, the Indian Department, and the army. The fur trade supposedly created the need for the army, which was sent to protect the Indians and bolster the fur trade but became the major customer itself because the troops needed food and other supplies. Together the Indians and soldiers provided a market for colonial produce as well as imports and returned about £650,000 sterling annually in bills of exchange and peltry plus payments for transportation. The ultimate customers north of the Ohio River were about 40,000 Indians. An Indian family purchased or received as presents merchandise worth at least £15 sterling ($3,000) per year. The obtained their own food but by 1765 were dependent on European manufactures. The assortment of merchandise followed the general pattern of the contents of a Canadian master canoe, £325 sterling worth of dry goods from England and 200 gallons of liquor worth £50 sterling for a total value of £375 sterling ($75,000). A canoe under the leadership of an experienced voyageur that went to the Indian country was a floating model of the general store that was part of every small town in America a hundred years ago. As in the general store, the trader supplied practically everything that the Indian consumer could not make for himself—clothing, liquor, guns, knives, blankets, ammunition, kettles, and other hardware.

The cost of transporting the cargo to Grand Portage on Lake Superior was £250 sterling ($50,000).[1] The smaller Albany canoes carried ten barrels of rum valued at £71 New York and 300 pounds of dry goods valued at £300 New York for a total value of $371 New York ($46,800). The cost of transporting the merchandise to Detroit was £85 New York ($10,710).[2] In both cases the dry goods, most of which were shipped from England, was valued at about five times the liquor that was produced in the colonies. From scattered data we know that a Pennsylvania Indian trader plus several horse drivers carried a stock worth about £580 sterling ($116,000) on a string of about thirty horses.

An average of one hundred canoes went to the upper lakes and the Northwest each year, and about thirty went to the Detroit area. Exports of fur from Canada were about £70,000 sterling annually. The Canadian fur traders obtained their merchandise from Scottish merchants in Montreal but purchased their rum and provisions from colonial merchants. The Illinois market produced more furs and deerskin than the Canadian market and therefore would have absorbed more merchandise. The French in Illinois traded actively in the Ohio, Mississippi, and Missouri Valleys and gathered furs worth in excess of £100,000 sterling. They purchased most of their merchandise from French merchants in New Orleans and their provisions from French farmers in Illinois. The Indians on the fringe of the frontier acted as mediaries for the tribes farther west and therefore absorbed far more goods. New guns were purchased from the traders, and the old guns were traded for fur from tribes farther west. The total demand for goods in Illinois exclusive of army rations was about £75,000 sterling. Baynton and Wharton expected to sell in Illinois £20,000 Pennsylvania worth of goods in 1765.

Table 6.1 provides an overview of the flow of merchandise, fur, and cash. In 1763 British army expenditures were £430,000 sterling ($86,000,000), most of which was spent in Canada and on the frontier for pay and rations. The average for the period 1765 to 1768 was about £400,000 sterling. Included in the army total was the Indian Department, which spent nearly £27,000 sterling in 1764 for presents to the Indians, but the average in this period was about £20,000 sterling.

Table 6.1 Balance Sheet for North America
(£ sterling in thousands)

| Area | Can. | Lower Lakes | Ohio Valley | Ill. | Fla. | Total |
|---|---|---|---|---|---|---|
| Assets in | | | | | | |
| British goods | £40 | 38.5 | 7 | 20 | | £105.5 |
| Colonial produce | 15 | 3.5 | 3 | 25 | | £46.5 |
| French Produce | 10 | | | (24) | | £10 |
| Rations | 120 | 52 | 23 | 38 | 67 | £300 |
| French goods | | | | 30 | | £30 |
| Total | £185 | £94 | £33 | £113 | £67 | £492 |
| | | | | | | |
| Assets out | | | | | | |
| Fur to Britain | 70 | 11 | 4 | 5 | | £90 |
| Illegal fur | | 18 | 15 | 95 | | £128 |
| Goods to Illinois | 20 | | | | | £20 |
| Army bills | 160 | 70 | 30 | 50 | 90 | £400 |
| | | | | | | |
| Total | £250 | £99 | £49 | £150 | £90 | £638 |

The frontier market was worth around £543,000 sterling annually after subtracting the fur exported to France from New Orleans. The frontier business was of considerable importance to the colonial economy; in comparison, imports from Britain to the thirteen colonies in 1765 were only £2 million sterling ($400 million). The merchandise purchased by the army (£300,000, more than 60% of the total of all the markets) was almost entirely colonial produce, provisions, and liquor. The Indian market (£192,000) was supplied by the colonists, Britain, and France. Only one-fourth of the value (£46,500 sterling) was colonially produced; £105,500 was from Britain; £30,000 from France; and £10,000 from the French in Illinois. The army was the major customer on the frontier, consuming products from Canada, the thirteen colonies, and French farmers in Detroit and Illinois.

The colonial merchants competed vigorously for the fur and bills of exchange to pay for colonial imports. The army business was divided between the colonists and the British merchants in Canada, who supplied the troops in Canada and the Northwest plus the four regiments on the Atlantic coast. The colonial merchants competed for the army business in the lower lakes, Illinois, and Pennsylvania. The receipts from the army business were divided, with about £160,000 sterling going to the Canadian merchants and the remaining £240,000 to colonial merchants, although the French in Illinois competed to supply the regiment there.

The returns on the fur were divided among the French in New Orleans, who received the bulk of the Illinois trade; the British merchants in Canada, who took most of the pelts from the Northwest; and the colonial merchants, who received the others. Over and above the heavy expenses, merchants usually received double the value of the goods traded to the Indians when the furs were sold in London. The returns for the merchandise traded in the five areas were furs worth about £220,000 sterling, with about £95,000 going to the French in New Orleans, £70,000 to the British merchants in Canada, and about £55,000 to the colonial merchants. The colonial merchants failed to maintain their share of the trade in the area between the Great Lakes and the Ohio River and in addition could not capture a share of the Illinois and Northwest markets.

The demand for supplies in the west was a stimulus to the colonial economy. At least £105,000 sterling in goods was imported from Britain specifically for the western trade, and £350,000 sterling in products for the fur trade and rations for the army was produced in America by local manufacturers and farmers. Additional profits were derived from transporting the goods. The net result was a livelihood for thousands of colonials. Canada sent provisions valued at about £135,000 sterling to the frontier and the army annually; New York sent about £55,000; Pennsylvania sent about £26,000 to Fort Pitt and £58,000 to Illinois, producing a total of £274,000 sterling ($54,800,000). In return, £123,000 in furs and skins and £400,000 in bills of exchange yielded an ample margin for the payment of transportation and other overhead costs plus a generous profit.

The merchandise was moved to the interior and the peltry was returned by canoe, wagon, boat, and pack horse. The Seven Years War had changed the transportation network. After 1760 the colonists theoretically had free use of the Mississippi, Ottawa, and St. Lawrence waterways. As a result, Quebec, Montreal, and New Orleans were added to the old trade centers, New York City and Philadelphia. Although moving cargoes west was less expensive on the old routes from New York and Philadelphia, the new routes, the Mississippi, the Great Lakes, and the Ottawa River, were more suitable for the export of furs.

The Ottawa route led from Michilimackinac and Lake Superior, the best sources of fur during this period. The Ohio River route was cheap and efficient westward but was impractical eastward and boats were seldom returned. The Mississippi, though difficult to ascend, was a quick pathway to the sea, but Spanish control led to the shipment of much of the fur to France. From a logistical point of view, the most advantageous routes were the Ohio River and the Great Lakes for import of cargo, and the Ottawa River and the Mississippi for export.

The Ohio River and the Great Lakes remained the cheapest routes for sending cargo to the frontier and gave the Philadelphia and New York merchants an advantage in supplying the troops with rations. Although the French in both Canada and Illinois retained the greater share of the Indian trade, the New York and Philadelphia merchants, who faced problems in returning peltry, profited more from supplying the army for bills of exchange.

Regardless of the apparent profits, the fur trade remained a risky business based on a sophisticated credit system that extended from the agents in London to the hunters in the forest. The costs of transportation and credit steadily increased the cost of merchandise from the time it left the factory in England to the point of exchange with the Indians. The possibility of great profit or great loss increased as the goods moved west, and fortunes in frontier business were made and lost by the big merchants. Several options were available to the merchant with substantial capital and credit. New York and Pennsylvania merchants could sell in New York and Philadelphia for local use if the price were high or the demand for cash great. The Canadians also sent peltry to New York and Philadelphia when the price was right. The merchants could send their furs out via the Mississippi, and there was also an opportunity to sell furs to the French and Spaniards in New Orleans for shipment to the Continent rather than to England.

Despite the diversion of large numbers of pelts to France via New Orleans, an estimate of the legal export of peltry, including deerskin, was £91,000 sterling in customs value. This amount was small, compared to the £900,000 sterling worth of tobacco exported to England, but fur and deerskin still ranked third behind rice among the major exports of the colonies to England. Moreover, these records cover only the legal trade. Fur was a highly valued commodity, light in weight and convenient to transport, and therefore was easy to smuggle. There is reason to believe that a considerable quantity was handled illegally.

Although the internal use of furs and skins increased as the number of

Americans increased, the exports of beaver and deerskin from New York and Philadelphia were only slightly affected because of the local demand by the hat makers, glove makers, cobblers, and other tradesmen producing leather goods for the local market. There were only 2,000,000 Americans and 70,000 Canadians in 1760, and fewer than 5,000 of the expensive beaver hats were sold annually in America. The precipitous decline in legal fur exports can only be explained by the diversion of the fur to pay for smuggled goods carried in by ships from southern Europe and the West Indies.

Whereas the fur trade was ostensibly the prime market on the frontier, in fact the army spent far more money than the fur was worth. Three regiments were sent to the frontier. Originally the London government had expected that soldiers would be needed to control the French inhabitants as well as the tribes and to prevent Spanish intrusion. The matter of containment of the French was over-emphasized because most of them were disinterested subsistence farmers who had little concern for life outside their village and were accustomed to abiding by European rules. The Spanish posed no threat to the British. The protection of colonial traders from the Indians and the converse became the major tasks of the British army. If furs were to be obtained, the British government reasoned that the safety of the traders from the Indians had to be assured by strategically located posts.

The three regiments on the frontier and the twelve regiments in Canada, Newfoundland, and Florida became a major market and had a beneficial effect on the American economy by encouraging business development on the frontier. The economic return to the colonies made the army one of the major industries. Most of the money appropriated to the army in America before 1768 was spent by purchases in Canada, Illinois, and Florida.

Because the army was seen as a boost to the American economy, many elements of colonial society were pressing to maintain military spending near the wartime level. There was little objection to the presence of the army on the frontier because it was a valuable market. The tremendous expenditure of government funds to control the fur trade occurred during a period when any expenditure and the accompanying tax burden on English landowners were politically disastrous. Governing this new territory cost additional money that England could ill afford. A series of wars had left England with serious monetary problems, increasing the national debt to almost £140,000,000 sterling in 1763 with annual interest at £5,000,000 sterling. Because of the high cost of the army, there was political pressure from London to manage affairs on a tight budget to prevent increases in English taxation. American expenses made up a fifth of the money spent on the army and a tenth of total British imperial military expenses.

Parliament continually pressed for the reduction of the cost of the army and the Indian Department. The Indian Department, a small part of the army budget, distributed presents and regulated trade. Immediately after the fighting ended in 1760, attempts to economize included reduction of the number of gifts to the

Indians that they expected as part of a deeply rooted custom. The curtailment of this practice was seen by the tribes as evidence of ill will. The French government had accepted this expense as part of the cost of obtaining fur, which went to a government monopoly. In contrast, under British rule, the government was expected to provide gifts and pay agents, but the furs went into private hands. Had the Indian superintendent been routinely supplied with funds for gifts from a tax on the trade, the Indians might have been pacified. After Pontiac's Uprising the average amount spent annually by the Indian Department was increased but still insufficient to satisfy the demand.

The fiscal problem in Great Britain was the underlying pressure that influenced many of the decisions made between 1765 and 1768. The British tax issue was not mere politics nor an attempt of George III to curry favor with the wealthy landowners. When the Stamp Act was passed, the tax rate was decreased from five shillings on the pound to four shillings on the pound, still high as 20% of the assessed value of every estate in Britain collected annually. The new money being made by manufacturing for the most part escaped taxation; the burden fell on the landowners, who were not necessarily wealthy. Even the continuation of the 20% tax on the value of the estates in the 1760s led to the sale to the newly wealthy manufacturers of many estates that had been in families for centuries.

As a frame of reference, a large farm in Wisconsin of 2,000 acres was assessed at $6,000,000 in 2001 and the owner paid about 2%, or $120,000 a year, in real estate tax. An English landowner in 1763 with 2,000 acres assessed at the equivalent of $6,000,000 would have paid £6,000 sterling ($1,200,000) in taxes. The British total revenue, most of which was from the tax on land, was £9.8 million sterling. Many members of Parliament very likely did not manage their estates well enough to produce enough profit to pay the tax and maintain the standard of living of a country gentleman. Many borrowed money and fought hard in Parliament to reduce the burden; others were forced to sell.

The total annual expense of the British government in 1763 was around £14.2 million sterling. The interest on the debt was £4.7 million sterling ($940 million). Either a heavy burden of taxation or a sharp reduction of expenditures was absolutely necessary simply to pay the interest. The British debt had increased from £77,800,000 sterling ($15.5 billion) in 1757 to £132,100,000 ($26.4 billion) in 1763. In 1763 Britain had a deficit of £4.4 million sterling. By curtailing expenses in 1764 to £10.7 million sterling and increasing taxation, the British nearly balanced the budget with only a £500,000 deficit. From 1765 to 1768 the budget had a surplus in three of the four years.[3]

Reduction of expenses in America was one of the most significant areas. The cuts in military spending made across the empire after 1766 had a proportional effect on the American forces. After the retrenchment of 1766, less money was available to repair the frontier posts and pay for extraordinary expenses. As the army was moved east to more economical quarters in 1768, an increasing amount was spent on the seaboard to the great loss of the western merchants.

Because of Britain's economy measures total military expenses in America decreased from £430,000 sterling in 1765 to £332,000 in 1768. The impact on the colonial economy was serious. Combined military expense and exports to Britain were £1.6 million sterling in 1765, compared to imports from Britain of £1.9 million, a deficit of £300,000 sterling. In 1768 the combined military expense and exports were still at £1.6 million sterling, but the imports had increased to £2.2 million sterling, a deficit of £600,000 sterling. The decrease in military spending of £100,000 sterling was a significant factor in the increasing deficit in America.

The men in business on the frontier were deprived not only of Indian Department purchases to create tribal goodwill, but of the profitable trade of provisioning the army. The effect of reduced expenditures on the military establishment and the Indian Department is dramatized when British military expenditures are added to the value of exports to Great Britain. The period 1765 through 1769 was one of comparative balance in the colonies when military expenditures are added to exports. In contrast, after 1769 the balance was extremely adverse for the colonies and in two years exceeded £1,500,000.

To satisfy Parliament's demands to reduce the budget deficit, the British government began to enforce existing laws that either prohibited imports of foreign goods or required the payment of duties for the import into the colonies, including French West Indies molasses and Dutch gin, brandy, and tea. In addition new taxes were imposed, including the Stamp Tax and the Townshend duties, which aroused strong opposition in America. The failure of the colonists and the British government to find some compromise in exploiting the frontier by 1768 led to a hardening of attitudes and eventually open conflict.

The failure to capture the fur trade from the French was a second factor that produced a deficit in the balance of trade with Britain. The total value of the fur and deerskin exported to Britain in the period was around £100,000 sterling. If colonial merchants had been able to take a portion of the Canadian trade from the French Canadians and a share of the Mississippi and Missouri Valley business from the French merchants in New Orleans, colonial fur exports would have more than doubled.

Presenting an alternate scenario may help the reader to comprehend the factors involved and the impact of various decisions. The decision to seek a victory in America on land in 1754 was arbitrary rather than obligatory. Had Britain chosen not to fight in America, the Royal Navy and a few troops would have been able to retain the status quo in the thirteen colonies. One can only suspect that the latent desire to acquire New France was a basic motive in the energetic prosecution of the campaigns in North America.

The next decision was to maintain an army in America. To do otherwise in 1765 would have carried a risk, considering the uncertainty of the attitude of the French and their influence on the Indians, who could pose a fearful threat to the colonists, as during Pontiac's Uprising in 1763. However, the decision of

General Gage to send only three of the fifteen regiments to the frontier may not have been wise. The other twelve regiments were placed in locations that were less expensive to maintain but where they had little if any mission to perform. If Gage had sent six or more regiments to the frontier rather than three, he would have had ample manpower to restore the French forts and replace their French garrisons at Miami, Sandusky, Vincennes, Green Bay, and St. Joseph, as well as to build additional forts at strategic locations to intercept the illegal French traders from Illinois. With at least a company of fifty men in each of these forts, the army would have been able to confiscate the goods of any conniving Frenchmen trying to trade without a license from a colonial governor.

If colonial traders could have conducted business from this network of well fortified posts, they could have competed with any French traders who did slip past the British army. Restrictions on colonial traders could have been modified to give them a better opportunity to meet the Indian demands. Most of the tribes were within a few days' travel of one or more of these posts. Given the ease of reaching the colonial traders and the better prices offered for their furs, most Indians would have been willing to transfer their trade from the French to the colonials. The net result might have been equal sharing with the French of the Illinois trade, giving the colonial merchants from Pennsylvania an additional £50,000 sterling in fur and deerskins. The relaxation of the rules and the additional posts in the Great Lakes area might have diverted half of the furs from Montreal to colonial merchants from New York, adding another £50,000 sterling to the colonial business.

Doubling the number of troops on the frontier would also have increased the profitable business for the New York and Pennsylvania merchants at the expense of the London-based ration contractors. Gage could have approved the substitution of buffalo meat for beef, and the colonial merchants could have obtained flour from the French farmers in Illinois and Detroit, thus diverting another £100,000 sterling to colonial pockets. The payments for the regiments in Canada and Florida were about £250,000 sterling. Moving three of them to the frontier in addition to the three already there would have transferred a good share of the ration business from British to colonial merchants.

With an additional £200,000 sterling in trade, the colonial merchants might well have considered the £50,000 to be raised by the Stamp Tax simply a cost of doing business, especially if the army was playing a more positive role in protecting the colonial traders and obstructing the French. A tax paid in colonial currency (rather than sterling) that would be spent in the colonies would have been more palatable. With £50,000 sterling in fur from Illinois diverted from France to Britain, continental hat makers and others who used fur and deerskin would have been forced to buy on the London market, increasing the price of the fur sent by the colonists to Britain.

All of these suppositions, though quite meaningless, do highlight the significance of the decisions to enforce rules that were beneficial to the French in both Canada and Illinois at the expense of the colonial merchants.

Gage, under pressure from the British government to reduce army expenses, repeatedly made decisions that reduced the ability of the army to protect the colonial merchants. Gage's decisions sacrificed too much to maintain peace with the Indians under French terms. The pressure from the British government to reduce costs at the expense of accomplishing the mission leads to the conclusion that the regiments were stationed in America not to protect the colonies or newly won territory, but to disguise their true mission of maintaining a large peacetime military structure that could be expanded quickly in the event of a new war in Europe.

As it was, the colonists continued to import large quantities of British manufactures. The deficit from 1765 to 1768 was absorbed in the short term by running up credit in Britain, while the colonists searched for legal and illegal means to obtain sterling bills of exchange to balance their accounts in England. The sale of provisions and lumber to the West Indies and southern Europe and of rum to Africa covered about half of the colonial deficit, and the sterling bills from the army covered most of the remainder. The Stamp Tax threatened to reduce some of the benefit from the army, and after 1768 the move of the army to the coast cut the total expense as the ration contractor was able to supply some needs directly from Britain. Not only did moving the regiments upset the tenuous balance of trade, but their presence in the coastal cities provided the British government with the means to enforce the collection of taxes, which further upset the trade balance.

The fur trade and the army were both factors in colonial prosperity. The army was an economic asset, and the colonists did not object to its presence until it was transferred to the coast to quell riotous behavior. The reduction of the military market and the failure to expand the Indian markets in Canada, as well as the lower Great Lakes, the area west of Fort Pitt, and Illinois, were major blows to the colonial economy and hurt the wealthy merchants most of all.

The net result was that the colonists obtained fewer furs after 1765 than in the period before 1760. England won the war, but the colonists lost the fur trade. With the loss of the fur trade, along with the reduction of army expenditures and the curtailment of smuggling, the colonial merchants turned to land speculation and were blocked again by the British government. Hemmed in on all sides and facing increasing deficits in the balance of trade, the colonial merchants joined in the opposition to British taxation.

## NOTES

1. Charles Grant to General Haldimand, 24 April 1780, *Canadian Archives Report, 1889* (Ottawa: Canadian Archives, 1889), p. 60.
2. Schedule of Prices, 1765, *Illinois State Historical Collections* (Springfield: Trustees of the Illinois State Historical Library, 1903–) [IHC], vol. 10, p. 403.
3. Walter S. Dunn, Jr., *The New Imperial Economy* (New York: Praeger, 2001), pp. 14–15.

# SELECT BIBLIOGRAPHY

Alvord, Clarence W. *The Mississippi Valley in British Politics*. 2 vols.
  Cleveland: Arthur H. Clark, 1917.
Alvord, Clarence W., and Clarence E. Carter, eds. *The Critical Period,
  1763–1765*, vol. 10. Illinois Historical Collections. Springfield: Illinois State
  Historical Library, 1915.
Askin Papers in the Burton Historical Collections of the Detroit Public Library.
Baynton, Wharton & Morgan Papers. Microfilm. 10 Rolls. Original in
  Pennsylvania Historical Commission.
Byars, William V., ed. *B[ernard] and M. Gratz*. Jefferson City, MO: Hugh
  Stevens Printing, 1916.
Chevalier, John, and Peter, Daybook. Pennsylvania Historical Society.
Colden Papers. *New York Historical Society Collections*. 1876.
Dunham, Douglas. "The French Element in the American Fur Trade." Ph.D.
  Dis., University of Michigan, 1950. Microfilm in State Historical Society
  of Wisconsin.
Dunn, Walter S., Jr. *The New Imperial Economy*. New York: Praeger,
  2001.
Dunn, Walter S., Jr. "Western Commerce, 1760–1774." Ph.D. Dis.,
  University of Wisconsin, 1971.
Edgar, William. William Edgar Manuscripts, 1760–1769, vol. 15 in the Burton
  Historical Collection. Detroit Public Library.
Fleming, R. H. "Phyn, Ellice and Co. of Schenectady." *Contributions to
  Canadian Economics*, 4 (1932).
Gratz, Michael. Letter Book, Etting Collection. Pennsylvania Historical Society.
Harrington, Virginia D. *The New York Merchant on the Eve of the Revolution*.
  New York: Columbia University Press, 1935.
Hazard, Samuel, ed. *Pennsylvania Archives*, 1st Series, 12 vols. Philadelphia:

Joseph Severns, 1851–1856.

Hough, Franklin B. *Diary of the Siege of Detroit.* . . Albany, NY: J. Munsell, 1860.

Hutchins, Thomas. *A Topographical Description of Virginia, Pennsylvania, Maryland, and North Carolina Reprinted from the Original Edition of 1778.* Cleveland: The Burrows Bros. Co., 1904.

Innis, Harold A. *The Fur Trade in Canada.* New Haven, CT: Yale University Press, 1930.

Jensen, Arthur L. *The Maritime Commerce of Colonial Philadelphia.* Madison: The State Historical Society of Wisconsin, 1963.

Johnson, Sir William. *The Papers of Sir Williams Johnson.* 14 vols. Albany: The State University of New York Press, 1921–1965.

Lawson, Murray G. *Fur, A Study in English Mercantilism, 1700–1775.* Toronto: University of Toronto Press, 1943.

Lees, John. *Journal of [John Lees] a Quebec Merchant.* Detroit: Society of the Colonial Wars of the State of Michigan, 1911.

McClusker, John J. *Rum and the American Revolution, The Rum Trade and the Balance of Payments of the Thirteen Colonies.* 2 vols. New York: Garland Publishing, 1889.

*Michigan Pioneer and Historical Collections.* 40 vols. Lansing: Wynkoop, Hallenbeck, Crawford Co., 1874–1929.

O'Callaghan, Edmund B., ed. *Documentary History of the State of New York.* 4 vols. Albany: Weed, Parsons, & Co., 1849–1851.

O'Callaghan, Edmund B., and Fernold Berthold, eds. *Documents Relating to the Colonial History of the State of New York.* 15 vols. Albany, NY: Weed, Parsons, & Co., 1853–1887.

*Pennsylvania Colonial Records.* 10 vols. Philadelphia: J. Severns & Co., 1851–52.

Phillips, Paul C. *The Fur Trade.* 2 vols. Norman: University of Oklahoma Press, 1961.

Russell, Nelson V. *The British Regime in Michigan and the Northwest, 1760–1796.* Northfield, MN: Carleton College, 1939.

Short, Adam, and Arthur G. Doughty. *Documents Relating to the Constitutional History of Canada 1759–1791.* 2 vols. Ottawa: J de L. Tache, 1918.

Shy, John. *Toward Lexington: The Role of the British Army in the Coming of the American Revolution.* Princeton, NJ: Princeton University Press, 1965.

Sosin, Jack M. *Whitehall and the Wilderness: The Middle West in British Colonial Policy, 1760–1775.* Lincoln: University of Nebraska Press, 1961.

Stevens, Wayne E. *The Northwest Fur Trade, 1763–1800.* Urbana: University of Illinois, 1928.

Wainwright, Nicholas B. *George Croghan, Wilderness Diplomat.* Chapel Hill: University of North Carolina Press, 1959.

Wilson, Charles H. *Anglo-Dutch Commerce and Finance in the Eighteenth Century.* Cambridge: The Cambridge University Press, 1966.

# INDEX

## About the Author

WALTER S. DUNN, JR. has published numerous works in the areas of 18th century fur trade, museum administration, local history, and military history. His books include *Second Front Now, 1943* (1981); *Hitler's Nemesis: The Red Army, 1930–1945* (1994); *Kursk: Hitler's Gamble, 1943* (1997); *Frontier Profit and Loss: The British Army on the American Frontier, 1760–1764* (1998); and *The New Imperial Economy: The British Army and the American Frontier, 1764–1768* (2001).